Maguire
summer '16

D1236206

The Johns Hopkins University Press
Director's Circle Book for 2014

The Johns Hopkins University Press gratefully acknowledges
members of the 2014 Director's Circle for supporting the publication
of works such as *True Yankees*:

Anonymous
Dominic and Helen Averza
John and Bonnie Boland
Richard Burgin
Charlotte G. and William R. Cronin
Jack Goellner and Barbara Lamb
John T. Irwin
John and Kathleen Keane
Cindy Kelly
Ralph S. O'Connor
Anders Richter
Daun and Patricia Van Ee

The Johns Hopkins University Studies in Historical
and Political Science

131st series (2014)

1. Dane A. Morrison, *True Yankees: The South Seas and the Discovery of American Identity*

Magerie
Summer 2016

True Yankees

The South Seas and the Discovery
of American Identity

Dane A. ...

DANE A. MORRISON

Johns Hopkins University Press   *Baltimore*

© 2014 Johns Hopkins University Press
All rights reserved. Published 2014
Printed in the United States of America on acid-free paper
2 4 6 8 9 7 5 3 1

Johns Hopkins University Press
2715 North Charles Street
Baltimore, Maryland 21218-4363
www.press.jhu.edu

Library of Congress Cataloging-in-Publication Data

Morrison, Dane Anthony.
True yankees : the South Seas and the discovery of American identity / by
Dane A. Morrison.
pages cm
Includes bibliographical references and index.
ISBN 978-1-4214-1542-0 (hardcover : alk. paper) — ISBN 978-1-4214-
1543-7 (electronic) — ISBN 1-4214-1542-9 (hardcover : alk. paper) —
ISBN 1-4214-1543-7 (electronic) 1. National characteristics, American—
History. 2. Ship captains—United States—History. 3. Merchant
mariners—United States—History. 4. Oceania—Discovery and
exploration—American. 5. South Atlantic Ocean Region—Discovery and
exploration—American. 6. Travelers' writings, American—History and
criticism. I. Title.
E164.M86 2014
917.3—dc23   2014008716

A catalog record for this book is available from the British Library.

Special discounts are available for bulk purchases of this book.
For more information, please contact Special Sales at 410-516-6936
or specialsales@press.jhu.edu.

Johns Hopkins University Press uses environmentally friendly book
materials, including recycled text paper that is composed of at least
30 percent post-consumer waste, whenever possible.

CONTENTS

ACKNOWLEDGMENTS

A number of inspiring people have helped to move this book along its voyage to its own final port. I suppose that it began with a conversation with John Brooke in a cafeteria at Tufts University, where I first broached the idea of a connection between American voyages to the East and the formation of a national identity, and John argued that this issue deserved further study. Along the way, two engaging National Endowment for the Humanities seminars introduced me to both thoughtful and articulate colleagues and the bodies of knowledge that inform the book. One was an institute on "Maritime History and Culture," led by the astute team of Benjamin Labaree, Edward Sloan, John Hattendorf, and William Fowler and situated on the enchanting grounds of the Mystic Seaport Museum. The other, led by Wayne Franklin and held at the American Antiquarian Society, was a seminar in the history of the book in American culture, "Re-Reading the Early Republic: From Crèvecoeur to Cooper," revealing the world of print culture and challenging me to think about books, authors, and audiences in entirely new ways.

I have certainly benefitted from inspiring conversations—and pointed critiques—from a number of friends and colleagues, among them Cindy Larson, Matthew MacKenzie, Katrina Gulliver, Michael Feener, Emily Murphy, Nancy Schultz, Al Andrea, and Carolyn Neel. My dear friend and colleague, Thomas Doherty, has been influential in the direction of this project at early and important stages in its development, and his support is truly and deeply appreciated. Parts of the work withstood the trenchant evaluation of my department's writers group, organized by Michele Louro, and I benefitted from the guidance of Michele, as well as Annette Chapman-Adisio, Avi Chomsky, Andrew Darien, and

Erik Jensen. Important in this regard, also, was the guidance of an anonymous reader for Johns Hopkins University Press.

The project received generous support from several sources. I am particularly indebted to the American Philosophical Society, where Linda Musumeci skillfully oversees the grants and fellowships programs, for a Sabbatical Fellowship. A George Washington Fellowship from the Massachusetts chapter of the Society of the Cincinnati was also instrumental in supporting this work, and I owe particular appreciation to Renny Little for navigating the arrangements and organizing a keynote talk. Several seed grants from the Salem State University School of Graduate Studies sustained both the research and supported the acquisition of illustrations for the book. Colleague and current department chair Donna Seger has been a staunch supporter since we both arrived on the Salem State University campus two decades ago.

Where would scholars be without the careful guidance of research librarians and archivists? At the Peabody Essex Museum's Phillips Library, Kathy Flynn and Irene Axelrod were invaluable pilots through these boundless collections. Andrea Cronin likewise generously offered her expertise on the China Trade materials at the venerable Massachusetts Historical Society. Several curators and staff at the Peabody Essex Museum have been of inestimable help, and I am especially appreciative of the support I have received from Daniel Finamore, Karina Corrigan, Lynn Francis-Lunn, Sam Scott, and George Schwartz.

When we think of the China and Indies trades, the evocative artwork of this domain is one of the first things that springs to mind. I am grateful to a number of people who have helped me navigate this field and acquire striking reproductions for the book. They include Robin M. Tagliaferri at the Forbes House Museum in Milton, Massachusetts, the brilliant Patrick Conner of Martyn Gregory Gallery in London, Anna J. Clutterbuck-Cook at the Massachusetts Historical Society, Susan Drinan of the Philadelphia History Museum at the Atwater Kent, and William Reese at the William Reese Company in Philadelphia (one of my favorite sources of Indies trade texts and art). I owe particular thanks to Kathy Fredrickson and Claire Blechman of the Peabody Essex Museum, who made their expansive collections available and who spent countless hours in identifying and delivering wonderful copies, including a favorite image for the book cover.

I have never enjoyed working with a press as much as I have with Johns Hopkins University Press. The people at JHUP managed this disorganized and often forgetful author with both remarkable professionalism and laudable grace.

The very wise and very patient senior editor Bob Brugger was instrumental in helping me to conceive of the project as a set of stories that humanized the history of America's entry into the Great South Sea. Catherine Goldstead, Mary Lou Kenney, Hilary Jacqmin, Juliana McCarthy, Sara Cleary, as well as copy editor Michael Baker shepherded the manuscript into a readable form.

Finally, the grace and wisdom of two women have sustained me along the course of this project, fostering a home life that is both supportive and studious. To my dear, brilliant wife, Kimberly, and my precocious and vibrant daughter, Abbie, I owe more than I can say.

DANE MORRISON
Newmarket, New Hampshire

INTRODUCTION

[handwritten annotations in margin: "It is interesting that she was named at the beginning of 1783 and the end of the Revolutionary war."]

On the 11th of May 1785, the American ship the *Empress of China* slipped into her berth along the wharves of New York's East River, to the calls and "huzzahs" of astonished merchants, sailors, and dockworkers. Hundreds of curious on-lookers dropped their ledgers, tools, and carts and raced to observe her arrival. Even in the midst of a staggering economic depression, New Yorkers were used to seeing ships returning from distant Europe and the West Indies or coastal ports like Boston, Philadelphia, and Charleston. But the arrival of this vessel drew exceptional notice because her port of call had been particularly exotic and her cargo was not the usual store of sugar, molasses, and grain carried on a conventional voyage. The *Empress* was the republic's first Indiaman, the first American vessel to sail "eastward of Good Hope" into the waters of the Indian Ocean and South China Sea. Fifteen months earlier, she had departed New York with a cargo of Appalachian ginseng and Spanish dollars, and onlookers now gaped to see the wares she had brought back from the East. *[handwritten: "where did they get ginseng?"]*

Extraordinary, too, was the publicity that surrounded the *Empress*'s arrival. As soon as the customs documents had been signed, ledgers and daybooks filled out, and cargo assigned to auction, her supercargo, or business agent, Major Samuel Shaw, sent a hurried message to Samuel Fraunces's tavern at the corner of Great Dock and Broad Streets, where the country's secretary of foreign affairs, John Jay, maintained his department office. Shaw believed it a matter of urgent business to document the journey to China and to frame it as an historic achievement that catapulted the new nation into the ranks of the community of civilized nations. Across the country, the popular press erupted in the same celebratory spirit, often quoting at length from Shaw's letter. The *Salem Gazette*, the *New Hampshire Gazette*, and South Carolina's *Columbian Herald* praised the enterprise, courage, and ingenuity of the American officers and crew, extolled the voyage as a "judicious, eminently distinguished, and very prosperous achievement," and asserted that all had been blessed by a kind Providence. Such traits, their readers reassured themselves, were the marks not of a loose set of dependent provinces but the character of an independent nation. Shaw himself believed that the Congress should recognize the introduction of Yankees at Canton as a great American holiday, a moment of national celebration as historic even as the country's independence day. It was for many Americans the most important event in the history of the new nation.[1]

Yet currents of anxiety churned beneath the hurrahs and congratulations that greeted the *Empress* in May 1785. In fact, Americans' responses to their country's first steps onto a global stage revealed a paradox of pride and doubt. Shaw himself captured the sense of uncertainty when he prefaced his letter to Jay with the words, "It becomes my duty to communicate to you . . . an account of the reception its citizens have met with, and the respect with which its flag has been treated in that distant region." Questions of reception and respect, of how Americans would be regarded, as individuals and as citizens of a republic, haunted public discussion of the *Empress*'s voyage. The loose confederation of separate nations called the United States of America was entering a critical era in which many doubted the country's capacity to "form a more perfect Union, establish justice, ensure domestic Tranquility, provide for the common defence, promote the general Welfare, and secure the Blessings of Liberty." Jay fretted for a government that was "fundamentally wrong," Alexander Hamilton complained that he wept over the country's myriad weaknesses, and George Washington lamented that the nation was "always moving upon crutches and tottering at every step." The new nation had won its independence but had not secured its legitimacy. Its first encounters with the East were important, then, because Americans looked to them not only to establish the country's reputation but also to define the character of the new nation.[2]

In 1785, the voyage of the *Empress of China* helped to quell Americans' concerns about the legitimacy of their republic and how their countrymen would be received in a postcolonial world. The question of their national identity lingered, however. How they discovered their character in the South Seas is the subject of this book. This study is intended as an examination of some of the ways in which Americans' first contact with the East inflected their sense of national identity. It is, then, a cultural history of the Old China Trade, or Indies Trade, as it is more accurately named, that focuses on the American experience of travel to and residence in Asia during the early years of the republic. The China Trade, or Indies Trade, has been a part of our language and consciousness at least since the *Empress*'s return. As the province of economic historians, museum curators, and collectors of antiquities, particularly, the terms convey proprietary meaning. Consequently, I want to be clear about the areas that this study does not attempt to cover. First, it is not an economic history. There are a number of worthwhile studies that attempt to estimate the volume of trade or patterns of consumption. A necessary starting point is James Fichter's *So Great a Profitt: How the East Indies Trade Transformed Anglo-American Capitalism* (Cambridge, MA, 2010). Second, this is not a history of East Asian export goods. Excellent introductions can be found in Carl Crossman's *The Decorative Arts of the China Trade* (Easthampton, MA, 1991) or, more recently, in Caroline Frank's *Objectifying China, Imagining America: Chinese Commodities in Early America* (Chicago, 2011).

   This study draws from the rich field of print culture, a broad area of study that encompasses both published texts and private accounts. The work of scholars such as Richard Brown in *Knowledge Is Power: The Diffusion of Information in Early America, 1700–1865* (New York, 1989), William J. Gilmore in *Reading Becomes a Necessity of Life: Material and Cultural Life in Rural New England, 1780–1835* (Knoxville, 1989), John Rogers Haddad in *The Romance of China: Excursions to China in U.S. Culture, 1776–1876* (New York, 2008), and Lawrence A. Peskin in *Captives and Countrymen: Barbary Slavery and the American Public, 1785–1816* (Baltimore, 2009) has demonstrated the importance of print in the everyday lives of ordinary Americans, whether delivered through very public newspapers, broadsides, books, and pamphlets or by way of somewhat private journals, diaries, and letters. They have emphasized the important idea that scholars need to examine a more expansive range of writing than the conventional "great books" if we wish to understand the transmission of ideas throughout early America. "Private" journals, diaries, and letters were seldom recognized as the property of the individual writer but were shared with family, neighbors, associates, and, sometimes, the wider community. They have revealed, as well, the complementary relationship between print and word-of-mouth forms of communication, pointing out how oral communication often fed letters, diaries, and journals that were incorporated into newspapers that then filled the taverns and parlors with further conversation. This study builds on these ideas to show how new understandings of the national character were formed in the early republic through the reception of published and "private" writings from the men and women who traveled throughout the East.

In *True Yankees*, I have selected five voyagers to convey the story of America's early encounters in the East, from initial contacts in 1784 through the culmination of the Old China Trade with the Treaty of Wangxi in 1844. Merchant Samuel Shaw spent a decade in Asia, 1784–1794, scouring the marts of China and India for goods that would captivate the imaginations of his countrymen, dying suddenly of tropical fever off the Cape of Good Hope. Mariner Amasa Delano toured much of the Pacific as an explorer and seal hunter in the 1790s and early 1800s. Edmund Fanning circumnavigated the globe as another sealer, explorer, and trader, touching at various Pacific and Indian Ocean ports of call well into the 1830s. Harriett Low was a reluctant twenty-year-old when she accompanied her merchant uncle and ailing aunt to Macao, residing there between 1829 and 1833 and recording her observations of expatriate life. Merchant Robert Bennet Forbes's last sojourn in Canton, 1838–1839, coincided with the eruption of the First Opium War.

I had sifted through hundreds of narratives before deciding to organize this study around these five. The strategy has necessitated leaving out many accounts and eliding a few. One might ask, for instance, why I did not devote a chapter to Charles Wilkes, whose exploits with the United States Exploring Expedition (1838–1842) garnered enormous national attention and coincided with the eruption of the First Opium War. Why not David Porter, whose *Journal of a Cruise* was published in 1815 and repackaged in 1822, and who gained international fame for his foray into the Pacific Ocean during the War of 1812? And, of course, why not any of the hundreds of others who sailed into, and often resided in, Asia?

While the narratives published by Wilkes, Porter, and the rest certainly touch on several of the experiences that framed the American foray into the Great South Sea, none equal Shaw, Delano, Fanning, Low, and Forbes in the breadth, complexity, and resonance that these travelers' tales achieved. Few Americans wrote as compellingly or explored the essential themes of Eastern contact as well as these writers. Few examples echoed the national mood and reflected its changes.

I decided to organize *True Yankees* around the experiences of Shaw, Delano, Fanning, Low, and Forbes because their writing satisfied several essential criteria. First, cumulatively, these five figures wrote testimonies that provide both a chronological and geographic comprehensiveness that is seldom attained in similar narratives. Shaw's travels of 1784–1794 marked the first direct American contacts with China and India. Amasa Delano's three voyages overlapped those of Shaw, carrying him into the South Seas from 1790 up through 1806. Edmund Fanning made numerous voyages and circumnavigations and financed a number of others between 1793 and 1833, when he published the first edition of his *Voyages Round the World.* Harriett Low spent the years 1829 to 1834 abroad. Finally, Robert Bennet Forbes's second residence in China, between 1838 and 1839 coincided with the onset of the First Opium War and the culmination of the Old China Trade. As their travels spanned the period of early American contacts with the East, so, too, did their journeys span the East, from Africa's Cape of Good Hope to the Pacific coasts of North and South America, ranging farther than the travels of Porter, Wilkes, Herman Melville, or others. Shaw saw the environs of Macao, Canton, Batavia, Bombay, and Calcutta. Delano's and Fanning's travels coursed much of the Great South Sea. Harriett Low was an involuntary resident of Manila, Macao, and Cape Town. And, Forbes saw most of the East as a sea captain and on two tours of China for Russell & Company. Simply put, they traveled farther, stayed longer, and recorded more than other, more renowned Yankee travelers.

Second, their writing constitutes a significant record of Americans' first experiences in what they knew as the Great South Sea. It is curious that this corpus has been so thoroughly neglected by historians. Yet, few accounts echoed so clearly the anxieties and ambitions of their age. Few probed the paradox of discovery as these did in describing the first American encounters in the South Seas and the consequent reimagining of a Yankee identity. Few provided a vocabulary of global proportions that reverberated through an emerging national culture. To paraphrase Linda Colley in her studies of British imperial identity, these five narratives appeared at a time when Americans were forming their new nation and as they questioned the elements of their national character. They ended with the gelling of modern attitudes toward other peoples, and, of special concern, views that were more fully racist. In between, they transcended the confines that held other writers. Porter wrote in terms of national honor, and Wilkes touched on the natural history of the Pacific and the cultures of its peoples, but to a great extent they were captives of these parallel themes rather than explorers of the interrelationships between them or their influence on American character. As I describe in this book, it was in this rich and complex sea of imagination that Shaw, Delano, Fanning, Low, and Forbes reimagined themselves and their countrymen.[3]

Third, and perhaps a bit surprisingly, writings about encounters with distant lands, seas, and peoples resonated deeply with the cares and concerns of ordinary Americans. Many of the histories penned in the last century, and much popular writing today, situates early American encounters with an imagined East as the province of antiquarian interest and bombastic nationalism. These earlier collectors and historians created a mythology of the Old China Trade that was focused around exotic goods and heroic adventure. None of our protagonists saw themselves as particularly heroic, however. Theirs was a squarely ordinary, middle-class struggle, a bourgeois battle for everyday matters of economic security and reputation. They were Benjamin Franklin's idealized "rising generation." They were also, paradoxically, history's declining bourgeoisie. Their narratives echoed the lives of ordinary men and women of the early republic who began in humble, often desperate circumstances who rose or fell as fortune would allow. They died young, as Samuel Shaw, or in obscurity, like Amasa Delano. Or, they passed away as septuagenarians, esteemed by the public, comfortable in wealth, and surrounded by family, as Edmund Fanning and Robert Bennet Forbes. They left the East, abandoned by the loss of a protector, as Harriett Low, later to find fortune but not security. Their tales are stories of struggle, disappointment, and loss as well as achievement, and in this, too, they mirrored the lives of ordinary Americans. *? really?*

Their writing resounded with the American public because they were such ordinary people. Or so they presented themselves—ordinary people whom fate had sent to extraordinary, indeed, exotic, places. Their countrymen could easily identify with them, also, because their accounts were so accessible, speaking in the language of vernacular republicanism and available in a variety of venues. Their tales appeared in the newspapers that could be found in taverns and coffeehouses. Their books were reviewed in the national and international magazines of the literati. Their adventures were appropriated and repackaged by the most popular writers of their time. Their drawings and lithographs graced countinghouses and sailors' homes. They gave lectures at athenaeums and marine societies. In each site, they transported Americans abroad to the East of their imaginations and, in turn, transformed their countrymen into "true Yankees."

In selecting Shaw, Delano, Fanning, Low, and Forbes as representative figures of this China Trade writing, from its origins in 1784 through its culmination with the Treaty of Wangxi in 1844, I do not assert a direct causal connection between their individual experiences or texts and the construction of a national identity. Nor do I believe that this group was singular in its influence. Rather, I am trying to show how, cumulatively, the "news from the East" carried by hundreds of American men and women contributed to the construction of that

I disagree. Attend they appealed because their lives were exotic! Were not-ordinary; their lives were exotic!

identity. That Delano first published in 1817 or that Fanning published in 1833, well after the formation of that identity was well underway, is not really the point, either. Rather, it is significant that they and hundreds of others brought their experiences vicariously to the American public through lectures before marine societies, historical societies, and athenaeums, in testimony before Congress, and in newspaper reports and magazine articles. The books they published later summarized their experiences and were the culmination of their careers. Despite the dates of publication, they represent the perspective and values of a first generation steeped in a republican vision of their nation and the world.

Americans' voyages to the East raise questions for our own age as well. It is surprising that the nation so often disparaged today for high-handed imperialism, for foisting its web of culture, commerce, and geopolitical strategies onto the disadvantaged peoples of the globe should have entered an age of globalism with such self-doubt. We would do well to ask, what did these first contacts mean to early Americans? How in their eyes did these encounters legitimize the status of the new nation? How did they use these encounters to form a national character? And, why, if at the time observers considered this a defining moment in the American experience, are these encounters largely unnoticed today?

Early American historians may have chanced across Samuel Shaw, but likely only in passing. His name, along with those of other world travelers like Amasa Delano, Edmund Fanning, Harriett Low, and Robert Bennet Forbes would be even less familiar to general readers of mainstream American history. Their stories are forgotten because the world they knew has passed—was passing even as they wrote of it—and has been replaced by a vision of America framed in the dusty hues of the Alamo, Indian wars, and covered wagons. Ohio editor and booster of Western expansion William Turner Coggeshall understood the power of frontier mythologies to sweep aside the realities of American life as early as 1859. He lamented "the popular idea of Western Literature" as a pastiche of "tomahawks and wigwams, sharp-shooting and hard fights, log cabins, rough speech, dare-devil boldness, bear-hunting and corn-husking, prairie flowers, bandits, lynch-law and no-law-at-all, miscellaneously mixed into '25 cent novels,' printed on poor paper and stitched between yellow covers." But, in the early years of the new nation, America faced East. The newspapers of the republic celebrated encounters in Cochin, Canton, and Calcutta, mourned losses in Feegee, Mocha, and Madagascar, and rushed reports from Constantinople, Bombay, and Bencoolen to their presses. In the nation's capital, politicians pored over dire dispatches from Barbary, Malacca, and the Ladrones. Along the

Appalachian foothills, in the Carolina backwoods, and sounding George's Bank, frontiersmen and fishermen picked ginseng, smelted lead, and pulled cod for the markets of India. In seaports like Salem, it was said, one heard shopkeepers telling boys to run *chop chop* to the *bazaar* for a *chow* of *dungaree, madras,* and *bandana,* for which they were to be rewarded with a *cum shaw.* In the green hills of Vermont, along the cobbled streets of Philadelphia, in the wainscoted drawing rooms of Charleston, anxious readers shared letters, diaries, journals, and logs from sons and daughters, fathers and husbands, employees and masters who had been last heard of in the waters of the Indian Ocean, the Arabian Sea, and the Great South Sea. We have forgotten what they knew, that the fundamental American experience during the formative years of the new nation was lived on the waters that led to China, India, and Java.[4] *to end the new-War*

In the years between the Treaty of Paris (1783) and the Treat of Wangxi (1844), that is, between the end of the War for Independence and the Mexican War, Americans' first contacts in the Great South Sea—the term that early Americans used to describe the expanse of oceans, lands, and peoples situated between the Cape of Good Hope and the coasts of North and South America—contributed to the economic recovery of their new nation and to the consciousness of their countrymen. Hundreds of merchants, shipmasters, and expatriates shared their experiences in published books and private journals, logs, letters, and newspaper reports. Yankee travelers introduced their countrymen to the ports of Algiers and the bazaars of Arabia, the markets of India and the beaches of Sumatra, the villages of Vietnam *Indochina* and the factories of Canton. But it was also the particular opportunity, and special burden, of American travelers in the East to defend their nation's honor and to define its character. And in this forgotten aspect of the American experience was a paradox: Their encounters with other peoples in what they called the Great South Sea offered their countrymen the most salient means of understanding their own national identity. Because national identity can be most clearly defined in contrast to the behaviors and beliefs of other peoples, their contacts with European expatriates and native Asians and Africans enabled Yankee travelers to triangulate the character of their countrymen among them. And, because they navigated poles of civilization between the perceived decadence of Europe and the "barbarism" of Asia and Africa, they could envision their republic neatly between these extremes and characterize the new nation as among the most civilized in the world.

In truth, many of the stories of American travels in the South Seas have been told. But the ways in which historians have remembered these narratives have been partial and popularized, cast as "the record of a brilliant era of American achievement" and overshadowed by the overland tales of the Western frontier. Consequently, our understanding of the ways in which postrevolutionary American culture formed a national identity has been obscured by the multiple mythologies of the early republic—mythologies of the sea, mythologies of the early republic, mythologies of the China Trade, and mythologies of the broad sweep of American history. Not all those who voyaged into the Indian Ocean or South China Sea, however, were true China traders, became the scions of eminent merchant houses, or sowed the fortunes and spawned the great dynasties of American society. Most of those who sailed to the East did so in the desperate attempt to establish even a bare "competency" to support their families at home. They were impoverished military officers like Samuel Shaw, drifters like Amasa Delano, and cast-off children like Harriett Low. Few returned with great wealth, and many did not return at all.

Although unfamiliar to Americans today, these accounts were among the most popular reading in the early republic, heard as lectures in the athenaeums of Salem and Philadelphia, passed from friend to friend in Boston, read aloud in taverns and inns along the stage route to Alexandria, pondered in coffeehouses in New York, discussed over dining room tables in Charleston. They filled the library shelves of Portsmouth's wealthy merchants, Newport's marine societies, and Philadelphia's museums. And they were popular, not just because they relayed interesting yarns, but because they addressed the central concern of Americans everywhere—both throughout the republic and within the republic of letters. In the succinct language of French immigrant turned "American Farmer," Hector St. Jean de Crèvecoeur, the question of the age was, "What then is the American, this new man?"

The formation of a national identity was a conundrum for citizens of the new republic. Before independence, most colonists thought of themselves as British. Following the Revolution, Americans struggled to create an American identity from the thirteen strands of disparate colonial identities. The period between the end of the Revolution and the War of 1812 was a time when the name "American" as a national label was still unfamiliar to many ears; when people described themselves as Carolinians and New Yorkers, Rhode Islanders and Marylanders, when Thomas Jefferson still referred to his home country as Virginia. Americans were sensitive to their *arriviste* status, and in the struggle for recognition that ensued alongside their earliest encounters with the East they searched for signs of legitimacy. Despite the success of their Revolution and the formation of a nation, Americans were aware that their character as a people remained in question. Among the intellectuals of literate Americans and Europeans, few political observers, here or abroad, gave its survival much hope. When the Massachusetts politician Fisher Ames, in 1800, looked back on the years since the Revolution, he recalled, "Until that contest, a great part of the civilized world had been surprisingly ignorant of the force and character, and almost the existence, of the British colonies . . . They did not view the colonists so much as a people, as a race of fugitives, whom want, solitude, and intermixture with the savages, had made barbarians."⁵

"Voyages of commerce and discovery" to distant lands introduced Americans not only to uncharted sources of goods but also to unfamiliar places, peoples, and experiences. The prospect of sending the Stars and Stripes to unknown places excited their imaginations. The accounts that carried these tales back to the Republic depicted "new worlds" in Americans' consciousness and presented them with images of the fascinating, the curious, the frightening, the revolting. Through the travelogues of the mariners, merchants, expatriates, and emissaries who wrote of their travels throughout the East, places such as Bencoolen, Huang-po, or Jolo Island became as familiar to American readers as Salem or Newburyport. Through the literature of exotic commerce, the community of maritime adventurers engaged the community of American readers and vicariously shared such adventures as trading blows with pirates in the Straits of Bangka, negotiating through Moslem harems in Malaysia, or retreating before a bellowing army of sea lions off Patagonia. In the process, Americans' "discovery" of markets in the Pacific and Indian Oceans following the American Revolution not only helped to rescue the national economy from a devastating depression; it also launched a buoyant celebration of American character. Commercial exploration of the East seeded a flowering of literary and journalistic constructions that explored the themes of discovery and identity. And these encounters "eastward of Good Hope" contributed to the development of a nascent national character—the "true Yankee."

This true Yankee was not a one-dimensional figure. The elements of national identity evolved over time and in response to the challenges that the country faced between independence and the Mexican War. We can trace these changes in the travels of Shaw, Delano, Fanning, Low, and Forbes. Shaw's voyage to Canton aboard the *Empress of China* in 1784 not only inaugurated American trade with the East but also publicized the republic's entry onto the world stage. For Shaw, the American was a citizen who carried the values of a free republic into the world, who strived to ensure that other peoples respected the new country as a legitimate member of the civilized nations, and who represented the dignity and virtues of his fellow citizens. Delano's encounters with the people of the Palau Islands, New Guinea, the Moluccas, the Philippines, Sumatra, Hawai'i, China, India, the Iberian Pacific, Australia, and South Africa introduced his countrymen to "India" and the Great South Sea, as he described the expanse from Cape Town to the Pacific coasts of the American continents. For Delano, this American was a citizen of the world for whom the spirit of a practical Enlightenment distinguished his character and showed him to be a man of gentility, scientific inquiry, and tolerance of other peoples. Like Melville, later, he saw his travels across the world's seas as the school through which Americans earned the particular regard of both Europe and India for their exceptional spirit of enterprise and openness. Edmund Fanning's travels marked a more mature phase in Americans' global encounters. Representing the new nation as a legitimate partner in the community of civilized nations, Fanning's repeated circumnavigations around the world carried him to the Marquesas, Canton, and "sundry voyages to the South Seas." He sponsored over forty voyages that established the United States as a commercial force in the world. The American he depicted was a man of adventure, perseverance, and courage yet, like Shaw and Delano, a gentleman whose refined ways and tolerant views of other peoples polished the "green Yankee" of the colonial period. Together, Shaw, Delano, and Fanning represented the concerns of a first cohort of South Seas voyagers whose postrevolutionary consciousness framed their encounters with Chinese compradors and Indian banyans as well as British ambassadors and French commodores.

Low and Forbes were part of a second diaspora of Yankee South Seas voyagers. Harriett Low's travels marked a significant transition from the world of Jeffersonian republicans inhabited by Shaw, Delano, and Fanning toward a society of Jacksonian democrats, for whom consumption and entertainment replaced civic consciousness and enterprise. Low's American had reverted to the kind of parochial consciousness that we associate with her Puritan forbears, and her intolerance of Asians and Europeans reflected the consciousness of the Jacksonian world of the Trail of Tears, fears of a Masonic conspiracy, and anti-abolitionist riots. Like Low, Robert Bennet Forbes's experiences were those of a different kind of American traveler, the sedentary expatriate of the second generation, who reflected a steadier, more stable, more confident America that had weathered the storms of the early republic. For residents such as Forbes, the national struggle for legitimacy within the community of civilized nations was largely over, and the liberalism they embraced was one of "an individualistic and competitive America, which was preoccupied with private rights and personal autonomy." His American was a man driven from home by financial embarrassment, bent on making his competency, and determined to limit his time abroad and to constrain his concern for the non-Western peoples who surrounded him.[6]

Drawing on letters hastily scribbled amid the bustle of "speaking" a passing ship in the South China Sea, or in ships' logs diligently constructed in quiet moments of reflection aboard a rolling brig in the Indian Ocean, or in florid journals dreamily sketched in the sultry, fetid February air of sumptuously appointed apartments in a Canton factory, the encounters of these five world travelers present a particularly American experience—yet one that few Americans recall. They describe this country's first contacts with the lands and peoples of the East. And they document the development of an American identity that began as tentative and tolerant and grew into a national character both more confident and less empathetic to the peoples who inhabited a region they regarded as the Great South Sea. This was the true Yankee.

The First
Generation

CHAPTER ONE

Samuel Shaw's Polite Reception

1784-1794

O N THE 19TH OF MAY 1785, sitting at a borrowed desk along the bustling wharves of New York harbor, a thirty-year-old merchant from
Boston named Samuel Shaw dispatched a letter that would transform
American consciousness. Shaw had just returned from a voyage unlike any previously undertaken by an American. In fifteen months, he and forty-one of his
countrymen had sailed across the globe, anchored in the Pei-ho River, traded
Appalachian ginseng for Cantonese teas and porcelain, and had just returned to
their berth above the Narrows that led into upper New York harbor, boasting
an impressive profit. It was a remarkable feat. Although the great European East
India companies had traded in China for three hundred years, no American ship
had even ventured beyond the Atlantic before. Indeed, there was no "America"
in 1785, not as a unified nation. The United States was divided into thirteen
separate republics organized into a loose alliance called the Confederation, and
Europe's capitals gave the nascent country only grudging regard. Consequently,
when the *Empress of China* triumphantly settled into her anchorage eight days
earlier, one of the first responsibilities addressed by the former Continental
army major was to send a report to Foreign Minister John Jay, observing, "It
becomes my duty to communicate to you . . . an account of the reception its
citizens have met with, and the respect with which its flag has been treated in
that distant region." For the most part, his countrymen could be pleased.[1]

Samuel Shaw was born in Boston's North End on 2 October 1754, at the
beginning of the French and Indian War, a conflict in which British Americans
fought for a nation whose capital lay three thousand miles across the Atlantic.
He was the third son of Francis Shaw (1721–1784), a merchant "distinguished
for intelligence and enterprise," and Sarah Burt Shaw (1726–1799). Like his

Sketch of Samuel Shaw (1754–1794), attributed to John Johnston (1753–1818), from Shaw's *Journals* (1854). Courtesy of the Massachusetts Historical Society.

brothers, John and Francis, Jr., Samuel would die at an early age, and like younger brother Nathaniel, he would die on the homeward passage from China. Still, Shaw was a fortunate son. Educated at Boston's renowned Latin School under the distinguished scholar James Lovell, he impressed his teachers with a passion for history and poetry. As the boy grew into a tall if somewhat portly manhood, he would become accustomed to adorning his correspondence with quotes from Horace and Virgil, Shakespeare and Pope. Yet, as a merchant's son, Samuel was destined for his father's countinghouse, and it appears that he spent much of his youth deciphering ledgers and daybooks. No doubt he would have followed the path of his father and brothers had not the struggle against the "tyranny" of George III and Parliament disrupted the mundane rhythms of provincial politics. The Shaw family was ardently pro-Whig, and their antipathy toward "impositions" such as the Sugar Act and Stamp Act was likely fanned when parliamentary decree required them to accept British officers within their household, among the three thousand soldiers who invaded Boston homes in the spring of 1775. In later years, family legend recounted that the impetuous Samuel challenged one boarder to a duel over some insult the latter had vented against the patriot cause, an imprudent action that was halted only when Major John Pitcairn, who would later command Royal troops at Lexington and Concord, secured an apology from his officer.[2]

Following the hostilities of April 19, twenty-year-old Samuel received his father's permission to enlist in Washington's Continental army, then forming across the Charles River in Cambridge. By December, he was commissioned a second lieutenant in the artillery unit of Henry Knox, who had operated a bookshop in Boston before joining the rebel forces and was then busying himself reading from the military manuals that had laid on his bookshelves just months before. Shaw remained in the army throughout the duration of the war, sending home a steady stream of letters that reveal a man who self-consciously fashioned his personality around the constellation of republican values that were transforming British provincials into independent Americans.

Shaw's letters to Boston describe both the character he was forming and the perspective he would bring to the Eastern trade. They reassured his family that he would husband the little money that they could spare to send him and the irregular salary he received from Congress, a sentiment advised by Benjamin Franklin in his popular pamphlet *The Way to Wealth* (1757), a tract familiar to every colonial merchant. And they described the young officer's efforts to cultivate the genteel deportment that he learned in Boston's mercantile community and that was requisite for an officer in Washington's army. As an up-and-coming young Virginia planter, Washington himself had famously copied "rules of civility" from various gentlemen's guides, and his deportment served as a model for rising young officers such as Shaw. The underlying tension between simplicity and gentility posed a particular challenge, however. He would "rub along" as best he could, but given "the stress which the world lays on external appearances," he did not want to be perceived as a "Joe Bunker." Duty was another virtue evident in Shaw's correspondence, and he chose to remain in uniform throughout the war, even as he saw "sunshine" patriots melt away to their comfortable hearths and prosperous shops. This sense of responsibility to an emergent country was a virtue ĥe shared with many of the men who would sail to the East when the war ended, their wartime memories knitting an imagined community of expatriate Yankees scattered across the globe and discovered in places as distant as Bencoolen and Bombay. Shared sacrifices had forged a bond that men such as Shaw extended even to comrades for whom "a continued series of ill-luck has constantly attended," like his esteemed companion Thomas Randall (1757?–1811). On learning of Randall's capture at Philadelphia, Shaw had written in September 1777, "His good conduct on all, and the most trying, occasions, joined with my long acquaintance and friendship, interests me exceedingly in his behalf." This tendency to create bonds among comrades, to create at least "one valuable or agreeable connection" in a distant port, would serve him well in his efforts to trade in the East. Shaw was becoming a sophisticated citizen of the world, albeit a world bounded by the confines of white gentility. Amasa Delano, second mate on Shaw's third voyage to the East, described him as "a man of fine talents and considerable cultivation; he placed so high a value upon sentiments of honour that some of his friends thought it was carried to excess."[3]

Unlike those who served in the state legislatures and militias, and who maintained a parochial view of the country, many of the men who served in the Continental forces and in the Congress developed a broader, more expansive view of the new nation. Shaw adopted this "continentalist" vision, espoused by such leaders as Washington, Hamilton, and Jay. Disdaining the "pitiful exertion" that he had witnessed among the populace of New York and Pennsylvania, he remarked, "It would be well if every distinction of this or that colony or province could be buried in that of *American.*" The military duty that brought him to New York in 1776, where Shaw would return nine years later to board the *Empress of China,* foreshadowed his complicated constructions of the peoples he would encounter in Calcutta and Canton (modern-day Guangzhou, China). While the war raged, he had stigmatized the Indians who attacked vulnerable frontier settlements as "savages," a term for Native Americans that was common to the colonial lexicon. But, after 1775, he likewise described the British as "barbarians." In another reversal, he found that he was even learning to like the French, whose Catholicism had been abhorred by earlier generations of New Englanders. Such was the kaleidoscopic lens through which he would gauge the peoples he encountered in the Indian and China seas. He would observe indigenous customs and foreign communities in the manner of an Enlightenment gentleman but rarely allowed them to speak for themselves in his accounts. It was a complicated view of the world, testing Europeans and Asians alike against the standard of the republican values of a new nation.[4]

Like so many of his countrymen who traveled to the East at the end of the war, Shaw was driven more by a sense of desperation than of adventure. Eight years away from the countinghouse had left him with a sterling reputation, but with little money and few prospects. By 1779 he had risen to a staff position, as aide-de-camp to General Knox, and had attained the rank of major. He had earned distinction as a reliable organizer in Knox's office and for courage on the fields of Trenton (1776), Princeton and Brandywine (1777), Monmouth (1778), and Yorktown (1781). He served as secretary for the corps of officers who sponsored the formation of the country's first veterans' group, the elite Society of the Cincinnati. But Congress had no money to pay those veterans and was locked in acrimonious debate over funding the pensions it had promised the Continental army. What Shaw wrote of Thomas Randall—that his wartime comrade would go to China "because he has at present no prospect more promising"—described his own situation and that of many Americans who would sail to China and India in their wake.[5]

The spirit of triumphant nationalism that adorned Shaw's letter to John Jay in May 1785 was as much testimony to the raft of crises that confronted the new republic as it was a statement of the country's achievement. The nascent United States was in trouble, and seasoned political observers gave the experiment little chance of holding together. At home, Hamilton, Jay, and Washington fretted over the republic's future, and abroad, realists predicted imminent collapse. Prussia's Frederick II famously stated, "I am much persuaded that this so-called independence of the Americans will not amount to much." Just two years earlier, Shaw's countrymen had defeated the mightiest nation in the world. The far-flung British Empire had arguably boasted the best-trained army, the largest navy, the wealthiest treasury, and—despite repeated miscalculations and misguided policies—the most modern administration the world had seen. Yet, as candlelight illuminations were snuffed, bonfires burned out, banquet tables emptied, and toasts silenced, Yankee mariners returned to empty wharves, rotting hulks, and decayed fishing nets. When in 1783 a compatriot remarked that the war for independence was successfully concluded, Franklin cautiously replied, "Say, rather, the war of the Revolution. The war for independence is yet to be fought."[6]

As Franklin feared, the Treaty of Paris produced neither national nor cultural unity. Instead, the Confederation faced myriad challenges—economic depression, rampant inflation, local insurrections, and boundary controversies. In the same month that Franklin signed the treaty, John Holroyd, Lord Sheffield, penned his venomous *Observations on the Commerce of the American States*, which called for a virtual blockade of American shipping to Jamaica, Barbados, Nevis, and the other West Indies islands on which the American economy had depended for nearly 150 years. Parliament enacted Sheffield's proposals into vindictive policy, plunging the country into a long spiral of stagnation and recession.

As Britain held steadfastly to its regressive Navigation Acts and even former allies resurrected traditional restrictive policies, the weight of mercantilism again placed a staggering premium on American exports. By the spring of 1784, the Confederation's economy began a descent from which it would not recover for seven years—almost as long as the war itself. To the southwest, imperial Spain blocked access to New Orleans and prevented American farmers along the Mississippi River from shipping their produce to Atlantic and Caribbean markets; to the northwest, Britain refused to vacate illegal forts in the Ohio Valley, instead using the sites as staging areas to launch Indian raids against the western frontier; to the east, the Barbary states of the Mediterranean dispatched corsairs against American ships, eventually capturing and holding hundreds of Americans for ransom. Europe's return to mercantilism triggered the severe depression that wracked every region of the country, and, exploding in episodes such as the 1786–1787 agrarian revolt, Shays's Rebellion, threatened to undo the newly won political gains.[7]

Sectional jealousies both undermined the possibility of coordinated action by the states and hindered the formation of a national identity. Reflecting on the question "Would an extension of the Union be politic?," Yale University president Timothy Dwight observed, "People in a great measure ignorant of each other, with no strong feeling of common interest, and separated by a wide distance, naturally have but little sympathy for each other; and the mere fact that they are under one government may not prove a sufficient bond of union."[8] For some of the deepest political thinkers of this age, the calamities of the so-called Critical Period were manifestations of a deeper and more troubling problem: the nature of American character. In this atmosphere of uncertainty and crisis, an "experimental voyage" for an experimental nation seemed a lifeline at which merchants up and down the coast had begun to grasp.

The impetus for the China project lay with Philadelphia's enterprising merchant, Robert Morris, who hoped both to make a profit and "to encourage others in the adventurous pursuit of commerce." Morris was in a strong position to galvanize this new kind of American voyage, but he was not the only visionary. As superintendent of finance for the Confederation, he was connected to a commercial community that stretched from Portsmouth to Charleston. He knew there was an American market for Eastern wares—"The inhabitants of America must have tea," Samuel Shaw would later write—and anticipated his countrymen's pent-up hunger for calico, pepper, porcelain, and other luxury goods. The consumer revolution that had swept through the seaports since the second quarter of the eighteenth century now accelerated and washed over the countryside, as British merchants dumped their stockpiled wares and Americans poured over advertisements for "the latest goods from England."[9]

Morris was intrigued also as he listened to the dreamy visions of John Ledyard, a Dartmouth College dropout who had sailed as a corporal of marines on Captain James Cook's final voyage (1776–1780). Ledyard had returned to his Connecticut home just as the war was winding down and had been peddling his own unauthorized account of the expedition in the coffeehouses of New York and Philadelphia. To anyone who would listen, he touted an idea for sending ships around Cape Horn and bringing otter pelts from America's Northwest Coast to Canton's trading factories. Morris was well aware, also, that the prescient Colonel Isaac Sears was making plans to send a cargo of ginseng from Boston to the Cape of Good Hope in southern Africa.

Ledyard's scheme was too ambitious for the calculating Philadelphian, and Sears's voyage was too modest. Morris combined the best features of each design in an enterprise that would send a single ship around Cape Town to Canton and directly back to the United States. A network of former revolutionary and prerevolutionary business associates coalesced around the project, and from the start it took on the cast of a national mission, with planning and financing centered in the ports of Philadelphia, Boston, and New York. Morris owned half of the vessel, with the other half held by a consortium led by Daniel Parker of Boston. Parker's financing came through the son of a British émigré living in Paris, John Holker, Jr., who served as France's consul to Pennsylvania.[10] Across the country, the news journals celebrated—and embellished—the national character of the enterprise. "Many eminent merchants from different parts of the Continent" were invested in the project, the *Salem Gazette* proclaimed. It was too modest a revelation for the *Virginia Journal and Alexandria Advertiser*, which reprinted Daniel Parker's assertion that "the ship . . . belongs to citizens of the . . . United States." They hailed the revolutionary service of the ship's officers and crew, catapulting Captain John Green (1736–1796), technically on a leave of absence from the Continental navy, to national notoriety. Like many of the Americans who sailed to the East in the early years of the republic, Green had been captured aboard a rebel privateer during the "late War." He had been confined among South Carolinians and New Yorkers at Mill Prison, where they all had "really suffered" together as Americans. The journals lauded both his patriotism and his "character as an able and spirited navigator."[11]

Most of the *Empress*'s officers, in fact, hailed from Pennsylvania. Like Green, they had previously served aboard privateers, or like the captain's clerk, Frederick Molineaux, had fallen into British hands. The ship would carry two supercargoes, Shaw and Randall, from Boston. After recovering from injuries sustained at the Battle of Germantown in October 1777, it seems that Randall had sailed privateers, operating out of Philadelphia in partnership with Thomas Truxton, a future China trader and naval hero, during the final years of the war. Randall's inclusion in the voyage came about through the intercession of his wartime comrade, although Shaw described their partnership as merely coincidental: "My friend, Daniel Parker, Esq., agent for those concerned, having offered me the appointment of supercargo, I followed the advice of my friends in accepting it; and finding that Thomas Randall, Esq., my intimate friend, had an inclination to go the voyage, we agreed to try our fortunes together." To provide diplomatic cover, on 23 December 1783, Daniel Parker wrote to Congress to request sea letters.[12]

The republic's newspapers flaunted this patriotic construction. Some editors even projected the traits that they hoped would appear in the national character onto Morris's ship. The 360-ton ship *Empress of China* had not been built for an "experimental voyage" like this, but Yankee ingenuity adapted the vessel to the needs of the times. "Built on the new invented construction of the ingenious Mr. Peck"—John Peck, a successful Boston merchant who designed ships as a hobby and was later father of a famous Harvard College entomologist—she had been launched in 1783 in Boston as the *Angelica*, designed for the familiar winds and currents of the Atlantic and Caribbean trade. The crew was depicted as a familiar trope, the simple, honest tar, "all happy and cheerful, in good health and high spirits" who behaved "with a becoming decency." The journals further asserted that these men were "elated on being considered the first instruments, in the hands of Providence, who have undertaken to extend the commerce of the United States of America."[13]

In March, the *Virginia Journal and Alexandria Advertiser* reported Parker's request to Congress for sea letters, although literally, the ship had already sailed. A host of journals announced the departure of the "handsome, commodious and elegant ship," which carried "several young American adventurers," and they played up the fanfare that accompanied the historic moment. On passing Fort George, the *Empress* had fired the "United States salute," it was reported. In contrast to the isolationist impulse of later periods, this early form of national-ism embraced the opportunity to encounter and engage the wider world and to carry the republic "to that distant, and to us unexplored country." In sum, then, the newspapers represented a national character that was enterprising, patriotic, and cosmopolitan. As Congress toasted two months later at its Independence Day banquet, "May the Simplicity of Manners, Industry and Frugality distin-guish the Character of an American" and bring "Liberty, Peace and Happiness to all Nations."[14]

On Washington's birthday in 1784, the *Empress* cleared the East River for Canton. Only three months earlier the last British warship had departed from New York. The city remained "a neglected place," and even as late as April 1789 visitors found the environs still "in a state of prostration and decay." The weather was inauspicious. A dreary winter of heavy snow and biting cold, "more severe than any that had happened for many years," as Benjamin Franklin de-scribed it, matched the desolation of the city. Because of the Little Ice Age, winters in the late eighteenth century commonly brought distress to American shipping. In June of the previous year, Iceland's Laki volcano system had ripped open an extensive fissure across southern Iceland, spewing lava across the land and toxic ash into the atmosphere over the next eight months. Across the north-ern latitudes of Europe, India, China, Canada, and the United States, the effects were devastating, as airborne poisons felled livestock in their tracks and choked tens of thousands of people. Consequently, the winter of 1783–1784 was bitterly cold, and not until late February did the Hudson expose enough water to allow for a departure. The southeasterly course that Green followed pushed the ship and its crew toward warmth, but before long the men of the *Empress* were com-plaining of the debilitating heat of the Asian tropics. They steered toward the world's markets but remained largely ignorant of the global interconnections that would influence the cruise and the fate of the new nation.[15]

For the most part, the *Empress* carried the kind of diverse cargo that was com-mon to colonial voyages—cordage, wine, lead, iron, Spanish dollars—but this was not an ordinary voyage. Morris's consortium had invested $120,000 in the enterprise, ten times the cost of a conventional voyage to Europe, and one item among the cargo revealed the "experimental" character of the voyage. Following the advice of Ledyard and a library of travelogues, including James Cook's *A Voyage to the Pacific Ocean* and treatises such as William Hebreden's "METHOD of preparing the GINSENG Root in China," the merchants had loaded 242 casks of the herb. The four-pronged *Panax quinquefolius* grew wild in the Appalachian foothills, and the consortium advertised for it throughout the country. Much of the cargo had been collected months earlier by Dr. Robert Johnston, the ship's surgeon, in the "back park of Virginia." In addition, the ship's officers had purchased more ginseng for their private "adventures," the modest allotments of space in the cargo hold allowed officers and crew.[16]

On March 22, the *Empress* anchored at St. Jago in the Cape Verde Islands. The stopover violated the instructions that Daniel Parker had carefully prepared two months earlier, urging Green to push his vessel to Canton as quickly as possible in order to secure the best market for the ginseng. However, when the captain found some leakage in the ship's upper works and in the casks that held the crew's drinking water, he took advantage of a loophole in Parker's letter to make repairs and replenish their provisions. The need for fresh water was particularly urgent in light of the course that Green had plotted. The *Empress* would bypass the customary sojourn at Good Hope to expedite the voyage to Canton's markets and avoid alerting the enterprise's chief competitor, the British East India Company. In the bay of Port Praya, the *Empress* encountered the French slave ship *La Jengut*, which had just arrived from Senegal and was bound for Cape Francois. The sight of a slaver was nothing new for Yankees plying the waters of the Atlantic, but Shaw may have never seen a slave ship before. He lamented the plight of the "poor creatures," naked and bound in chains, who overflowed onto the main deck. Yet, he did not acknowledge his countrymen's own complicity in human trafficking. Eighteenth-century observers commonly constructed social problems in personal rather than structural terms, and Shaw followed middle-class conventions only to lament, "Good God! . . . is it man, who . . . can become a fiend to torment his fellow creatures?" Even so, the Americans gave three cheers to the French brig as she departed on her course.[17]

Slipping out of Port Praya on March 27, Green steered the *Empress* southward, into waters that none of the crew—with the possible exception of his clerk, Molineaux—had navigated before, hoping that his charts, sextant, and copy of Samuel Dunn's *New Directory for East-Indies* were accurate. By May 13, the captain calculated that the *Empress* still lay a thousand miles west of Cape

Town. The ship maintained a southeasterly course, turning northward only when Green was confident that the ship was well past Good Hope. The passage through the Indian Ocean during the months of the summer monsoon was tedious. "One dreary waste of Sky and water," purser John White Swift described it. Finally, on July 17, a lookout spied Java Head looming at the entrance of the Sunda Strait, and with great relief, Green turned the *Empress* northward toward Mew Bay. He and his crew had now been away for five months, had traveled some sixteen hundred miles, and were still almost a month and over a thousand miles from their destination. They were homesick and "exposed to hotter sun than I ever before experienced," as Swift complained. But, the reception they received at their first Asian anchorage shored up the crew's spirits.[18]

In a fortunate coincidence, as Captain Green piloted the *Empress* into the roadstead at North Island on July 18, he came to alongside two French naval ships, the *Triton* and *Fabius*. In command were officers who had served under Admiral de Grasse off Yorktown in October 1781, the definitive final battle of America's War for Independence. The three crews had come a long way from the Virginia Capes to Sunda Strait, but the fires of common cause burned brightly between them. Aboard the *Triton*, Commodore d'Ordelin welcomed the newcomers "in the most affectionate manner," relayed the news that Lafayette had received the order of the Society of the Cincinnati, and confided that his countrymen were "much pleased with the honor done to their nation." And he complemented his good wishes with offers of practical support. To Shaw's relief, d'Ordelin "gave us an invitation to go in company with him" and "expressed a wish to render us every service," even providing his ships' signal pennants. The French commander had made eleven voyages to Canton previously, and the guidance he could provide through the reef-strewn strait and pirate-infested China Sea was invaluable. The bonds of friendship were further cemented through shipboard banquets. At dinner, the company was "exceedingly polite, and very glad at meeting us." For his part, Captain Green was relieved to hear the French officers validate the charts he used and "commended the sailing of our ship highly."[19]

Although Shaw intended to furnish a detailed record of the Chinese reaction to the arrival of the Yankees, he expended much more ink on the responses of the European expatriate community. Canton potentially offered a new market for American wares, but Americans would not measure their nation's legitimacy by Eastern standards. It was the European community of civilized nations that was the benchmark of acceptance in the world arena, particularly in the spheres of gentility and diplomacy, to which Americans sought acceptance. Ironically, the first practical signs of Europe's approval came half a world away, along the coast of Sumatra. It was the particular support of "our good allies the French" that Shaw reported as "exceedingly beneficial" and "no small addition to our happiness." Captain Green also recorded the "polite attention," "every civility," and "constant advice and assistance" of the French in his ship's log.[20]

On August 23, the *Empress* and her French consort anchored off Macao, the eleven-square-mile peninsular port that guards the passage upriver to Canton. For the Americans, it had been an especially long journey, traversing some 18,000 miles over six months, at a time when a conventional Atlantic voyage spanned six weeks. Green recorded in the ship's log that on anchoring in Lark's Bay, Shaw and Swift "had the honor of hoisting the first Continental flag ever seen or made use of in those seas." Macao was ostensibly a colony of the Portuguese Empire; in reality, it was one of a slew of new world cities that European colonizers were opening in the early modern world, a cosmopolitan enclave that operated under an often chaotic pastiche of Chinese and Portuguese regulations. D'Ordelin had already advised the Americans of the diplomatic rituals they would need to perform before they could proceed beyond Lark's Bay. Chinese regulations mandated that foreign captains apply to Macao's Hoppo, or customs officer, for a *chop*, the document that gave permission to enter the Pei-ho River. To expedite matters, the French advised offering a modest gift, a *cum shaw* to the Hoppo and his staff. Everyone understood this for what it was—a bribe. The new vocabulary signaled to Shaw that he was entering a world very different from the Atlantic community he had left behind. He had already begun to describe it as exotic, a mixture of the strange and curious that distanced the place and objectified its inhabitants. If the voyage were to be successful, he would need to curry the favor of the Chinese mandarins and depend on the European expatriates who made up Canton's commercial community. There were auspicious signs. At Lark's Bay, the French consul, Monsieur Vieillard, "came on board to welcome us to that part of the world" and "kindly undertook the introduction of the Americans to the Portuguese governor." Merchants from the Swedish and German factories followed. What awaited at Canton, where the other delegations had gone to prepare for the 1784 trading season, remained to be seen. Taking on the mandatory Chinese pilot at Macao, the *Empress* covered the next sixty miles in a few days. It passed miles of banana and bamboo "plantations" and "padda" fields of rice that stretched as far as the crew could see. As the Pei-ho turned westward, it took on the name Tigris, bounded on each side by the island

Painting of the Bocca Tigris, c. 1810. Courtesy of the Peabody Essex Museum.

fortresses of Anung Hoy, or Ladies' Shoe, and Tiger Island. Centuries earlier, the Portuguese had dubbed this point the Bocca Tigris, or "Tiger's Mouth." Missing the obvious decay of the site that closer inspection would have revealed, Shaw recorded that the stronghold appeared to be an imposing obstacle—an observation that later China traders would find amusing.[21]

On August 28, the *Empress* anchored at Whampoa, as Westerners awkwardly pronounced the name of Huang-po Island, the main anchorage for foreign vessels. The image of the Stars and Stripes sailing into Whampoa in company with the fleur-de-lis established a measure of legitimacy for the new nation. French aid was critical to the success of this first American foray into the East, and the importance of its timing cannot be underestimated. The Americans would soon discover that French assistance did not come without complications, particularly with the British community, but at this point the companionship of their former allies helped to secure a place of respect within the European community. Still, the Americans would have to learn quickly how to conduct themselves in this cosmopolitan world. As the *Empress* came to anchor, Green ordered a thirteen-

Fan, showing *Empress of China* at Whampoa, c. 1784, said to have been a gift from Chinese officials to Captain John Green. Courtesy of the Philadelphia History Museum at the Atwater Kent, The Historical Society of Pennsylvania Collection.

gun salute to announce its arrival, "which were answered by the several Commodores of the European nations." Soon, the Danish factory sent an officer "to compliment" the visitors, and the English sent an officer "to welcome your flag to this part of the world." They were followed by the Dutch factory, which offered a boat "to assist." The "French ships sent two boats, with anchors and cables, under an officer, who assisted us in getting into a good berth, and staid on board till we moored." Protocol required the visitors to return these visits, and here, too, Shaw was pleased to report, "The behavior of the gentlemen on board the respective ships was perfectly polite and agreeable."[22]

Western vessels were not permitted beyond Whampoa, for reasons both practical and cultural. The Pei-ho became too shallow for the great Indiamen to proceed beyond this point, narrowing to an average of 150 yards across; Chinese restrictions narrowed as well, the Americans learned, allowing only ships' officers to approach China proper. Here the *Empress* would berth until her departure, offloading her ginseng and lead and taking on teas, silks, and porcelains. The crew would be kept busy in repairing the wear and tear that the vessel had sustained during her transoceanic journey. Over the next two days at Whampoa,

Shaw and Randall learned more about the procedures for doing business in Canton. They would need to contract with a Hong merchant before they would be allowed to trade at Canton. Under imperial regulations, this person could be only one of a dozen or so merchants of the Co-hong, the guild charged with ensuring Western compliance with Chinese laws and customs. The tortured history of the Co-hong suggested how difficult it was for imperial bureaucrats to develop a policy for dealing with any foreign presence in the Celestial Empire. An imperial decree had established the guild in 1720, another dissolved it in 1771, and yet another had reestablished the group just two years before the *Empress*'s arrival. The Hong merchant, sometimes called the security merchant, or *fiador*, managed most of the commercial arrangements while the ship remained at Whampoa. He paid the myriad customs duties, which Shaw estimated at $4,000 per ship, brokered the exchanges of cargoes, introduced craftsmen and shopkeepers, and intervened with imperial officials on behalf of the foreigners. He recommended the comprador, or purser, and the linguist, or translator, who ostensibly facilitated transactions in Canton, secured the sampans for carrying freight between Whampoa and Canton, and performed a thousand other tasks. Shaw was told that the services of these intermediaries were essential, but later Americans complained, often bitterly, about their dearth of knowledge and lack of skills. The linguist's knowledge of Western languages was so primitive, it was said, that it was necessary to foster a patois of business terms, or pidgin English. The Chinese and European merchants who descended on the *Empress* at Whampoa determined that the American would be assigned to the Hong Merchant Puankequa, a fortunate choice, as he was one of the most experienced and reliable of the guild.[23]

Two days later, Shaw and Randall left the *Empress*, covering the twelve miles upriver to Canton in a ludicrously named fast boat. Progress was slowed over the last five miles, as their craft maneuvered between the thousands of egg-shaped sampans, crab boats, and serpentine dragon boats that filled the river. The din of a million voices created a low roar, and the sensory onslaught must have intimidated the Yankees, whose Boston comprised fifteen thousand people and whose Philadelphia held thirty thousand. Their destination was Jackass Point, a spit of land whose name belied what awaited. As they approached, they gazed upon what seemed an array of gleaming palaces, whitewashed and built in the classical European style. The imposing two-story structures were marked by pediments, with tall, arched windows and verandahs on the upper floors and porticos projecting from the Dutch and English factories. Before each structure, like sentries at attention, waved the flags of each nation atop extended poles.

This painting *Foreign Factory Site at Canton*, c. 1810, shows the "federal flag" centered in the expatriate enclave. Courtesy of the Peabody Essex Museum.

The whole image gave the Americans the impression of a dominating Western presence.

Shaw and Randall settled into the French factory until they could find lodgings for themselves. Almost immediately, they began receiving guests, a procedure that continued over the next two days. In Shaw's thought, the moment of encounter was as historic as the new nation's day of independence, later asserting that the federal government should recognize the 30th of August as a great national holiday. As the Bostonian described the situation, "circumstances had occurred" that had "attracted the attention" of the Chinese and had placed his country "in a more conspicuous point of view" than ever before. More notice greeted the American visit "than has commonly attended the introduction of other nations into that ancient and extensive empire."[24]

Actually, the imperial officials and Hong merchants who welcomed the Americans did not know quite what to make of them. Shaw found that the first order of business would be to identify his country. As he greeted silk-robed mandarins and waistcoated Western merchants, the *Empress*'s supercargo must have suppressed a smile upon learning that the Chinese had "styled us the New People" and the "flowery flag people," mistaking the thirteen stars in the ship's pennant for a floral pattern. The Chinese seemed to know almost nothing about this former part of the British Empire. The Americans met their inquiries with letters of greeting from Congress and the president and a map that "conveyed to them an idea of the extent of our country, with its present and increasing population." For their part, the Hong merchants "were not a little pleased at the prospect of so considerable a market for the productions of their own empire." It was an introduction that would be repeated throughout the entire sixty years of the China Trade encounter, as Yankee merchants and sailors stepped onto the world stage. Three years later, when the sloop *Experiment* returned from Canton, several American journals carried a similar message: "It was a matter of surprise to the natives and Europeans, in that quarter, to see so small a vessel arrive from a clime so remote from China." As late as November 1800, when the USS *George Washington* anchored at Constantinople, the first American vessel to call at the capital of the Ottoman Empire, the "new people" were required to introduce themselves yet again. As sailor Samuel Patterson recalled, Ottoman officials boarded the *Washington* "to enquire what ship that was, and what colors she had hoisted. They were told that it was an American frigate and an American flag. They said they did not know any such country. Capt. Bainbridge then explained that America was the New World . . . by which name they had some idea of the country." Debuts in distant capitals like Canton and Constantinople became opportunities to celebrate, and to legitimize, the Yankee entry onto a global stage, as Shaw observed. He and Randall had been "treated by them in all respects as citizens of a free and independent nation. As such, during our stay, we were universally considered."[25]

Over the next two weeks, the Americans commenced their operations. By September 6, accommodations in the Austrian factory had been readied to receive them, and the *Empress*'s supercargoes and officers moved their possessions into rooms there. Ironically, the men who boasted their republican sympathies could now be found at the site that styled itself the Imperial *hong* and flew the double eagle flag of the Hapsburg Empire. A week later, on September 14, the ceremony of "Cumshaw and Measurement" took place. A delegation of Chinese customs officials and Hong merchants boarded the *Empress* and measured the length of the vessel, which determined the duty owed. The Hoppo, the "grand mandarin" of the customs office, then provided the *chop* for opening the ship's hatches, and now the business for which the *Empress* had come could proceed.

Immediately, chop boats began to carry the *Empress*'s cargo upriver and fill the *godown*, or warehouse, in the imperial factory.[26]

Settled into their lodgings, Shaw and company found that the Canton expatriate community took on a whirlwind pace of business and socializing. The September-to-April tea season had commenced, and during these six months, there were cargoes to be loaded, goods to be purchased, and money to be made. Their days were spent being ferried to silk, porcelain, and lacquer shops, where they were introduced to craftsmen, artists, silk makers, and tea growers and learned how to distinguish between "first chop," or highest-quality, goods and "third chop," or inferior products. Evenings were dedicated to socializing. Even beneath the relentless pace, there remained suspicions about the Yankees' legitimacy, in Shaw's words, "personally and nationally." The Americans, as they became known, were particularly anxious that their British cousins, especially East India Company officials and naval officers, would receive them favorably. Shared language and common culture, as well as the protection of the Royal Navy and the acquiescence of the Company, would be significant in establishing the American mission on a sound footing. But "Lord North's cruel war" would not be ignored by the Yankee contingent, and especially by men who had served in the Continental army and navy and who had been held as prisoners of war; nor would it be ignored by the English. It was incumbent on the Americans to present a measured demeanor, neither contrite nor proud, and presenting the recognized markers of gentility as well as nationhood as reference points; it was required, as well, in this extended expatriate community, that their British counterparts display a spirit of reconciliation rather than the petulance of retribution that the Sheffield government called for. Implicitly referencing his identity as an American merchant, Shaw noted with some pride that John Bull had not been "behindhand." Even the head of the English factory assured him, "As soon as it was known . . . that your ship was arrived, we determined to show you every national attention." Invitations to call, the signals of respect among Western gentility, came quickly and cordially. Shaw could write to Jay, "Besides the gentlemen of the factory, many of their captains visited us, gave invitations, and accepted ours in return." As to the war, the erstwhile enemies strove to make amends, and America's unofficial consul described the English overtures in glowing terms: "On board the English [ships], it was impossible to avoid speaking of the late war. They allowed it to have been a grave mistake on the part of their nation, were happy it was over, glad to see us in this part of the world, hoped all prejudices would be laid aside, and added, that, let England and America be united, they might bid defiance to all the world."[27]

Neither the press of business nor Shaw's preoccupation with the European reception of his mission dampened the American's curiosity about the Celestial Empire. Here was an opportunity to apply what he had learned in the pages of Herodotus and Tacitus, recording his own observations of a culture that intrigued his countrymen. In this, there could be rewards as well. From the example of Benjamin Franklin, Shaw was fully aware that a man born in humble circumstances could use the pen to establish himself in genteel society. He had read a number of modern travelogues and expeditionary accounts, and he now followed the literary conventions he found in the weathered volumes he had brought to guide his observations. He relied particularly on George Anson and quoted extensively from the English explorer's *Voyage Round the World* (1748) to demonstrate his own erudition.

Over the next four months, Shaw attempted to record his observations on Chinese religion, customs, politics, and anything else that might intrigue the public. But, he complained, his efforts were stymied by the hermetic policies of the Celestial Empire. "In a country where the jealousy of the government confines all intercourse between its subjects and the foreigners who visit it to very narrow limits," he wrote, one could learn little about the people or the place. The origins of this idea of China as *Zhongguo*, the Celestial Kingdom, standing above all other nations in matters of morality and cultural advancement, had been lost in traditions that reached back 3,500 years, but its influence on imperial policies toward the *waiguo*, or inferior kingdoms, had lost none of its potency. Even long-standing residents of the factories "have not seen more than what the first month presented to view," Shaw learned; consequently, his conversations with Western residents revealed only a few additional details. And, the infrequent invitations to the estates of Hong merchants across the Pei-ho yielded little more. The old men hid their wives and daughters for fear of contamination by the *fan quai* and concealed their knowledge of the empire for fear of retribution from the mandarins.[28]

Shaw had traveled across much of the American countryside in the buff and blue colors of the Continental army, but the China that he encountered in August 1784 was unlike anything he had seen. In comparison, his Boston was a parochial enclave of barely fifteen thousand souls, only two thousand of whom had remained after shots were fired at Lexington and Concord. Canton was a

bustling, congested global city two thousand years old and one million people strong.

Nor could his reading have prepared him. Shaw discounted much of what he had read previously—the accounts of the sixteenth-century Jesuit missionaries were particularly suspect for their "marvelous" tales—and was dubious of the extravagant yarns he now heard in conversation with European residents. Ironically, these were the most reliable sources he could have consulted. The works of the eminent philosophes of his day were remarkably imprecise, belying their pretended expertise. He had no doubt perused the benign representations of Sinophiles like Montaigne and Voltaire and the blistering critiques of Sinophobes such as Defoe, Diderot, and Montesquieu. As an adept of Enlightenment rationalism, he knew that he should rely upon his own observations to provide "sufficient data" for the journal he was composing, but these impressions simply mirrored the views of his times.[29]

By the time Shaw arrived in the East, the conventional wisdom that China was "the admiration of the world" for its ability to bring order to a population of millions over the course of a millennium was giving way to the opposite and equally flawed view of the Middle Kingdom as cruelly despotic. Over the next four months, Shaw's own views evolved, following this trajectory. Upon his arrival in Canton in August, he applauded the "striking evidence of the wisdom of its government." By December, he came to see the empire as less celestial, paling in comparison with his idealized American republic, and more like the decadent European monarchies he loathed—closed, tyrannical, and corrupt.[30]

Indeed, the Celestial Empire revealed traits that were disturbingly familiar. The emperor's decrees and edicts were all too similar to the proclamations and commands of George III, against whom the men of the *Empress* had waged a long and bloody war. Beneath the façade of order that China presented lay a culture that was remarkable for its intolerance, a counterpoint to the enlightened ideals the Americans embraced. For a "new people" who were sensitive to issues of acceptance and inclusion, the experience of being outsiders was troubling. And yet, nowhere else in the world would Americans be treated so much as outsiders. Indeed, the world of American expatriates in Canton was a "golden ghetto." It was made clear in the designation the Chinese reserved for all but their own people—the *fan quai*. As the English residents, who had resided there at least since the eighteenth century, would have explained to these new people, the Chinese considered a *fan quai* to be a "barbarian wanderer" or "outlandish demon." There was one significant difference for the Americans, however.

They now occupied a position that they shared with other expatriates, and this brought the Western populace closer together.[31]

The patina of order in this exotic, inverted world was symbolized in the façades of the factories themselves. The long bank of whitewashed brick that distinguished the European factories created an impression of expansive presence, but, in actuality, the *fan quai* merchants were shoehorned along barely three hundred feet of frontage between the river and the city's walls. Removed to the peripheries of China, pushed to the outskirts of Canton, perched along the banks of the Pearl River, theirs was a suffocatingly small world. The emperors had dictated that the *fan quai* should be few—there were rarely more than a dozen before 1820, frequently outnumbered by transient visitors—enclosed in a neighborhood of less than twelve acres. Surrounding the compound was a tall fence—later a wall—which held the "barbarians in and apart," a further reminder of their enforced separation and isolation. The most interesting immediate attraction, the execution ground, was sited within view of the factories. The design was meant to ensure that the factory residents would see China as a distant and all-powerful state and be reminded of their own dependent, precarious condition. The impression was not lost on Shaw, who observed, "The limits of the Europeans are extremely confined."[32]

A more serious "imposition" was the corruption that seemed to infect every aspect of Chinese life. From their earliest contacts, American writers depicted the Celestial Empire as a labyrinth of rules, procedures, and customs in which business could be moved forward only through the repeated applications of *cum shaw*. Samuel Shaw's journals set the tone for exploring the interwoven themes of Oriental decadence and Yankee virtue. Even Shaw, who as much as anyone sought to encourage American trade with the East, warned his readers, "The knavery of the Chinese, particularly those of the trading class, has become proverbial . . . it is allowed that the small dealers, almost universally, are rogues, and require to be narrowly watched." His partner, Thomas Randall, saw little recourse, however. Responding to calls to lodge a formal protest in 1791, he warned, "The idea of a representation, concerning the frauds and impositions of the Chinese to the Emperor, would deserve attention were there not the danger of making things worse." Under the imperial regime, even one's movements, so necessary to the regular flow of business activity, were constrained by the requirement that "every Chinese, excepting the co-hong and persons in office, is obliged to have a chop for visiting the factories, which is renewed every month, and for which servants, and even coolies, hired at three dollars a month, must pay half a dollar." Further expense was incurred in paying the linguist on business in the customhouse, as no foreigner at that time was permitted to enter the imperial structure; nor should the trader forget to bring to the Hoppo some "sing-songs," or articles of curiosity.[33]

Shaw and Randall, however, were not being entirely honest with their readers in their representations of the "impositions" they encountered in Canton. A merchant or mariner could expect to face some sort of corruption or inconvenience in nearly any port in the early modern era, and the colonial ports of the European powers were perhaps more egregious than anything they would encounter in Asia. At St. Jago, the *Empress* had met with the usual extortion. There, the commandant demanded one dollar for the duty of overseeing the ship's water casks and insisted on supervising the purser's purchases to ensure that the Portuguese monarch received his requisite tax on every sale. Shaw's journal recorded no complaint with the practice by the Portuguese king or colonial officials to tax trade indirectly.

The culture of corruption that Shaw and Randall found at Canton was not a local phenomenon, and their outrage was exacerbated by the knowledge that this miasma was abetted, indeed fostered, by imperial policies that emanated from Peking (Beijing). As Shaw discovered on his first visit to the factories, the Americans' expectation that they could trade freely and efficiently was dashed on the imperial restrictions that governed foreigners' conduct in Canton. Most infamous were the Eight Regulations. Established by the imperial government to protect the native Chinese from the corruption that necessarily came through contact with the *fan quai*, they were periodically reissued or expanded through the demise of the Old China Trade. These regulations precluded a variety of practices that were customary in virtually every other port in the world. Americans learned, for instance, that they were prohibited from year-round residence in Canton, riding in sedan chairs, owning firearms, employing Chinese servants, or loaning money to Chinese merchants. They were forbidden from learning any of the Chinese dialects and from teaching Western languages to native inhabitants. They were to be closely supervised by the Co-hong merchants, who would serve as intermediaries for all communication between the *fan quai* and the imperial government. Perhaps most grievously, foreigners were not allowed to bring their families to Canton.[34]

The China that Shaw observed was, in his terms, a tyranny. He heard it in the mandarins' frequent reminders that the republican ideas of the "flowery flag people" had no place in the Middle Kingdom. "The Chinese let slip no opportunities of laying new impositions," the consul reported. In describing the invasive measures imposed by imperial authorities, he suggested policies reminiscent of a modern totalitarian government: "The mandarins on the quay are very vigilant, and every servant in the factories is a spy."[35]

It was unlikely that Canton's *fan-quai* could have avoided such displays of state power, particularly when the imperial authorities were determined to demonstrate theirs. Nor were the expatriates themselves immune from what Shaw described as the excesses of an arbitrary and brutal government. Most egregious, perhaps, was the fate of a cannoneer who served aboard the British Indiaman *Lady Hughes*. On November 24, the unfortunate sailor had obeyed an order to fire off the traditional salute for a departing ship, but when the cannon misfired, several Chinese subjects, including a mandarin's servant, were killed. Canton's governor demanded that the gunner surrender to imperial authorities for trial. When the culprit failed to appear before the mandarins, they seized the ship's supercargo, triggering a "general alarm" among the foreign community. That the events occurred during the height of the trading season sealed the fate of the unfortunate gunner. Outmaneuvered, British officials turned him over to the imperial police. When Shaw returned from his second voyage to Canton in 1786, he reported, "It must occasion pain to every humane mind to reflect that this poor fellow was executed by the Chinese, on the 8th of January following."[36]

The diplomatic imbroglio that came to be known as the Canton War opened an opportunity for Shaw's nationalist aspirations. When the British consul solicited support from the expatriate community, the former Continental soldier used the request to describe the role that he saw for his country in world affairs. Americans, Shaw predicted, would sit within the community of those who "considered the rights of humanity deeply interested in the present business."

By interpreting the *Empress*'s mission in nationalist terms, Shaw made the Canton War an object lesson in the progress of liberty for "every humane mind." He used incidents such as the *Lady Hughes* affair to distinguish his countrymen's own national character as a people who embraced Western notions of justice, honor, and liberty. The republican community that they imagined conveniently ignored their own oppression of African American and Native American peoples and the inequalities that confronted American women. Their observations brought "useful knowledge," a favored phrase of the time, because it served the political moment as Americans struggled to define the character of their own national experiment.[37]

"After remaining near four months at Canton, and experiencing, from all hands, every possible attention, we set sail for America the 28th December," Shaw wrote. Much preparation was needed before the *Empress* could leave China, however. Captain Green supervised the myriad of mundane details required to get the vessel ready for her departure, securing the exotic cargo in the ship's hold, with porcelain as ballast and teas firmly packed in jute. He had to inspect the vessel's hull, sails, and rigging to ensure that she could manage another crossing. For their part, the supercargoes went through another parade of diplomatic courtesies. Shaw informed his countrymen, "Invitations from every nation followed, and we were obliged to receive from each another public dinner and supper." Monsieur Vieillard, the French consul who had played an important role in introducing the Americans to Canton's commercial community, now insisted "upon paying us this honor in his separate right," another offer the American company could not refuse. Likewise, a visit to "the respective chiefs" of the European factories was "a ceremony not to be omitted."[38]

Amidst the balmy breezes of a Canton winter and the booming of thirteen cannon, which was returned by the European ships, the *Empress* raised anchor and departed from Whampoa. It is not clear how the mandarins regarded the demonstration, in the wake of the *Lady Hughes* affair and the Canton War. Captain Green had to await permission to leave Macao, in the form of a Grand Chop, which signified that they had met the obligations due to the empire and were free to sail for *Hwa-ke*, the flowery flag country. Finally, on the last day of 1784, nine months after leaving New York, the *Empress* departed China. The following day, she joined the Dutch ship *General de Klerk*, and they sailed in tandem for North Island to the southwest.

In the four-month sojourn at Canton, the *Empress* had immediately fulfilled important elements of its mission. The voyage to China had secured a form of diplomatic recognition that was unattainable in the Atlantic community. The influential East India companies had accepted Americans as respected members of the expatriate society and had recognized the United States as an equal partner in the community of civilized nations. Shaw summarized America's first encounter in the East: "The attention paid us at all times by the Europeans, both in a national and personal respect, has been highly flattering."[39] The voyage succeeded, as well, in answering the doubts about a national identity. Chinese authorities had welcomed the flowery flag barbarians in part out of curiosity, in part because the Yankees acted like a new people. When Shaw traded with the locals as well, he reported, he "treated [them] politely every time"; one seller observed, "I see very well you no hap Englishman. All China-man very much love your country." Even decades later, well after the novelty of their arrival had worn off, this idea of the Americans as a new people, somehow distinct from the Europeans in their treatment of the Chinese, seemed to linger. In 1823, British missionary Robert Morrison mentioned it, acknowledging the mercenary reputation his countrymen had acquired among the Chinese: "These opinions are nourished not only by what they sometimes see; but also by what they hear from Europeans. They are told that 'England will do or suffer any thing for the sake of the trade: that without the China trade England would be ruined.' &c." China's merchants and traders saw the Americans differently, as a people who generally treated them with respect.[40]

The economic results would not be known until New York's auction houses appraised the value of the tea that the *Empress* carried home. Shaw and Randall had loaded the ship's hold with teas, chinaware, lacquerware, 248 Malacca walking canes, 20 pairs of "Crystal Spectacles," window blinds, and 24 bamboo fishing rods. The officers and crew made their own purchases. Captain Green's "adventure" appears to have included a fan and punch bowl that depicted the *Empress*. Shaw ordered so much porcelain—120 chests and several tubs—that much of it had to sit in the imperial factory's *godown* until Randall could charter a second vessel. A number of these China pieces were monogrammed with the insignia of the Society of the Cincinnati—the Angel of Fame in flight—underscoring the theme of national purpose in which Shaw had cast the voyage.[41]

In fact, there were indications of the *Empress*'s success even before the vessel berthed in the East River. On the return leg of the voyage, Green decided that it was now prudent to bring his ship into the green waters off Cape Town, the strategic way station held by the Dutch East India Company since 1652 (it would be captured by the British in 1795). Francis Drake had called this "the most stately thing, and the fairest Cape in all the whole circumference of the earth." Anchoring in Table Bay on 9 March 1785, on the western coast of Africa, the *Empress* spied another Yankee vessel anchored there, the *Grand Turk* out of Salem. Under Captain Jonathan Ingersoll, the *Turk* had left Massachusetts the previous November 27 and took three months to reach Table Bay, in February 1785. The *Turk*'s primary investor, Elias Hasket Derby, had expected to trade West Indies rum and sugar, Virginia tobacco, barreled pork and beef, as well as flour and cheese, and 10,000 Spanish dollars for cheap Bohea tea and ginseng. So unfamiliar was the Indies Trade even to astute American merchants that Derby did not realize that East India Company ships were not authorized to "break bulk"—sell a portion of their cargoes—at Cape Town. Fortunately, a

Company captain was willing to trade from his private adventure, and, when the *Grand Turk* departed on April 13, she carried two hundred chests of teas and assortments of nankeen and sateen cloth.

By this standard, the *Turk*'s voyage would garner significant profits for Derby. Shaw saw something else in her voyage that would benefit the reputation of his country. Ingersoll had intended to sail to the Guinea coast to find a market for his rum, but "without taking a single slave," then to the Caribbean islands to purchase sugar and cotton. Shaw commended the captain and the merchant. "Notwithstanding the disappointment in the principal object of the voyage," Ingersoll would not engage in the slave trade, on orders from Derby himself. This resolution to suffer failure rather than participate in the nefarious business of human trafficking "did the captain great honor, and reflected equal credit upon his owner." The idea that Derby was in fact complicit in the slave trade, as he had been at St. Jago, through the purchases of goods produced by slaves, seems not to have dawned on Shaw.[42]

The possible success of the voyage could not ameliorate the devastating news carried in Ingersoll's sea chest, however. Francis Shaw had died the previous autumn, October 18, just as his son was settling in to business half a world away, and Samuel now read of his loss through the Boston newspapers. Reflecting on the cruel ironies of global travel, he pondered: "How precarious is all earthly happiness! and how liable are we to be disappointed, even in our fondest and most virtuous expectations! The American papers brought by Captain Ingersoll announced to me the death of the best of fathers, and destroyed the pleasing hope I had entertained of meeting that dear relation, and cheering his declining age with the society of a beloved son."[43]

On 11 May 1785, the *Empress* entered upper New York harbor as she had left it fourteen months and twenty-four days earlier, to the joyful booming of cannon from the Castle. It would take months for Morris and his partners to determine just how much profit the voyage had garnered, but almost immediately they knew the gamble had paid off. The final tally came to $37,727. Shaw thought this a modest return on the consortium's investment of $120,000, yet it represented a profit somewhat above 25 percent, after deducting the cost of the voyage, a respectable showing at a time when the country needed some positive news. Greater encouragement followed in August, when Thomas Randall brought the *Pallas* into New York harbor with $50,000 worth of teas in her hold. The *Pallas* was an English country ship that Randall had chartered at Canton, commanded by John O'Donnell, an Englishman and former India merchant who had taken American citizenship and now pursued the East India Trade from a base in Baltimore. Together, the *Empress* and *Pallas* carried 880,100 pounds of tea into New York.[44]

Within days, ports up and down the seaboard were abuzz with the news of the *Empress*'s success. The *Salem Gazette* called the voyage a "judicious, eminently distinguished, and very prosperous achievement." Other journals exulted over the cornucopia of exotic goods carried home under Yankee sails, crowing, "On the 9th instant, arrived at Baltimore, directly from China, the ship *Pallas* . . . She has on board a most valuable cargo, consisting of an extensive variety of teas, china, silks, satins [*sic*], nankeens, &c. &c." Throughout the summer and autumn of 1785, the *Virginia Journal and Alexandria Advertiser* carried advertisements for "fresh Hyson and Gunpowder teas" and other goods "received by the Empress of China, directly from Canton." The news sparked a virtual ginseng boom, as journals such as the *Massachusetts Centinel* advertised, "Wanted, a quantity of GINSENG, for which Cash, and a good Price, will be given." To educate the public, editors printed essays on the cultivation of the herb that was held "in such high estimation with the inhabitants of [China], that they never found it too dear."[45]

The significance of the *Empress*'s "experimental" voyage lingered well past the boom of the last cannon blast or the last dinner toast. It encouraged other merchants to consider the potential rewards to be worth the risk and spawned a myriad of proposals and projects. Even the future Anti-Federalist Virginian William Grayson could appreciate the national moment, and he conveyed this excitement to James Madison in a letter of 28 May 1785: "I imagine you have heard of the arrival of an American vessel at this place in four months from Canton in China, laden with the commodities of that country . . . Most of the American merchants here are of the opinion that this commerce can be carried on, on better terms from America than from Europe, and that we may be able not only to supply our own wants but to smuggle a very considerable quantity to the West Indies. I could heartily wish to see the merchants of our stage engage in this business."[46] *Does he mean slavery of Chinese?*

The backers of the *Harriett* of Boston and the *Grand Turk* of Salem had been prepared to send ships to the Cape of Good Hope; the voyage of the *Empress* made it clear that Americans could pursue voyages to India and beyond with confidence. Consequently, later that year, fourteen Yankee vessels sailed to the Indian Ocean and reached Mauritius, Batavia, Calcutta, Bombay, and the Northwest Coast of the North American continent. On her return trip to Canton for the 1786–1787 season, the *Empress* berthed with four other American vessels, including the *Experiment* and the *Hope* out of New York, the *Canton* out of Philadelphia, and, once again, Elias Hasket Derby's *Grand Turk*. Within five years, twenty-eight American vessels had voyaged to Canton, and within a decade American trade with the Orient was an established practice.[47]

"The reception our citizens have met" in China helped to transform the nascent nation from an awkward, impotent confederation of republics into a confident economic power. The lure of new markets in distant seas came at a critical moment, as the grip of economic depression had reached beyond idled seaports into the farms and homesteads of the countryside. It did not come soon enough or in enough quantity to salvage the fortunes of men like Daniel Parker or Robert Morris, and it would not save the homesteads of desperate farmers like Daniel Shays in western Massachusetts. Yet, news of the *Empress*'s voyage prompted Derby of Salem, Stephen Girard of Philadelphia, John Jacob Astor of New York, and a host of other merchants to invest in ships destined for Good Hope, Calcutta, and Canton, providing work for countless shipyards and wharves, rope works, sail lofts, instrument- and mapmakers, bookshops, and grocers as well as an outlet for the country's lead, iron, and agricultural products.[48]

Beyond contributing to the economic recovery of the republic, the voyage was a compelling demonstration that the new republican experiment would survive and, as a sign of the times, an indication that trade with the East Indies would become a new standard for confirming national legitimacy. American newspapers noted with distaste a British claim reported in Boston's *Independent Chronicle* that "the Americans have given up all thought of a China trade which can never be carried on to advantage without some settlement in the East Indies."[49] Such slights in the public sphere brought vigorous retorts. The *Salem Gazette* of 4 March 1784, offered "a PROPHECY respecting America, not unlikely to be fulfilled . . . In the year 1800 they will have opened a trade to the East-Indies." In the emergent public sphere of the new republic, it became important not just to promise achievement but also to show the world what American merchants and mariners could accomplish.

The excitement surrounding the arrival of the *Empress* came at a particularly sensitive moment in the Confederation's standing among nations. While Morris's ship lay berthed at Whampoa, the pashate of Morocco was capturing another American vessel, the *Betsey*, out of Philadelphia, demanding ransom and recognition. Weeks after Shaw's return to New York, Americans would learn that two more Yankee ships, the *Maria* out of Boston and the *Dauphin* of

So what happened?

Philadelphia, were taken by Algerian corsairs. Painfully aware that Congress was incapable of either ransoming the captives or mounting a rescue, American minister to France Thomas Jefferson hoped to forge a league of minor powers, including Naples, Rome, Venice, and the German Hanseatic towns, anchored by the naval might of Portugal, Spain, or Russia, to mount a blockade of North Africa. Now, the prospect of voyages that could bypass the roiled waters of the Atlantic, Caribbean, and Mediterranean blunted the sting of these national insults and gave further proof to the claim of American legitimacy.

Even before the *Empress* returned to New York, Shaw weighed the possibility of a return to China. He had hoped to recover the "competency" he had sacrificed during the years of the Revolution, and the experimental voyage to the East achieved his purpose, putting him on a more secure footing. But, as many later China traders found, the long awaited arrival home was attended by disappointment and loss. Shaw's return to New York had been triumphant nationally but bittersweet personally. Complicating the devastating news at Cape Town that his father had died while he was in China, he now learned that his older brother, John, had died in Gouldsboro, Maine, leaving a widow to tend for two sons and several daughters. Although younger brothers, Nathaniel and William, could be counted on to relieve the family's distress, the major's sense of duty required him to find employment nearer to home, in "an office the duties of which would allow me sufficient time to attend to my private concerns and the settlement of my father's estate." His friend and mentor Henry Knox, now minister of war in the Confederation government, secured him the office of first secretary. Shaw called for his nephews to come to Boston and took on their support. "Situated as I found myself on my return, by the death of my father and of my eldest brother," he was forced to abandon "the idea of pursuing the China business," he confided to his journal.[50]

To make matters worse, Shaw's hopes for a second voyage under Morris and Parker evaporated. The consortium of New York and Philadelphia merchants had failed. His friend and mentor, Daniel Parker, "became bankrupt, and [had] gone to Europe." Robert Morris was still solvent, although not for much longer, and was putting together a more ambitious plan. He wanted to organize another voyage of the *Empress* to China, which called for Shaw and Randall to settle as residents at Canton. The Bostonians, however, demurred at the idea of an extended commitment abroad, Shaw observed, and "as he was pleased to think the terms we required were too high, the matter dropped." Morris would send the *Empress* to China once more, but his project was scaled down to a single voyage.

original by of Dennis

Still, Shaw and Randall were able to sell their teas to the Philadelphian. In November 1785, fortune favored them again. Another consortium, this time a group of New York investors led by Isaac Sears, invited Shaw "to take a concern with them in a voyage to Canton." Shaw could write to his surviving brothers in December, "I am now certain that this undertaking will answer my most sanguine expectations." The agreement satisfied Shaw's concern about regaining a competency. If he survived the voyage, he would be "in easy, very easy circumstances." If he did not, his heirs would still be entitled to full compensation for his services, and this legacy he left to his mother.

The tone of Shaw's letters and journals during this shore leave reflected his disappointment; his correspondence grew more serious and even petulant. Personal disappointment had not dashed Shaw's national spirit, however, and he imbued the next voyage with as much patriotic significance as the first. Congress bestowed upon him the honorific title of consul and made Randall vice consul. Although the offices brought no salary, they gave the merchants a public position, and this mattered to these veterans and members of the Society of the Cincinnati.

The *Hope* weighed anchor from Sandy Hook, New Jersey, on 4 February 1786, almost two years after the departure of the *Empress*. Shaw's second voyage to "India" began on an even more secure footing than that of the *Empress*. He again had the services of his trusted business partner Thomas Randall, and the vessel would be piloted by a master mariner, James Magee, an Americanized Irishman who had commanded privateers during the Revolution and who would go on to captain voyages for Elias Hasket Derby to Canton and the Northwest Coast. Shaw's younger brother Nathaniel was on board also. This time, too, the lead investor in the sponsoring syndicate, Isaac Sears, accompanied them, along with one of his sons. The *Hope* followed the same course that the *Empress* had opened, the tedium of the voyage broken only by the need to flee the occasional privateer.[51]

The *Hope* anchored off Batavia (modern-day Jakarta) on the 4th of July, but there was little to celebrate there. The dreaded tropical sicknesses that made Batavia a notorious biological killing field had taken the ship's steward and, during the two-week layover, sent Magee and Sears to their cabins with fever. Still, Shaw could record that the Americans were received with the same displays of civility that he had recorded aboard the *Empress*. The Dutch governor-general gave them permission to trade in the city and hosted a supper in their honor, as

Indonesia a Dutch colony.

did Mr. Bynon, secretary to the Council of Justice, and they were invited to visit several of the suburban estates, or "county seats."[52]

On this voyage, Shaw filled his journals with the usual economic and diplomatic considerations, but he also paid more attention to his surroundings and included in his journals the social and cultural observations that would satisfy the curiosity of his countrymen—orphans' colleges, the exotic fashion of expatriate women, and the sumptuous lifestyles of wealthy colonists. The Batavia that he described was an enterprising global city of Dutch, creole, Armenian, Jewish, Islamic, Malay, and Chinese merchants and shopkeepers. The streets were wide, the houses ample, and the estates of the wealthy were "far superior in point of elegance to anything of the kind I have ever seen." Even so, the "great emporium of the Dutch in India" was no experiment in social harmony. Batavia offered the Yankee visitor another opportunity to consider the toll of European conquest abroad and to situate his new republican country as the exemplar of liberty in a world of tyrannical rule. Java was "a striking example of [European] wealth and energy," but progress came at a horrendous cost—"the lives of at least a million of the innocent natives, whom we ought to suppose equally dear to the Supreme Father of all."[53]

The *Hope* put Batavia behind it on July 23, navigating the Sunda Strait and South China Sea on its own, reaching Macao on August 10, and anchoring at Whampoa on the 15th. This time, there was no welcoming boom of cannon to greet the Americans as the *Hope* glided into her berth. The fate of the "the unfortunate gunner" of the *Lady Hughes* had abruptly curtailed the Western practice, "and that affair entirely abolished the custom of the ships at Whampoa saluting, on any occasion whatever." The supercargoes immediately repaired to Canton, where they secured a factory, leaving the ailing Sears and Magee downriver. In the factory compound, they renewed the spirit of cordial camaraderie that cemented the bonds of the expatriate community. The consul reported favorably, "The reception we experienced on this second voyage, both from the Chinese and the Europeans, if we except the English, was exceedingly proper. The former were pleased at the increase of our trade, and the latter, with whom Randall and I were on the footing of old acquaintance, behaved to us in a polite and friendly manner; and the gentlemen of the other ships, I believe, were equally pleased with their reception."[54]

Anticipating the eventual publication of his "private" journals, Shaw took on the role of historian to document rites of inclusion when he arrived in August. In this capacity, he reported, "Respecting the intercourse between the Europeans and the Americans at Canton, it would be only to repeat . . . Nationally and personally, we have abundant reason to be satisfied." Especially satisfying—and often amusing—for the republic's new consul, "nationally and personally," were the myriad of little rituals of inclusion that diplomatic conventions required. Shaw could report again that the factories generally provided a warm welcome and "that the etiquette between the English and me has, at last, been happily adjusted." Invitations, calls, and dining followed in good order. At times, Shaw recorded ceremonies that paid particular respect to the American visitors and told Shaw's readers that their country had a place of prominence within the community of civilized nations. One of these moments came during a dinner held in his honor at Macao in 1786:

> A circumstance that occurred at the entertainment given us by the Portuguese ought not to be omitted. The dessert, which was very elegant, was prepared in a room adjoining that in which we dined, and the tables were ornamented with representations, in paper and gilt, of castles, pagodas, and other Chinese edifices, in each of which were confined small birds. The first toast was Liberty! and in an instant, the doors of the paper prisons being set open, the little captives were released, and, flying about us in every direction, seemed to enjoy the blessing which had just been conferred upon them.[55]

Shaw's journal is silent on what the Americans thought of this nod to American ideas of liberty from representatives of the Portuguese Empire. It does not tell us if there were Hong merchants or mandarins in attendance, nor does the entry offer a glimpse into Chinese reactions to the festivities. In these lapses, however, the journal underscores a striking observation about the way in which Americans experienced China. In Shaw's writing, as well as in that of the Yankee voyagers who followed him, China was a stage setting in a national drama, the expatriate community constituted the actors, and the public sphere of the literate West—Europe and especially America—was the audience. And, although they occasionally played bit parts, the "other"—Indians, Malays, Parsees, and especially the Chinese—were largely props. The China Trade experience was part of a larger drama, the search for an American national identity and acceptance within the community of civilized nations. And it was one that played out at home and abroad, but especially wherever Americans found themselves among other peoples.

Shaw's second sojourn at Canton was not all business, but an economic per-spective dominated his thoughts, and he framed his report soberly: "Any ob-servations, on occasions succeeding a first visit, must be mainly confined to the foreign commerce." As the new American consul to China, Shaw noted that his countrymen had made significant progress in opening the Indies Trade. As the *Hope* drifted into its anchorage at Whampoa in that August of 1786, Shaw spot-ted the pennants of other American ships hoisted among the fleet of European Indiamen, including those of his *Empress of China* and the *Experiment* from New York, the *Canton* out of Philadelphia, and Elias Hasket Derby's *Grand Turk* from Salem. Indeed, over the 1786–1787 trading season, more Western ships had sailed into the Pearl River than in any previous season, and the markets were consequently glutted and the price for teas ran 25 percent more than in 1784. Yet, Shaw identified this moment as an economic turning point for his country. Not only were the "advantages peculiar to America in this instance" impressive, but also the American approach to the Indies Trade had "not a little alarmed the Europeans." And he assumed that he had acquired experience enough to offer some recommendations. But he was wrong about what constituted the American advantages. Perhaps his nationalist fervor obscured his merchant's view; perhaps he had not accrued enough experience as a merchant to under-stand the essential elements in overseas trade. The accumulated exposure that he brought to his position, after all, was modest—perhaps four years in his fa-ther's countinghouse and a year as Knox's aide-de-camp. It is not known if Shaw ever sailed as a supercargo before the voyage of the *Empress*. Consequently, he misunderstood the cargoes and the ships.[56]

He assumed that his previous experience in Canton positioned him to ad-vise other Yankee captains, and the *Grand Turk*'s new captain, Ebenezer West, found him especially helpful. He turned to Shaw repeatedly to explain the pe-culiarities of doing business in Canton. Under the Eight Regulations issued by the emperor, West learned, he would first have to find a Hong merchant as agent for the vessel. Shaw recommended Pinqua, with whom he had dealt previously, and made the necessary introductions. He also found a comprador, or local steward, to provision the *Grand Turk* while she lay at Whampoa. With the arrival of the Hoppo, West studied up on the intricacies of Canton's trading customs, which included an elaborate fee structure: 100 percent for the Hoppo's *cum shaw*; another 50 percent to cover his "opening barrier fee"; 10 percent to the superintendent of the treasury; 10 percent for "transport of duty to Peking and weighing in Government scales"; 7 percent to account for the difference in weights used in Canton and Peking; and one-fifth of 1 percent "for work of converting." West's log reported repeated disappointments and tribulations on this voyage, but when the *Grand Turk* returned to Derby Wharf in June 1787, her hold carried enough Bohea teas, chinaware, cinnamon, silks, and nankeens to bring a handsome profit to the merchant owners, captain, and crew. West attributed much of this success to the careful supervision of the new American consul.[57]

Shaw believed that the key to American success in the East—indeed, the recovery of his country's economy—was ginseng. An historic example underlay his reasoning. Recalling how the gold of Aztec Mexico and the silver of Inca Peru had filled Spain's treasuries and made her the most formidable power in sixteenth-century Europe, he predicted that ginseng would be "as beneficial to her citizens as her mines of silver and gold have been to the rest of mankind." And, the Chinese demand for the root, like the American demand for tea, would go on indefinitely: "It is probable there will always be a sufficient demand for the article to make it equally valuable."[58]

Furthermore, Americans would benefit "from making the voyage circuitous," by which he meant ad hoc, voyages directed not by theory but by expediency. Where the East India companies had the resources to organize dedicated voyages that sailed between Europe and Canton, stopping only at Good Hope and Batavia, the Yankees did not. This was the experience of other Americans, which Derby's *Grand Turk* would confirm, and even France did not have the commercial culture to support an East India company. Although Shaw dreamed of organizing an American East India company and would commission the construction of an 800-ton Indiaman for his third voyage, other merchants were embracing a more practical strategy, based on the conditions they saw. Through the 1790s, Americans were rebuilding the economy, and merchants lacked the capital and organization to build sizable ships. Business was still conducted through proprietary owners or impermanent partnerships, and the kind of corporate organization that would sustain investment was decades away. At the moment that Shaw conceived his strategy—in January 1787—none of the conditions that would support this approach were in place. Yet, Shaw was a visionary, and some of his suggestions would, in time, be embraced by American business leaders.[59]

Shaw's strengths as a nationalist propagandist outweighed his abilities as an economic strategist. In promoting the practicality of an American Indies Trade, he contributed to the emerging idea of American exceptionalism. "On the whole," he committed to his second journal, "it must be a most satisfactory consideration to every American, that his country can carry on its commerce with China under advantages, if not in many respects superior, yet in all cases equal, to those possessed by any other people."[60]

In the interim, conditions forced an alteration of the *Hope*'s mission. On October 28, Sears finally succumbed to the tropical fever he had contracted at Batavia, and the New Yorker's remains were buried on French Island, the verdant heights that overlooked Canton from across the Pei-ho River. The loss of their chief backer "deranged our intended plan of business" and sent Randall and Sears's son back to the United States. Following his own advice for "circuitous" trade, Shaw would remain to seek out fresh opportunities, trying the markets at Bengal on the Coromandel, or east, coast of India and the next year testing the markets at Bombay (modern Mumbai) on the west coast. Such was the nature of expatriate life. Death and departure were the only constants that visitors to the East could count on.[61]

Shaw's itinerary was even more circuitous than he anticipated. The *Hope* departed Macao on 2 February 1787, carrying his lengthy description of the Canton trade to Foreign Minister Jay, "conformably to [his] instructions" as consul. He had decided that he would explore the markets at Bombay and Calcutta first, but the only ship taking passengers for India was sailing to Madras. Shaw wanted to avoid the inconvenience and delay of booking another passage out of Madras and decided to wait for another India-bound vessel. Negotiating transit to Bengal at the end of the season proved more difficult than he expected. When the British country ship *Ganges* arrived at Macao the next day, Shaw was told there was no room for him. This he construed as an affront to his nationality, rather than accepting the fact that his gamble had not paid off. "The Europeans say it is an unheard-of thing to refuse a gentleman a passage in a country ship, and perhaps, had I been a European, there would not have been an exception in my case," he complained. Regardless, Shaw had to remain at Macao for another six months. He had "lost the whole season," and patience was now his "only remedy."[62]

Shaw spent his time as any number of stranded China traders had done and would again, composing a description of the natural history and "manners and customs" of his place of exile. He had at hand the extensive canon of European travelogues and exploration tracts to guide him, and he relied on these, especially Anson's *Voyage Round the World*, from which he quoted extensively, to guide his observations. Perhaps he drew consolation for his own plight from

Anson's closing line, "Though prudence, intrepidity, and perseverance united are not exempted from the blows of adverse fortune, yet in a long series of transactions they usually rise superior to its power, and in the end rarely fail of proving successful."

By July, Shaw began committing his observations to paper. The second journal of travels that came out of his exile served him as a set of reflections upon the palette of customs and values that paraded before him, and Shaw used it to situate his country's national character against the poles of what he perceived as European decadence and Asian barbarism. He reserved his harshest criticism for the "injustice of the Portuguese" in Macao. As a dedicated Whig who had railed against the imposition of the Stamp Act, Quartering Act, and Intolerable Acts, he was beginning to form a theory of international relations based on free trade and global cities. He found "extraordinary," for instance, the Portuguese claim to a monopoly of Macao's Typa roadstead, and he was appalled to witness the imprisonment of the captain of an English country ship who sought to escape a storm by anchoring in the Typa, gaining his freedom only after acquiescing to "considerable concessions." Portuguese "injustice" extended into the most mundane facets of expatriate life. In Macao, the colonial government mandated that only Portuguese subjects could own homes, while everyone else was required to rent housing, often in "a wretched condition," from them. A tenant who had the temerity to pay for improvements to a property soon found that he faced a rent increase or eviction. The Portuguese even tried to extend their regulation of colonial life to the afterworld, refusing permission to bury Protestants in a Catholic cemetery. Instead, Shaw lamented, "a bargain must be made with the Chinese, who own all without the walls, before he can be conveyed to his long home." Shaw had at hand a language, acquired in Boston's newspapers and pamphlets during the years of resistance that led up to his country's War for Independence, that he used to characterize Portuguese regulations: they were impositions, extortions, and usurpations that "a wicked and corrupt administration" employed to violate the "Liberties of mankind" and were designed to plunge "virtuous Freedom" into the "Gulf of Slavery and servile subjection."[63]

Shaw was even more surprised to discover acquiescence by the various European East India companies in the face of Portuguese impositions, "especially as it would be so easy to retaliate upon them in every port they frequent." His countrymen had overthrown such arbitrary rule, and it perplexed him to see that the Europeans had not yet learned from the American example. The dysfunctional relationship between Portuguese Macao and the expatriate community heightened his sense of Yankee exceptionalism.[64]

In spite of Portuguese "injustice," Shaw's six-month confinement to Macao was not especially onerous. Ocean breezes freshened its Praya Grande during the sweltering months of the summer monsoon that made Canton muggy, miserable, and mosquito-ridden. Each of the major East Indies companies maintained a residence downriver to accommodate its merchants in the offseason, from May to October; in addition to these "company houses," several of the English and Dutch merchants rented dwellings where their families lived in comfort. The arrangement strengthened cosmopolitan camaraderie, and Shaw found entertaining society in an expatriate community of "a harmony and good-fellowship." Over the spring of 1786–1787, the consul stood out as the lone American among European and Parsee merchants, mariners, and their families, and he could report that during his Macao detention, "every attention has been paid me that I could wish." The convivial Shaw displayed the genteel manners and talent for conversation that charmed the most sophisticated Europeans, and his company was in demand for every form of entertainment. Mr. Hemmingson of the Dutch factory offered an open dinner invitation, and the consul "went to their table whenever I pleased and without ceremony." He was "ever at home" with Mr. Vogelsang and the other Danes, and French traders included him in their repasts as well. The English residents did not leave their Canton factory until April, but then Mr. Browne, the head of the delegation, "gave me an invitation to their table, . . . and, putting his hand on my shoulder, in a familiar manner, added, 'And not only to-morrow, but every Sunday during the season, as we have fixed upon that day to entertain our friends.'" The handful of wives and other relations who resided in Macao softened the overly masculine tone of expatriate life, and "during their stay, the entertainments given them at different houses always comprehended a ball in the evening." In addition, passing ships brought fresh news and interesting company, including the Count de La Pérouse, whose expedition would vanish mysteriously the next year during his attempted circumnavigation of the world, and the officers of a quixotic French naval expedition that futilely attempted to slip past the Bocca Tigris. He could report home that again Americans would be welcomed as citizens of this small, confined world.[65]

As for the Chinese people who resided at Macao or Canton, there was little that Shaw could add to the descriptions penned in his first journal. They were,

This 1794 painting *Calcutta Port and Vessels*, by Balthazard Solvyns, depicts an Indian port as Shaw might have seen it. Courtesy of the Peabody Essex Museum.

he noted, a people "whose manners and customs may be considered like the laws of the ancient Medes and Persians, which altered not."[66] What did change, however, was his estimation of the imperial administration, an alteration in Shaw's perspective that challenged "the prevailing idea of the excellence of the Chinese government." In this more extended sojourn he realized how pervasive was the poverty he had witnessed two years earlier. He labeled it an abomination and laid its causes at the feet of the mandarins, who were "certainly culpable in suffering such things." For two years famine had stalked Canton and the provinces to the north and west, yet "a small exertion on their part would prevent the scenes of horror which daily present themselves." Ironically, at this moment the drama of Shays's Rebellion was being played out on the frontier of Massachusetts, and many of those revolutionary war veterans, former comrades of Shaw and Randall, attributed their economic distress to their own representative government in Boston, which was doing nothing to ameliorate the depression there.

As it turned out, Shaw was able to transact some business while at Macao in 1787. On July 28, the brigantine *Columbia* arrived from New York, and he shipped home a modest cargo.[67] He planned to invest the proceeds toward building "a large ship, in or near Boston, in which I purpose to return here in 1790." This enterprise would confirm both the wisdom of his vision for an American India company and the credibility of his position as consul. Not until the new year was a country ship available to carry him to India. Finally, he sailed for Bengal on the 23rd of January 1788, and arrived at Calcutta on March 15, where he would spend the next four months. Here, he took notes intended to describe yet another new world to his countrymen.

Shaw was not the first American to sail to India. In the late seventeenth century, Nathaniel Higginson had left Salem to work for the British East India Company; his brother reputedly became a pirate who cruised the Indian Ocean. More recently, William Duer of Albany, New York, went to India in 1765 to serve as Lord Clive's aide-de-camp before returning to support the Revolution and partner with Daniel Parker in supplying the Continental army. David Ochterlony left Boston in 1777 to become a cadet in the British army in India; he saw action at Koil, Aligarh, and Delhi and was eventually knighted. John Parker Boyd of Newburyport, Massachusetts, found employment as a mercenary leader for local rajahs throughout the subcontinent. India's cities were too well known to Americans to warrant an extended description, Shaw believed, and "a detailed account of them, by a person merely on a short visit here, could not be deemed very interesting." But Shaw's sojourn in Calcutta was significant because of what *he* represented. His travelogue was not intended to be a description of the subcontinent, but rather a recounting of the experiences of an American—one of the new people—in India. His purpose was to use the foreign setting as a backdrop, and against this exotic world he could more clearly trace the lines of a particularly American character, one who was urbane, cosmopolitan, and worldly and who challenged the conventional European wisdom of his countrymen as backward frontiersmen.[68]

Of paramount importance was the "cordial reception" he found in Calcutta's European community. Merchant Anthony Lambert "took every opportunity of introducing me to the best Company," Shaw was pleased to report. The social circle that accepted the Yankee consul included chief justice Sir Robert and Lady Chambers, who welcomed him with "easy politeness," and Mr. Wilton, "a gentleman of elegant manners, from whom I received repeated marks of attention and civility." A warm welcome from Mr. Addison, who had lost his father in the action at Bunker Hill and a brother in a later engagement of the Revolution, indicated that many wounds had healed during the four years that had elapsed since the end of the war. These contacts provided Shaw with more than sociability; they gave him access to information he needed in order to negotiate contracts. Lambert introduced him to the eccentric Mr. Johnson, who could claim "a thorough knowledge of Indian politics and intrigue" and who lived "somewhat in the style of a native prince." Johnson entertained the

American consul at his estate at Raspugly but kept his seraglio of twelve female companions hidden. Shaw well understood the importance of these contacts and procured the customary letters of recommendation from his Canton connections, which garnered "the usual attentions" and, of greater consequence, offers of funding and credit "as far as I might have occasion for either."[69]

Shaw criticized India's community of expatriate Europeans in only a few particulars. Although there was much to denigrate—its hedonistic extravagance and attachment to luxury, rigid class boundaries, and oppression of the indigenous peoples—the American consul muted his republican complaints. Throughout his travels along the Indian coast, in a newfangled contraption called a buggy or a sumptuous twelve-oared *budgero*, he emphasized instead the economic benefits of the European presence. Shaw praised the reliable European banking system he found there, and he approved of the opium trade that was then developing in Bengal. Stopping at Dueda on his return to Canton at the end of July, he again found a cordial reception. Shaw resided with two British merchants for almost a week, noting, "It was pleasant to observe the progress made in this settlement in the short space of six months."[70]

Curiously, an even more welcoming community awaited him in the cosmopolitan seaports of the subcontinent. It was in Calcutta that Shaw met an old Boston acquaintance, Benjamin Joy. This was a phenomenon of early American life, the diaspora of American expatriates across the globe. The dispersal was astonishing. In Calcutta also he found George Scott, a clerk who had come out on the *Hope* in 1786 with Shaw and Randall. At Bengal, he met up with Captain O'Donnell, the Irish American mariner who had commanded the *Pallas* from Canton in 1785 and the *Chesapeake* to India in 1786. Shaw provided him with a letter of introduction to General Knox. This image of India as an extended republic of Yankee expatriates presented in Shaw's journal was a curiously familiar one, designed to entice his countrymen out of the stagnation of the postrevolutionary economy and onto a world stage populated by friendly faces.[71]

Against this expansive view of global commerce, Shaw contrasted the parochial religious practices of Indian "devotees," presenting his countrymen with spectacles of behavior they were sure to regard as outlandish. He retold the now-familiar stories of a Hindu worshipper who crawled along the banks of the Ganges, "following it through all its windings, from its source to its mouth," another who allowed his fingernails to grow into the backs of his clasped hands, and others who impaled iron rods through their tongues or cheeks for days at a time. Shaw had his own firsthand stories to tell as well. He described a snake

[handwritten margin note: How about Philadelphia person who recreate the crucifixion who still carry the cross? Easter]

charmer who repeatedly infuriated a twelve-foot cobra with impunity. More sensationalist still was "the painful operation of the swing," in which a Hindu was impaled with an iron hook, then suspended and twirled around an extended pole. Beneath implausible anecdotes, Shaw did not attempt to analyze or under- stand the belief systems that drove such practices. His curiosity was limited to examining the wounds they endured until he "was satisfied that there was no deception." In his mind, Hindu believers made "the firmness with which they will bear pain" the sole measure of their faith. Nor did he seek out examples of quieter, more pietistic systems that could resonate with his readers, such as the meditative regimen of Buddhism, for inclusion in his journal. Rather, he confirmed, "the austerities practiced by them, at the present day, are sufficient to countenance the most seemingly improbable relations that have been given of what they will endure for the sake of their religion."[72]

Shaw finally left Calcutta on May 7 aboard an English country ship bound for Madras, where he spent two weeks observing economic conditions, making contacts, and extending his network of correspondents. Departing Madras on July 15, he finally returned to Macao aboard the British country ship *Clive* on September 8. On the 16th, Shaw was back at Canton, reviewing the cache of letters that awaited him, dating from the previous November. It had been a suc- cessful voyage, attendant with "many agreeable circumstances." He had made important connections and gained an invaluable understanding of the intercon- nected local economies of the eastern Indian Ocean. He could provide details of the British takeover of Pulo Pinang, now renamed Prince of Wales Island, two years earlier. The island had quickly become a major emporium for the trade in tin, pepper, and opium. At Dueda, on July 27, the two British merchants who hosted him appeared "to be making money fast" and were open to doing business with Yankees. He reached Malacca in mid-August, reported that this site, like the other Dutch establishments in the East, suffered from the growing English competition at Pulo Pinang and was now in eclipse.[73]

By late 1788, commerce in East Asia was in flux, in part because of a growing American presence, and Shaw could provide information about the economic activities of his countrymen there. Upon his arrival at Whampoa in September 1788, he found several American ships already there, ready to take advantage of the trading season. From Philadelphia had come the *Asia* and *Canton*, under Captains Barry and Truxton, respectively, and from New York, the *Jenny*, under Captain Thompson. Expected were the *General Washington* from Rhode Island, and the *Jay*—the newly rechristened *Hope*—from New York under his partner

Randall. He had heard rumors, also, of an expedition being organized in Boston and destined for the Northwest Coast to collect furs for the Canton market. This intelligence likely described the consortium of six Boston merchants who had financed the voyage of the *Columbia Redivia* and *Lady Washington*, an expedition that had been underway since leaving Boston at the end of September 1787. The vessels' names could be taken as markers of how far the Americans had progressed in the three years since they had won their independence. The *Jenny* and *Hope* harkened back to the familial traditions of a provincial world, the *Jay*, *Columbia*, and *Lady Washington* celebrated the struggle for independence, while the *Asia* and *Canton* marked the entry of the new nation onto the world stage.

Shaw was not oblivious to the significance of the historic events that were reshaping global commerce and that he had helped to initiate. Although Britain's twenty-one Indiamen dominated the trade at Canton that season, the Swedes, Danes, and Spanish each sent two ships only, and the French sent but one. Yet, the new nation had sent five vessels to Canton, comparable to the number, if not the tonnage, of the Dutch East India Company. The moment marked another kind of turning point for Yankee commerce. "Certain it is, that the ships from our country have never brought so large a portion of their funds in ready money," Shaw observed. The ginseng that had filled the holds of the American vessels was quickly losing its value as the West glutted Chinese shelves with the root, and Americans would soon replace ginseng with Spanish dollars. The problem raised important commercial questions: How should Americans pursue the Indies Trade? What goods could they ship? Should they continue the traditional provincial policy of free trade, opening competition to any number of small merchants or consortia? Or should they follow the European example "of managing their commerce with this country by national companies and with large ships," the result of two centuries of mercantilist regulation? For the new republic, the decision "must ultimately be determined by her own experience," he concluded, following the dictates laid down by the great philosophe Montesquieu in *The Spirit of the Laws* (1748). For his part, Shaw elected to experiment with the European strategy, sending orders to Boston for the construction of a single large Indiaman. He wrote to Randall and others in hopes of establishing an American India company. The decision nearly bankrupted him.[74]

As Shaw approached the end of his sojourn, he could again report his confidence that the new nation had been accepted by Europe's trading companies. "Nationally and personally," he concluded, "we have abundant reason to be satisfied." Yet, Shaw's preoccupation with diplomatic ceremony glossed over a harsh financial reality. The success of Randall's voyage was in doubt. His partner had sent letters aboard the *Washington,* which reached Whampoa on October 28, indicating that the *Jay*'s departure from New York would be delayed until December. Randall reported further troubles at Madeira, where complications with the local merchants brought further delays. It was not likely that the *Jay* would reach Whampoa before Shaw's departure and "could not, in common probability, be expected to save her season." It was now "absolutely indispensable" that Shaw return to Boston as quickly as possible to oversee the construction of his new ship. Consequently, it seemed, his decision to remain in the East and pursue opportunities in Canton and Calcutta "entirely independently" of the *Jay*'s voyage had been a wise one.

The *George Washington* left Macao on 28 January 1789. At North Island in the Sunda Strait, he learned that he had missed the *Jay,* carrying Randall and his brother, Nathaniel, by six days, an "aggravated disappointment." On February 17th, however, the *Washington* slipped into the harbor at Krakatoa Island, where Shaw spotted the *Jay.* The reunion was one of "inexpressible joy." Understanding that he could not catch the height of Canton's trading season, Randall had wisely elected to test the markets at Batavia then proceed to Bombay before turning to Canton to take advantage of the following season. Reassured, the partners made arrangements "for meeting again in America, in 1791, then to pursue our fortunes together." When the *Washington* raised anchor off Krakatoa on February 20, it carried both Shaw brothers home. On the afternoon of 5 July 1789, they passed Newport, Rhode Island, where they were saluted with seven guns, and by the evening anchored just below Providence.

In his three years abroad, Samuel Shaw had missed Shays's Rebellion, the Constitutional Convention in Philadelphia, the ratification debate, *The Federalist Papers,* Washington's inauguration in New York, and a host of weddings, funerals, and anniversaries among family and friends. The United States to which he returned was a new nation; no longer a confederation, it had become a unified republic. And its national character was taking shape, as Americans navigated the contrasts between themselves and the Europeans, Chinese, Indians, and Sumatrans whom they encountered in the South Seas.[75]

Shaw resettled in Boston, having made some money in his Canton ventures, but not a competency—what later China traders called their *lac,* or the minimum $100,000 that it was said a man needed to establish a family in comfort. His attention was now directed toward the construction of a new ship, designed especially for the China Trade. Amidst overseeing the work in Daniel Briggs's shipyard in Germantown, south of Boston, and collecting a cargo, he found time for domestic pleasures among the expansive Shaw family. And the fame that he craved now came his way, curried by a network of supporters who had worked to stoke his reputation as he labored half a world away. In February 1790, Washington renewed Shaw's commission as US consul to China, in time for his anticipated departure the following month. He was honored again in July, when Harvard College awarded him an honorary master of arts degree at its annual commencement. In attendance were his correspondent John Jay, who was now serving as the country's first chief justice of the Supreme Court and who received an honorary doctor of laws degree, as well as graduates Thomas Boylston Adams, Josiah Quincy, and John Quincy Adams. Shortly after, he was elected a Fellow of the American Academy of Arts and Sciences, along with Jay and other eminent figures.[76]

Meanwhile, Shaw and Randall pursued their plans for a return to China. In September 1789, they joined a throng of thousands to watch the launching of his new vessel, which they christened the *Massachusetts*. It was a "Yankee-built" ship, of nearly eight hundred tons, constructed "expressly for the Canton trade." The vessel reflected Shaw's belief that American merchants should follow the approach established in Europe's two centuries of experience in the Indies Trade. His two voyages in modest vessels did not shake his conviction that an American India company, sending substantial East Indiamen directly to China, was the right course for his countrymen. Consequently, the firm of Shaw and Randall had ordered the largest vessel ever constructed in a Yankee shipyard. On 28 March 1790, Captain Job Prince set a course for Canton. The *Massachusetts* carried $15,000 in currency but no ginseng. Aboard were Shaw and his twenty-nine-year-old brother Nathaniel. The newspapers reported the departure prominently in their SHIP NEWS columns in April: "On passing the Castle, she saluted the flag of the United States with 13 guns—which was immediately returned from the Castle."[77]

This celebratory spirit was shaken when the *Massachusetts* reached Java. Landing at Batavia, the capital of the Dutch Empire in the East Indies, Shaw learned that the authorities there had suspended trade with all American merchants "on account of evil reports which had been circulated concerning them by persons unfriendly to their commerce." It was a severe national rebuke. Once again, Shaw was reminded of the tenuous status of American legitimacy among the great nations. Taking up his consular pen, Shaw wrote remonstrances to the shabandar of Batavia and to President Washington. There was little the

American administration could do, however. After 1783, the US Navy existed only on paper. Other powers, from the Barbary states along the Mediterranean to the Great South Sea, tested the new nation's ability to protect its citizens and its commerce in distant oceans.[78]

The *Massachusetts* pressed on, anchoring at Whampoa Reach on September 30 to discharge her cargo and make repairs. Although the ship had reached China near the beginning of the tea season, Shaw found the trading conditions were poor. He expected to meet up with Randall, who had gone ahead to make preparations for his arrival, but his partner had not been at Macao to greet the ship. He was still in Canton trying to make up a cargo for the return voyage and had contracted "a considerably large" debt. Worse still, the freight in the hold of the *Massachusetts* found no buyers, and Shaw had brought only $15,000 in specie. Even the ship itself was a loss. Despite the graceful lines that shipwright Daniel Briggs had designed into the ship, she had been built of unseasoned white oak and loaded with green masts and spars. Consequently, the *Massachusetts* and her cargo had begun to rot by the time she reached the tropics and, when the sealed hatches were opened at Whampoa, the air within was dead enough to snuff a candle. To ensure that the voyage would not be a total loss, Shaw sold her to the Danish company whose sole vessel had been damaged in one of the devastating typhoons that racked the South China Sea. The Americans' voyage would not be a complete loss. The ship had likely cost $40,000 to build, but European buyers were desperate for ships and the Danes reportedly paid $65,000.[79]

Finding the Canton market saturated, Shaw searched for other sites where he could invest his capital. India beckoned, as did Europe. He elected to disperse the firm's capital throughout the emerging global economy. He booked passage to India for Nathaniel and himself aboard an English country ship. From there, Nathaniel would return to Boston, where he would meet up with Randall and purchase another vessel to replace the *Massachusetts*. Shaw would sail on to Ostend, where his Dutch contacts could help to arrange shipments back to the East. On 12 January 1791, the brothers sailed for Bombay.

Once again, the debilitating climate of the East shattered the Shaw brothers' dreams. Nathaniel contracted tropical fever, and within a month, he was dead, at age twenty-nine. Samuel had no recourse but to continue on with his plans. He found an American ship that would carry a portion of his funds back to Boston; the rest he took in a Danish charter to Ostend. In January 1792, he sailed from Belgium for New York. With luck, he might return to China in time for the 1793–1794 season.

Again, his return to Boston was a whirlwind of business and social activity. Within months, he had a new ship, the *Washington*, and a new wife. In August 1792, he married Hannah Phillips of Boston, daughter of an eminent and wealthy Boston merchant; he was thirty-seven, she was a month shy of her thirty-sixth birthday and, it appears, a spinster. It was a notable enough pairing to warrant a notice in the *American Apollo*. Hannah fretted, but Shaw dismissed her concerns, observing that his fate was in the hands of Providence. Marriage neither changed his plans for a third voyage to China nor delayed his preparations for it; rather, it made the voyage to earn his *lac* more pressing.[80]

In February 1793, Shaw took the *Washington* to Asia, this time making directly for Bombay, in company with his youngest brother, Benjamin. The outward voyage was expeditious. Shortly before departure, he wrote to one of his new in-laws, "A better ship than we have need not be under any man's foot." In Bombay, however, he came down with the tropical disease that had felled Isaac Sears and Nathaniel. Doctors at the English factory diagnosed his condition as an ailment of the liver from which few Westerners survived, and they urged Shaw to sail to Canton, where he could find better treatment. The passage through the South China Sea was difficult. Fever tormented Shaw for much of the voyage and worsened when a typhoon battered the ship and drove her off her course. It took three months to reach China, where Shaw found refuge in a house at Macao that Randall had rented on 2 November 1793. There, Randall and Benjamin tended to their patient as best they could, helplessly watching the fever worsen, abate, and then return with renewed intensity. By the end of the trading season, they decided that Shaw stood little chance of surviving the disease if he remained in China.

On 17 March 1794, Randall commanded the *Washington* out of Macao, with the ailing Shaw and his brother Benjamin aboard. He had hired a surgeon for the voyage, James Dodge, who watched over the patient. They had come to China escorted by a French fleet and left with a British fleet escorting British East India Company ships. The world had changed dramatically in the previous year. Napoleon had broken the Peace of Amiens in 1793, and the world was now in flames. Washington had proclaimed a frail neutrality, and the "reception our citizens have met" among the now-warring powers remained a concern even ten years after American independence had been declared. In the East, the bonds within the expatriate community were tattered, but they often held. Randall found support among his British comrades. On his return to Boston he made sure to report the "polite attention" he had received from Admiral Gower and was "much indebted for favors rendered him." At St. Helena, he "received every

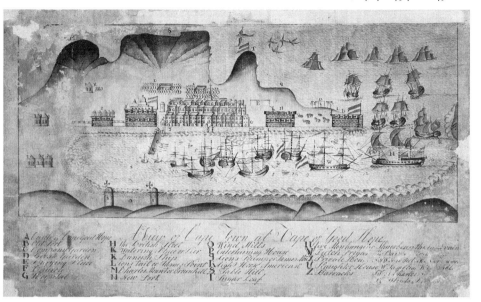

This *View of Cape Town at Cape of Good Hope*, drawn by a sailor aboard Elias Hasket Derby's *Light Horse*, c. 1788, depicts the South African roadstead as Shaw knew it. He was buried here in 1794. Courtesy of the Peabody Essex Museum.

mark of respect." Yet, on the American coast, the *Washington* was boarded by the English frigate *Blanche* and "treated with a degree of insult."

At Good Hope, the ailing Shaw received the best care the Royal Navy could provide. Dr. Gillon, surgeon to Lord Macartney's embassy, then stationed aboard the man-of-war *Lyon*, and Dr. Macrea, surgeon to the Indiaman *Hindostan*, tended to him. By this point, however, the disease was "too inveterate for medical aid," as Randall related. With his brother and partner by his side, Shaw expired at 3 p.m. on 30 May 1794, off the Cape of Good Hope. He was not quite forty years of age. Three days later, the *Washington*'s crew assembled, and his body was committed to the deep. By August 16, newspapers from Bombay to Boston were reporting the sad news. Hannah Shaw learned the details in a dispatch sent by Randall when the *Washington* reached Sandy Hook on August 24.[81]

Samuel Shaw's decade of encounters in the "Great South Sea" belie the mythologies of the "Old China Trade" and of early America. He was not part of a merchant elite who dominated the political and social life of his country. He did not pioneer new routes or discover new lands or markets. He did not establish a great commercial empire, build an elaborate mansion festooned with

Asian symbols, fill museums with exotic curiosities, or even earn his *lac*. Nor did he rise from poverty to the opulence of Newport or Cherry Hill. Rather, Shaw typified the far greater numbers of China traders who struggled to achieve middling respectability, and who died in a distant land or returned to America empty-handed. The story is mundane rather than heroic, and for this, Shaw's narrative reflects an important American experience, because it was so ordinary, so typical.

The many crises of the republic's "Critical Period," as Harvard valedictorian John Quincy Adams described conditions in July 1787—especially threats on the high seas—challenged the legitimacy of the new nation and accentuated the dilemma of an uncertain national identity. Americans' first contacts with the East, signaled through voyages of "commerce and discovery," opened new worlds (in the national consciousness), ushered in an era of economic recovery, and fostered a China Trade genre of writing through which Yankee travelers and expatriates began to fashion a national identity. Shaw's voyage to Canton on the *Empress of China* in 1784 not only inaugurated American trade with the East but also publicized the republic's entry onto the world stage. What the Americans found in the Great South Sea challenged their colonial assumptions about the world; it bound them closer together as one people; and it legitimized their status according to the criteria of their age—as an independent nation and men of character.

"Tempestuous Seas of Liberty,"
1785–1790

I N THE DECADE after Samuel Shaw's first voyage to China, an American exodus swept into the Great South Sea, carrying the word that a new people had arrived to take their legitimate place among the community of nations. They spilled out from the wharves of Boston, Philadelphia, New York, and countless smaller seaports into Calcutta, Pondicherry, Sumatra, Ceylon, and even insulated Japan and returned with cargoes of tea, pepper, coffee, and silks that provided a timely injection of capital into the withered economy and stimulated the recovery of the early 1790s. Their success did not come easily. Yankee merchants and mariners girdled the globe during a period of profound tumult and disorder, of real and quasi-wars, of embargoes and blockades, of piracy and privateers, and they found that the "tempestuous seas of liberty" continued to challenge both the country's overseas commerce and its national reputation. Consequently, ambiguity and clouded expectations continued to form the context for American encounters in the East and for the birth of the nation, and Yankee voyagers continued to demonstrate particular sensitivity to any question about the legitimacy of the United States.

Their early contacts with the peoples of Asia, Africa, South America, and Europe's Asian expatriates offered this "new people" a significant measure of their national character. They believed that Americans who traveled abroad, as much as those who remained behind, contributed to the creation of the republic and, especially, toward the formation of an authentic national identity. Indeed, contact with the regions beyond Europe, navigated between "civilized" Europe and the "barbaric" East, afforded Yankee voyagers a more nuanced palette from which to fill in the details of an emergent national persona. An essential step in acquiring membership into the community of civilized nations was gaining recognition in the expatriate enclaves of the distant outposts of Europe's empires in the East. If the advent of the new nation astonished Europe, it was especially surprising beyond the Atlantic, where virtually no one knew who the Americans were. The United States would continue to be a new world over the next half century, and its encounters abroad took the form of a long introduction. And it was in their reading of these introductions throughout the Southern Ocean that Americans at home celebrated their progress in gaining recognition of their nation's legitimacy.[1]

We do not know how many Americans traveled to the East during the height of the Indies Trade. Tabulating the number of Yankee ships that sailed to some part of Asia, from Constantinople to Cape Town to Hawai'i, the numbers of crew and passengers they carried, and the numbers of people they left behind in distant ports is complicated by the scanty records that have survived. But, historians are beginning to wrestle with the question. Caroline Frank, for instance, has estimated that some 2,900 Anglo-American "Red Sea men" sailed into the Indian Ocean as pirates during the seventeenth and early eighteenth centuries. After independence, hundreds of ships plied the waters of the East Indies each year; some of these left a record of their travels, but many—perhaps most—left little trace. It is, therefore, difficult to estimate how many Americans were residents of an Indian factory or beachcombers on a Pacific isle and for how long they stayed. Much of the evidence is necessarily anecdotal. There were the 700 men and women who languished in North African prisons, most taken during the Barbary crisis that lasted from 1784 through 1815, some taken after 1815. Others, like Samuel Patterson in Fiji or John Jewett at Nootka, were held captive for extended periods. Several hundred men resided voluntarily at Canton, of course, some, like William C. Hunter, remaining for decades. A few American women sojourned at Macao, as well, including "traveling spinster" Harriett Low and Salem matriarch Rebecca Chase Kinsman. Others lingered throughout the East as resident merchants, at Calcutta, Bombay, and Madras, or at Île de France and Bourbon, at Manila, or at Batavia and Sumatra in Indonesia. After 1812, missionaries in India, Burma, China, and elsewhere complemented the numbers. Perhaps a hundred missionaries traveled through these lands. There were, less famously, scores and perhaps hundreds of "alone men" or "lopers" on Más Afuera, Hawai'i, in the Ascensions and the Falklands, and throughout Polynesia and Micronesia. The impact of their writing on the formation of a national identity was more significant than the numbers of Americans who sailed to the East, the duration of their visits, or even the tons of goods imported in the Indies Trade.[2]

One month after the *Empress* plowed through the ice-choked East River for balmy Canton, the *United States* cleared Philadelphia's Delaware River for China. Hearing that the markets might prove more profitable in a closer destination, her supercargo altered course for India, reaching Pondicherry (Puducherry) in December 1784. So startling was the display of the Stars and Stripes in the waters of the subcontinent that British observers reporting to Governor Warren Hastings garbled the ship's name, reporting it as the *Independent States.* The feat was not lost on Americans back home, however. Soon, the public press carried the notice of the arrival of another Yankee ship from Bengal: "The *Chesapeake* was the first American vessel allowed to hoist the colors of the U. States in the river Ganges, and to trade there," crowed the *Salem Mercury* on 2 June 1789. Within three years, the *Columbia Rediviva* and *Lady Washington* had opened a fur trade for Americans between the Northwest Coast and China, and the nation's newspapers preened over the expedition in the same language of global achievement. When the *Columbia* returned to Boston in 1790, American journals lauded the ship and its crew as the first Americans to circumnavigate the globe. Within a year of Washington's inauguration as president of a new people, twenty-eight Yankee vessels had voyaged to Canton, and within a decade American trade with the exotic Orient had become an established motif in the nation's culture. Laurels—some given grudgingly, some bestowed more liberally—came even from skeptical Europe. Observers such as Alexis de Tocqueville described Americans' Indies commerce in heroic terms: "An American navigator leaves Boston to go and buy tea in China. He arrives at Canton, stays a few days there, and comes back. In less than two years he has gone around the whole globe, and only once has he seen land. Throughout a voyage of eight or ten months he has drunk brackish water and eaten salted meat; he has striven continually against the sea, disease, and boredom; but on his return he can sell tea a farthing cheaper than an English merchant can; he has attained his aim."[3]

Americans discerned the results of continual striving even in the new federal government they established in 1789 and in the economic recovery the country experienced over the next decade. On taking office in April 1789, Washington had hoped that Robert Morris would stay on as minister of finance, but when the Philadelphian declined, the president turned to the brash genius of his former aide-de-camp, Alexander Hamilton. In a series of reports on the country's finances that he presented to the new Congress beginning in January 1790, Hamilton construed the idea of public credit in terms of national character as well as economic policy. The country's ability to secure loans from foreign investors was contingent on its reputation for prompt and full repayment of its debts; however, the Confederation Congress had been consistently remiss, and in failing to meet its obligations had earned itself a contemptible reputation for its blithe refusal to address the nation's most pressing problems. In reestablishing the public credit through prompt repayment of its debts, then, Hamilton asserted, the constitutional government would also restore honor to the national identity.

The Indies Trade occupied a central place in Hamilton's economic planning, and the nascent Congress at last acquiesced to his program of financial recovery. To take full advantage of the profits now coming in from the world's bazaars and marts, Hamilton reestablished the customs offices that had fallen into disrepair, with the flow of revenue now channeled into a national rather than imperial treasury. In short order, Congress fell in with the country's sudden "rage for East India voyages" and passed its first tariff on 4 July 1789, encouraging the Indies Trade through a 10 percent discount for all goods entering on American vessels. This would play a supporting role, focused entirely on commerce, however, and in the early decades of the republic there was no talk of conquests and colonies. Six years later, the teas, silks, and porcelains carried from China were valued at $1,023,000 and by 1810 this had grown to $5,745,000, as Hamilton's plan achieved its purposes, although his archrival Thomas Jefferson, now president, reaped the benefits. By then, in a second irony, Jefferson and his colleague and accomplice James Madison had sown the seeds that would erode the country's participation in global trade.[4]

Still, in these early days, signs of resurgence could be seen in New York and Philadelphia, where the *Empress*'s voyage had been planned, and from the myriad of more modest ports along the coast. In Boston, there were faint indications of an improvement in maritime business conditions by 1791. The port's newspapers noted the uptick in the number of ship arrivals, especially from the new markets opened in the East, marking its emergence from the lingering depression of the 1780s. Federal officials at the old customhouse took in revenues of $450,000 in 1792, $600,000 in the next year, and $700,000 in 1794, and these figures grew after the completion of a new customhouse that abutted India Wharf. For the country as a whole, treasury officials tallied exports at $15,000,000 in 1789, $20,400,000 in 1790, and $42,105,961 by 1803, remaining more or less steady until President Jefferson imposed his infamous embargo in December 1807.[5]

The India Trade primed much of this recovery. On his subsequent voyages, Samuel Shaw had wisely tried his luck in the marts of Bengal and Calcutta, following the openings established by the *United States* in 1784 and preceding the voyage of the *Chesapeake* in 1789, and he took pains to identify the best sealanes for American merchants who had the courage to follow. This truly was an Indies Trade, spanning the globe from Jamaica to Japan, rather than strictly a China Trade. By the end of the eighteenth century, more American ships visited India than China, carrying principally cotton and silk textiles, as well as more modest cargoes of sugar, indigo, and spices. Cinnamon, cardamom, and Malabar pepper filled the shelves of early American pantries. Shaw was one of those who had even envisioned an American Indies company that could compete side by side with the great European East India companies. Most Yankee merchants preferred to trade as independents, however, "each ship pursuing its own advantage going wherever a profitable market could be found," and it was in this individualistic approach that Yankee ships found success. In the period 1795–1805, American trade with Bombay and Calcutta exceeded the India Trade of all the European nations combined. How much of this global trade fueled the economic recovery of the 1790s has been a source of some debate among historians. Of the $42 million of goods that Boston exported each year during the 1790s, only $217,266 worth was sent to the East. But the returns brought Yankee merchants valuable cargoes to reexport to Europe, and it was the revenues from this turnaround trade that filled the national treasury and the pockets of merchants and seamen. The timing of the income, if not the amounts, was instrumental in the recovery of a nation reeling from eight years of war and five years of economic stagnation. It quickened the revival of fishing and the advent of manufacturing. Still, the economic outlook remained troubled. Europe's monarchies had clung to their mercantilist policies, and even the country's former allies restored their traditional trade barriers once the Treaty of Paris was finalized in November 1783. In response, Yankee observers frequently described the seas before them as "boisterous," "turbulent," or "tempestuous."[6]

Britain would not relax its Navigation Acts until 1840, some sixty-five years after Adam Smith had published *On the Nature and Causes of the Wealth of Nations* and the Second Continental Congress had approved its Declaration of Independence. Immediately after the peace was proclaimed, American news journals described political conditions overseas as chaotic, frequently fretting that the accounts they received contradicted each other. The *Boston Magazine* for February 1784 sought reports from sources of "undoubted veracity" that could make sense of developments in the Caribbean, and it boasted that in the previous autumn "the harbor is crowded with American vessels, which are admitted to an entry on the same footing as their own vessels trading to that place." This news was intended to counter "what has been asserted to the contrary." American merchants and mariners desperately sought out reliable information to plan voyages and safeguard their cargoes and crews, but a steady current of contradictory reports presented an unsteady, kaleidoscopic image throughout the period. Like the *Boston Magazine* eighteen years earlier, the *Salem Register* for 11 March 1802 complained that reports from the French West Indies "have long remained contradictory." The long-anticipated arrival of merchant fleets—traveling in convoy for protection—was rumored to be again delayed until France and Britain signed a definitive treaty. It was unclear, but unlikely, whether a uniform system of government would be restored to the French possessions, especially as Toussaint L'Ouverture appeared to be in complete control of Haiti, a change the *Register* applauded. And so it would be eight years later, when war erupted again between England and the United States.

It was on these tempestuous seas across the globe that the challenges to national legitimacy smoldered, like embers that ignited into flames of war then settled as kindling for another flare-up. Amidst the unsettling reports of tensions with Britain, conflict in the Islamic Mediterranean, and the disturbing developments of the French Wars, Americans had to wonder if the republic could even survive. Up through the Treaty of Wangxi in 1844, Americans could expect only instability, and indeed turbulence, on the "seas of liberty," which they hoped to liberate. American vessels, far from home waters, underarmed and undermanned, all too frequently became caught up in foreign intrigues or claims controversies. European merchants could hope for succor from their powerful navies and ingenious diplomacy. How could American merchants hope to protect their own shipping, they wondered, when their pleas to Congress to reestablish a national navy capable of defending Yankee vessels and crews were met with handwringing sermons about the sad state of the national treasury?[7]

The first overseas challenge to American legitimacy came as early as 1784, out of the Ottoman East, when Morocco's emperor Malay Muhammad (Side Mohammed) ordered the capture of an American vessel as leverage to force Congress to sign a commercial treaty. Even after negotiators settled a peace, American ships bound for the Mediterranean found themselves subject to cap-

[handwritten: done to children in Egypt]

ture and confiscation. By 1790, nearly a hundred Americans languished in the cells of Morocco, Algiers, and Tripoli, many dying in grueling work camps and under punishments like the sadistic *bastido*, or foot beating. In time, the number of captives grew to as many as seven hundred, and the country's newspapers decried the situation as a national disgrace. When ambassador to France Thomas Jefferson beseeched Congress to raise a fleet against the Barbary pirates, he was told that the $400,000 in the national treasury would not accomplish the task. Given the country's lack of a navy and the regional divisions that prevented formulation of a coherent defensive strategy, American policy followed that of Europe—capitulation. The Washington and Adams administrations sent tribute in the form of money and even the Portsmouth-built warship, the *Crescent*. James Madison could only lament that the situation would "confirm . . . all the world in the belief that we are not to be respected, nor apprehended as a nation in matters of Commerce."[8]

A greater challenge erupted in the month after Washington's inaugural in New York City, emanating from Paris, London, St. Petersburg, and Vienna, but necessarily incorporating the sea lanes to Calcutta, Canton, and Bombay. In May 1789, revolution erupted in the streets of Paris, spread throughout the provincial countryside, and soon tore apart the peace in Europe. The instability benefited American trade in the early years of the conflict, as Yankee ships brought food to Europe and connected Western ports with their colonial dependencies. But global war came in March 1793, triggering the outbreak of an anticipated conflagration between France and the major European powers that would further roil the troubled waters of the Atlantic world. The news reached the United States that Louis XVI had been beheaded the preceding January. What Americans then called "the French war" and "the European maritime war"—what we know as the Wars of the French Revolution—quickly transformed the conditions in which American ships engaged the world.[9]

Through the next decade, Americans faced conditions overseas that were remarkable for their confusion and uncertainty. A maelstrom of conflicting commercial and maritime rules emanated from the European capitals and from their colonial dependencies, imposing, rescinding, and reasserting blockades of their enemies' ports. In the spring of 1794, war with Britain seemed imminent for a time as a result of a British Order in Council issued on 6 November 1793, which amounted to a total blockade of the French West Indies (to coincide with its military campaign to conquer French colonies). By the time news of the order reached American shores, the British had already captured over two hundred

Yankee vessels in the Caribbean. The British, however, revoked their dictate the following January, and in November 1794 emissary John Jay, Samuel Shaw's *Empress* correspondent, signed a treaty of amity and commerce with Britain, sacrificing the country's overseas commerce in the hope of securing peace. It worked. Although the Jay Treaty stood mute on the issue of impressment and prevented American ships from the "country trade"—the traffic carried between the South Asian ports of India and Ceylon and East Asian marts in China, Sumatra, Malaysia, and the Philippines, and held as a monopoly by the East India Company—the result was a respectable commercial boom.[10]

China traders could not avoid passage through the Atlantic and so were caught up in these wars. In June of 1793, the *Portland* was taken off the Scilly Islands, diverted by a British man-of-war from its destination of Le Havre with a cargo of Pennsylvania flour. First mate Edmund Fanning described the engagement in his widely read *Voyages Round the World* (1833). Fanning's developing sense of national identity, based on a constellation of traits that framed the American in terms of his authenticity, gentility, and patriotism, crystalized in the interaction, when the Royal Navy commander barked, "You d____d Yankee, hoist out your boat this instant and come on board, or I will sink you!" Carried to Falmouth, Fanning rescued his crew of impressed seamen aboard a Royal Navy frigate, denying his heroism as simply the act of a "true Yankee."[11]

Jay's efforts to improve relations with England only worsened matters with France. After Congress ratified the Treaty of Amity with Great Britain in mid-1795—the roundly excoriated Jay Treaty—the French retaliated with a declaration of war on vessels flying the Stars and Stripes, severing American commerce with the West Indies. By June of that year, when Washington learned that a French privateer had captured the American merchant ship *Mount Vernon*, the former president understood the loss as a portent of the inevitable deterioration of relations. Congress held hearings on the growing hostilities in June 1797, outraged to learn from Secretary of State Timothy Pickering that France had refused to receive US ambassador Charles Cotesworth Pinckney, and French privateers had seized 316 American merchant ships, mostly in Caribbean waters. Over the next year, as that number soared to more than 600 vessels, President Adams informed Congress that French agents had rebuffed his negotiators and demanded consideration—a bribe—before peace talks could begin. Congress and the public erupted at the so-called XYZ Affair and what they perceived as an intended insult to the nation's honor. In early July the legislature cancelled the 1778 treaties with its former ally and, in "an act further to protect the commerce of the United States," authorized both its warships and American privateers to retaliate against French attacks. Thus began the Quasi-War, which involved the country in the European conflict most of them had hoped to avoid and laid a foundation for similar retaliation against Britain in 1812.

Despite increasing provocations, the Yankee republic had not prepared for war. Instead, President Adams and Congress expected the nation's mariners and merchants to carry on naval operations until a navy could be rebuilt. In 1798, 452 merchantmen armed for defense; between 1799 and 1801 the number soared to 933. The result was to popularize the association between the republic and its people. As privateers fought off French warships and hauled vanquished ships into prize courts, their countrymen hailed their victories alongside those of the nascent national navy, banqueting on Canton porcelain and donning Indian silk that bore images celebrating the victories of merchant vessels like the *Herald* and *Grand Turk*.[12]

The world's newest republican powers concluded their disagreement in the Convention of Peace, Commerce, and Navigation in 1801, but it did not halt the depredations on American shipping. The French Wars that had come four years earlier and had expanded into a global war fought in the sea lanes of the Mediterranean, Caribbean, and Indian Oceans, as well as the Great South Sea, continued through another decade-and-a-half to challenge the young republic's fitful struggle to maintain its neutrality and ensure its legitimacy. Over the next few years, one source reported, French privateers seized more than five hundred American ships, and nearly another thousand were lost to British marauders. As Spain, Denmark, Naples, and the Netherlands fell before Napoleon's armies, the emperor marshaled their privateers against American trade with Britain as well. During 1809 and 1810, Danish and Norwegian privateers captured 160 American vessels.[13] *What a mess at sea!*

The Indies Trade merchants could not avoid these dangers, and the Indian Ocean and Arabian Sea became one of these tempestuous seas. The *Empress* had proven that the United States could send a vessel across the world to China, but in the years following that triumphant voyage, the nation could not protect its citizens or their property even in the familiar waters of the Atlantic, Caribbean, and Mediterranean. During the Quasi-War, French privateers filled choke points like the Bay of Bengal and the waters around Île de France (Mauritius) and Bourbon (Réunion). In one notable moment, Americans in Boston and Philadelphia read about their countryman on the far side of the world, Captain Nathaniel Silsbee, who led a convoy of five Yankee Indiamen out of Calcutta battling French privateers, even coming to the aid of the East India Company's packet *Cornwallis*. To offer some protection, the Adams administration sent warships beyond the Cape of Good Hope. In 1800, the USS *Essex* became first to show the flag in the Indian Ocean. Anchored off Cape Town in March of that year, Captain Edward Preble described the Dutch reception in the same language of national legitimacy that Shaw had used a decade earlier, confirming for Secretary of the Navy Benjamin Stoddart, that "this government has been uniformly friendly and obliging. They have treated me with distinguished attention and have uniformly tendered their best services."[14]

As the booming cannon of the *Empress* had introduced Americans to Canton and the world a decade earlier, the guns of the *Herald* and the *Essex* proclaimed the nation's legitimate status across the tempestuous seas that girdled the globe. Theirs was not a search for approval, however. They sought—indeed, they felt entitled to—the recognition that belonged to one of the world's great civilized nations. Americans were coming to believe that their early contacts with the peoples of Asia, Africa, South America, and Europe's Asian expatriates confirmed their nation's legitimacy and established their national character. In the world that lay "eastward of Good Hope," navigated between "civilized" Europe and the "barbaric" East, the new people were discovering who they were.

CHAPTER TWO

Amasa Delano
Opens the Great South Sea
1790-1820

(handwritten annotations: "This is the same Delano as in Franklin Delano Roosevelt well. perhaps a maybe line")

W HEN TWENTY-SEVEN-YEAR-OLD Amasa Delano of Duxbury, Massachusetts, embarked from Hancock's Wharf in Boston for the port of
Canton on a beautiful, crisp morning in March 1790, he was sailing
aboard the largest and most admired vessel of its day, the "Yankee-built" ship
Massachusetts. Delano had commanded vessels on his own, but now he berthed
as only second mate. Still, he had reason to be thankful for his posting. The
country was on the verge of release from the wrenching depression of the 1780s,
aided by Americans' entry into the China Trade just six years earlier. The opportunity to join the enterprise drew mariners from New Hampshire to Virginia,
with a few English and Irish thrown in, and the beautiful lines and workmanship
of the *Massachusetts* attracted multitudes of curious spectators. On her arrival
in Batavia and Canton, even European merchants and seamen, masters of the
India Trade and commanders of great Indiamen three times as large, were no
less impressed, and Delano would write that they became regular and admiring
visitors. She was acknowledged to be "the handsomest vessel in two ports."[1]

In Delano's time, Americans had a term for such displays of native ingenuity, clever innovation, and determined enterprise. They believed these qualities
represented the elements of the emerging national character that they associated
with the fictional namesake of Benjamin Franklin's almanac, and they called a
countryman who exhibited these traits a "poor Richard." Franklin, of course,
had epitomized such ingenious self-made men, but he was only the brightest
star in this constellation, a revolutionary generation of self-fashioned tinkerers,
inventors, and innovators who included Thomas Jefferson, Benjamin Rush, and
Benjamin Banneker. Delano's 1817 memoir of the China Trade, *A Narrative of
Voyages . . . in the Pacific Ocean and Oriental Islands*, contributed to the formation

of this American identity by representing the men of the *Massachusetts* as simi-
larly enterprising. In other passages, he described himself as the naïve and curious everyman whom his countrymen knew as the "real Jonathan," the truculent
nationalist they called "Yankee Doodle," and the cosmopolitan global traveler
whom Oliver Goldsmith and Samuel Johnson had popularized as a "citizen of
the world." Delano's concern with using his China Trade experiences to con-
struct the national character mirrored Samuel Shaw's preoccupation with "the
reception our citizens have met" in the East. And, in utilizing his three circumnavigations of the globe to tell his fellow Americans something significant about
their emergent identity, Delano helped to introduce a distinct body of writing
that we might call a China Trade literature.[2]

    Like other Americans who sailed to the East during the first decade follow-
ing the War for Independence, Amasa Delano was bred to the sea and "much
accustomed to the salt water." Born on 21 February 1763 in the "industrious,
enterprising" seaport of Duxbury, home of Separatist stalwart Miles Standish
and Indian-fighter Benjamin Church, he was descended from John Alden and
Philippe de Lannoy, who came to Plymouth on the *Fortune* in 1621. As the eldest
son of a ship's carpenter and later master builder, Samuel Delano (1739–1814),
and a mariner's daughter, Abigail Drew (1742–1811), young Amasa and brothers
Samuel and William were already learning about ships and shipbuilding virtually in the cradle.[3]

    As a boy growing up in a colonial seaport on the eve of the Revolution, Amasa
absorbed the rhetoric of Whig politics along with boatbuilding and sailing, and
he was impatient to go into battle. In 1777, as General John Burgoyne marched
to Albany in his failed effort to separate New England from the rest of the provinces, Samuel, Sr., was held as a prisoner of war on board the *Rainbow*, a British
man-of-war anchored at Halifax. The impetuous Amasa ran off to Boston to
enlist in the Continental army when he met his father returning from captivity.
To the boy's great embarrassment, Samuel Delano insisted that Amasa abandon
his comrades and accompany him back to Duxbury. "He was," his biographer
writes, "very much mortified in being thus deprived of an opportunity of performing the daring feats of a true blooded Yankee." But, in September 1779,
the sixteen-year-old Amasa returned to Boston and joined the crew aboard the
privateer *Mars*, which captured a single British vessel. Delano seems to have
experienced more adventure than he was ready for during the "terrible winter"
of 1779–1780, "suffering every hardship that was possible for men to endure."
Many of the early China traders had participated directly in the War for In-

dependence or knew its hardships vicariously through family and friends, and consequently they developed a frosty attitude toward Britain. Delano, too, came out of the war with strong views on privateering, embargoes, impressments, and debtors' prisons. Yet, he was not scarred by his experiences as others had been, and he seems to have developed at an early age a broad tolerance for the ambiguities of the world. Throughout the next decade, he knocked about the Atlantic, touching at Virginia, Bilbao, and various West Indies ports, working his way up from common seaman to mate and then captain. In 1786, he commanded his first vessel to Cayenne, off the coast of Brazil, and he made several subsequent voyages to the West Indies. When the opportunity came in 1789 to sail to China, he had already acquired the skills, experience, and confidence to embark upon the world stage. Looking back to his youth, Delano reflected, "At that period my mind was elastic and ready to draw agreeable emotion from every companion, every object and every event."[4]

"The voyage, with which I shall commence my narrative, was made in the ship *Massachusetts.*" Thus, Delano opened his *Narrative* of a *Voyage of Survey and Discovery*, recounting the ill-fated passage of the American Indiaman to Canton in 1790. In this introduction he inscribed several beginnings—that of a voyage, of a personal journey, and of a nation's history. In the China Trade literature of the early republic, these stories were interwoven.[5] This was the vessel commissioned by Samuel Shaw and Thomas Randall, and, for both merchant and seaman, a living symbol that Americans had achieved economic success in the East and, as a result, that the nation had turned the corner of the depression of the 1780s.

The *Massachusetts* was the pride not just of Delano but also of the public press, which celebrated the ship's departure with the kind of nationalist enthusiasm they had lavished on the *Empress of China* six years earlier. As she passed the fortifications known to Bostonians as the Castle, her cannon boomed thirteen salutes to the federal flag, which were returned from the shore, reported the *New Hampshire Gazette* for 7 April 1790. Other accounts touted her "as fine a ship, of her dimensions, as ever went to sea," both "an excellent sea boat" and a beautiful ship. Yet, the voyage was not without its risks. In September, as the *Massachusetts* entered Sunda Strait, she weathered a typhoon that tore other ships to pieces and swamped a Danish vessel and her entire crew. As the ship approached Batavia in August, three men who were painting the hull fell into the ocean and midshipman Thomas French plummeted from the main yard to his death. Delano's famous mortality chart in the opening pages of his

View of Foreign Cemetery on Dane's Island, attributed to Sunqua, c. 1840, was likely the final resting place for a number of Delano's comrades aboard the *Massachusetts*. Courtesy of the Peabody Essex Museum.

1817 *Narrative* detailed the fate of the officers and crew. Of the sixty-one men who boarded the *Massachusetts* in 1790, forty-eight (78%) were no longer living, many having died from disease and accidents at sea. The East, especially, had been a dangerous place for American mariners. They had "died at Macao" and "died at Canton," were "lost overboard off Japan" or "murdered by the Chinese near Macao," and enslaved in Algiers. Their remains were scattered across the East, "buried . . . outside of Batavia roads," "buried under the walls of Macao," and "thrown overboard in the Straits of Sunda." Shaw himself had contracted a liver disease at Calcutta and died at sea in 1794 off of the Cape of Good Hope. This was the less glamorous—and, in modern treatments, less noted—aspect of the Old China Trade. For their part, however, mariners like Delano would not only mythologize the superiority of American technology and skill but also celebrate the "decency and honour" of the men who sailed.[6]

The *Massachusetts* followed the track of the *Empress*, anchoring at Whampoa Reach (Huang-po Island) on September 30 to discharge her cargo and make repairs. Although the ship and men found a warm reception from Canton's Hong merchants and Europe's expatriate factors, Delano and Shaw found there the disadvantageous trading conditions that would doom this and many other China Trade voyages. Now, the crew scattered to the far corners of "India." Shaw fled to Calcutta, Delano's brother Samuel sailed to the Northwest Coast of North America, and others signed on with Danish or British ships.[7]

On 14 April 1791, sixteen years after the volunteer farmers at Lexington and

For true Yankees such as Amasa Delano, the sight of American vessels anchored at Whampoa served as a marker of his nation's legitimacy. Courtesy of the Peabody Essex Museum.

Concord had challenged the king's authority over them, Amasa Delano joined the British navy. It was a decision that warranted an accounting to his countrymen, and Delano framed his explanation in the terms that a self-conscious Yankee would appreciate. "Set adrift" at Canton after Shaw had sold the *Massachusetts* to the Danish East India Company, he accepted Commodore John Mc-Clure's invitation to join the Bombay Marine scientific expedition of the East Indies. He enlisted aboard the *Panther* "as a volunteer officer" and was "subject to none but the Commodore's command." After a shaky start—the British crew did not welcome an interloper, especially one from their former provinces—Delano's enterprising spirit won them over. As in other relationships that he later developed in his global travels, he injected a nationalist imperative. "My fellow officers jocularly called me Jonathan," invoking the common European term for a crude, unsophisticated American, Delano recorded, "and soon learned I had the curiosity which is considered as characteristic of my countrymen." As he discovered the following May, at San Pio Quito, in the Babuyane Islands, north of the Philippines, his new friends were happy to exploit his penchant for pranks and jokes. Yet, years later, he would recall that he had been happier on this cruise than in any other position he ever held. His description of the voyage of the *Panther* and *Endeavor* to the Pelew (Palau) Islands, Sumatra, Java, New Guinea, the Spice Islands, Otaheite (Tahiti), and Owhyhee (Hawai'i) presented his countrymen with an image of the American as, in Samuel Shaw's phrasing, the "new man." Those back in "Yankee land" who read his journals and heard him speak, those who would later read one of the editions of the *Narrative*, discovered in his recollections an American who left home as a real Jonathan and returned as a citizen of the world.[8]

Delano did not sail in the China Trade, as we think of it today. Nor did Edmund Fanning, Richard Jeffry Cleveland, or any number of renowned China Trade writers. For the seafarers of the early republic, the vast expanse from Cape Town to Hawai'i was known as India, and they sailed in the Indies Trade, touching at any tropical port that might bring a profit. Long after these scribbling mariners had first encountered the world, they portrayed themselves as guides to exotic lands. The books they composed were intended for several audiences and incorporated the elements of travelogue, gazetteer, navigational guide, and handbook to the Indies Trade. Delano seems to have had some kind of book in his mind even before the *Massachusetts* sailed, and toward this end he preserved his own journals and copied or appropriated other ships' logs. In his travels, he established a pattern of reflection and writing that steadied his mind through anxious times and occupied his thoughts through tedious journeys, "drawing from the adventure . . . lessons of wisdom and prudence." Like so many Americans who traversed the globe during the years of the early republic, he took up the pen "to relieve my mind" and "employed myself in making observations." In the end he wrote an account that would introduce these new worlds to his countrymen.[9]

In this role as literary guide to exotic worlds, the "true-blooded yankee" spoke both to and for his countrymen. Delano came to understand how writing a text of "useful knowledge" legitimized a man in the early republic, and he alerted his audience to this feature in the subtitle of his book, promising readers a *Voyage of Survey and Discovery, in the Pacific Ocean and Oriental Islands* much like that of James Cook, John Wallis, John Byron, and other pioneering explorers. In describing the East as exotic, he seems to have anticipated an audience of "readers generally" who were interested in natural history for its own sake as well as for its scientific promise and commercial potential. Consequently, the "character as an American" that he took on in the book was in part that of an enlightened man of commerce embarked upon voyages of commerce *and discovery*. Through page headings that read "from Sooloo to Macao," "from the Ilse [*sic*] of France to Bombay," and "from Calcutta to America," he carried readers in Philadelphia, New York, and Boston along to an imagined East that had been newly opened by American travelers. There was a freshness in his words, and even though he published a generation after Shaw's first contact with China, he wrote as if his voyages constituted the first American encounters in Asia. He advised his readers that Macao's weather was favorable from March to the end of October with temperatures between 62 and 79 degrees Fahrenheit, described the spring and autumn realignments of the monsoon winds, and warned of the "Typhon, which always happens at the shifting of the monsoon."

An essential element in Delano's project was the introduction of an Eastern vocabulary into American discourse, and he shared the exotic terms he had learned in Asian ports with his countrymen through eclectic descriptions of local customs. At Amboyna, he recorded that the Dutch residents threw a party by announcing they would "*smoke a pipe*." In Jakarta, adjacent to one of the country's mosques, one could fine a large hollowed log "which the natives call a tom-tom, and which is an enormous drum." On Jolo Island, in a meeting with a Malay *sunahdar*, Delano related, "We smoked a hubble-bubble of tobacco and opium, and were friends." In Sumatra, the traveler noticed that British officials rode in "a chair for two persons, drawn by one horse, [which] is also much used in their parties for pleasure . . . It is light and airy, and . . . is called a buggie." And, throughout the South Seas, the Malaysian people smoked bangue (hashish).[10]

Infused throughout his *Narrative* is the idea that the East described by an enterprising Yankee had to offer something more than the cabinets of curiosities that could be viewed in Rembrandt Peale's Philadelphia museum or the East India Society in Salem. As he traversed the Pacific and Indian Oceans during the 1790s, Delano kept notes on the commercial potential he found there, and his *Narrative* was designed to impress on its mercantile audience the image of lands of unbounded economic potential. In India, Delano noticed not only that the name of the Eastern coast—the Malabar Coast—meant "mountaineer," referring to the mountains of Hindustan, but also, for his more commercially inclined readers, that "pepper is a very important article of trade in this country," as were the areca nut, wild cinnamon, and cotton goods. This was both an observational technique and a writing style that he polished on later voyages. These descriptions of the bounty of the Pacific world recalled the awed discourse of seventeenth-century New World observers such as John Smith, William Wood, and John Josselyn. On the outgoing leg of one voyage, anchored off the South Atlantic isle of Cayenne in 1786, Delano discovered his own "new world": "The country along this coast abounds with the greatest variety of wild beasts, beautiful birds, serpents and reptiles of any country I was ever acquainted with." In a later description of the Bass Islands in the South Sea, he related, "A lagoon along the Storm Bay passage, in southwestern Tasmania, is one of the pleasantest places nature ever formed; all its shores are lined with beds of oysters . . . in such quantities, that one man may easily load a boat of a ton burthen in two hours."[11]

Inherent in Delano's construction of the East as a site of unconstrained bounty was a preoccupation with "useful knowledge" that was characteristic of the early republic, and his personal voyage of commercial exploration aboard the *Panther* and *Endeavor* moved in parallel alongside that of Commodore McClure's scientific expedition. Like Shaw, Delano had come to the East to investigate opportunities for trade, not as an amateur anthropologist or geologist, but to earn a competency—his *lac*, as Canton merchant Nathaniel Kinsman later phrased it—that would enable a man to retire from the perils of the sea, purchase land, perhaps a farm, provide for his family, and leave something to his children. needed at least 100 K.

Delano saw prospects for "a very profitable trade" throughout the region, and his journals, and the book they became, prescribed the way in which American merchants should conduct business in the East. He counseled sending a ship of 300–400 tons—much smaller than the *Massachusetts*—well armed, commanded by a competent trader and navigator, and freighting a cargo of Western manufactures, from a European or American port to Surat, Madras, or Calcutta, there to add local goods, and proceed to various ports throughout the South Sea. Because his was an age in which commercial news, even in the well-traversed Atlantic, came through sketchy rumor or thirdhand accounts that were weeks and months old, the driving principle in Delano's advisory was expedience. A voyage to the East was necessarily more desultory than one that sailed to Bristol, Le Havre, or Bilbao. Consequently, he learned to employ a language of contingency in his writing: "Proceed then eastward through the straits of Malacca: thence to the coast of Borneo, in latitude 2° north; try what could be done at Sadang in that island; what also in the vicinity; and then follow the coast to the north east, trying the trade as far as the river Borneo." From Borneo, one could sail northward to try the ports at the several harbors of Cape Misfortune, Sulu, and Mindanao, seeking especially pearls and mother of pearl, universal commodities in the Eastern markets. In these waters, the southwest monsoon was expeditous, but the northeast winds afforded a safer passage. If the mariner-merchant found the markets in the Philippines were depressed, he could sail eastward to the Celebes, "always inquiring of the natives for the best places of trade." The prudent trader would set his destination for Canton, of course, as goods fetched the best prices there, even better than in Europe or the United States. Critical to the success of the enterprise, even more than in Atlantic or Mediterranean commerce, were the character and capabilities of the commander. In particular, he should be possessed of those qualities that Delano and other China Trade writers associated distinctly with the national character—perseverance, enterprise, and promptitude. His reflections on the qualities of an effective merchant were deeply etched into the American consciousness, from Franklin's Poor Richard and Father Abraham to the names of the vessels Americans sent overseas—the *Enterprise, Commerce, Industry,* and the ship Delano built upon his return to Boston, the *Perseverance.*[12]

By 28 April 1791, the Bombay Marine expedition had reached its first stopover, Sumatra, where McClure could provision his ships and Delano could gather more data for the book that had begun to form in his mind. Fortunately, he was not "called to study . . . the sinister intentions" of men, as he would on too many later voyages. But here he did encounter the tropical fever that felled so many Western travelers, and the crews of the *Panther* and *Endeavor* "began to be sick, and to die, in a most extraordinary manner." They reached Batavia on September 16, already a familiar landfall for American ships pressing on to Canton or Manila. As the capital of Dutch outposts in the South Sea, Batavia boasted dockyards, hotels, and, like Macao, a remarkably cosmopolitan population of some 200,000 Chinese, Japanese, Africans, and indigenous Malays. Delano jotted notes on customs that mirrored the best and worst features of his own countrymen. The Chinese shopkeepers and customs officials were "enemies to idleness" but "deceitful to the last degree." The Javanese would "apply themselves" in farming and shipbuilding. The Amboynese constructed elegant houses with split cane windows "very neatly wrought in different figures." At times, others seemed to violate the republican principles that Delano extolled. He found Malaysian peoples "notoriously treacherous" and "void of morals." Early in the *Narrative,* he drew a very brief character study of Cockawocky, "a forward, officious, and blustering fellow" from the Palau Islands, who had represented himself as an able guide and interpreter but who repeatedly failed as a guide or negotiator. Yet, Delano depicted the true Yankee as a true citizen of the world who learned how to adapt and do business despite the blustering of officious natives, condescension of petty potentates, and conniving of mendicant mandarins.[13]

By 10 June 1791, McClure's expedition had sounded the Palau Islands. Here, Delano recorded the same displays of natural beauty and bounty, and the same kinds of natural dangers, he had observed earlier. It was along one of the Palaus' treacherous reefs that the *Antelope Packet* had wrecked in 1783, seeking the spices for which Europe's consumers paid dearly. And here he began to form the character studies that distinguished the *Narrative* as a new kind of American text, introducing the peoples and places of the wider world to his countrymen and enabling them to situate the national character between the poles of aged Europe and the exotic East. Whatever little his readers knew of the indigenous peoples of the Pacific before, as the killers of Cook and the crew of the *Antelope Packet*, Delano dismissed. The peoples of the Palau Islands were specimens of "interest, cordiality and happiness." They demonstrated a blithe curiosity and even "lively sympathy." Above this "truly amiable people" stood their king, Abba Thulle, whom Delano presented in terms that might have astonished his readers. He had seen a popular drawing of the king, which he included in his 1817 book, although he presumed that many of his readers already knew it well. It was, he thought, a perfect representation of the traits of the noble Polynesian, except that the man it portrayed was "too savage and ferocious." Rather, more than any man he had ever met, Thulle possessed "the very first natural abilities" and was a figure of "wisdom and benevolence." So magnanimous a figure was the king that he gave his enemies three days' warning before he attacked. Although a "naked savage," this was a figure that Delano held out as one whom Western leaders could emulate. Americans, he implied, could learn much from the character of leaders such as Commodore McClure and Abba Thulle.

Delano's East, then, was a complex place in which the conventions of backward natives and enlightened Westerners did not bear scrutiny. He complicated Americans' understanding of the world in other ways. Against the example of the enlightened Abba Thulle, he contrasted instances of Europeans such as Mandan Blanchard, whose "arrogant and licentious" behavior oppressed the indigenous peoples and corrupted their cultures. On an earlier voyage, an English commander had left Blanchard in the Palau Islands to assist the king and inculcate Western ideas of civilization among the people there. Instead, for three years, the avaricious European had used his authority to satisfy his lust and greed until

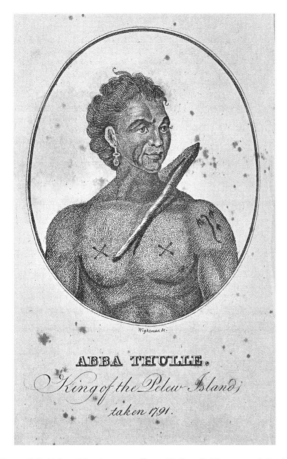

Abba Thulle, King of the Pelew Islands, 1791, from Delano's *Narrative* (1817). Courtesy of the William Reese Company.

he was ambushed and murdered. The example of Mandan and other would-be Western conquerors inverted the East that Americans had imagined.[14]

At the end of October 1791, the expedition reached New Guinea, and here Delano was introduced to the East as a place of dangerous waters and dangerous men. The *Panther* and *Endeavor* had followed the course set in Captain Cook's log, and continued to find his directions unreliable. Cook had suggested the existence of a strait that supposedly sliced the southern coast of the island, and they were there to plot its location. Almost immediately, however, the crews were engulfed in a "day of adventure" on October 26. With the tide turning against them and Delano on the morning watch, a fleet of nearly a dozen canoes approached. Although armed, the New Guineans displayed the universal signals of friendship in those waters—a white cloth for a flag and palmfuls of water scooped onto their heads. Assuming the New Guineans had come to trade, the *Panther*'s watch let down their guard and suddenly found themselves under a hail of arrows from the "false savages." The ship's doctor, who had gone out in the longboat to parlay, was butchered, the quartermaster shot in the hip, and Delano shot in the chest, a painful but not critical injury.

Delano used the episode to reflect upon treachery—the term commonly used in this age to describe assaults by indigenous peoples upon Westerners—and interviewed fellow officers about the massacre of twenty men from the *Queen Indiaman* in the same waters a few years earlier. This was not the East of Abba Thulle, certainly, but Delano's conclusions, gleaned from reviewing the journals of the *Queen Indiaman* and other Indies Trade vessels, were complicated. Introducing a theme to which he returned in later writing, Delano reminded his American readers, "The causes of this hatred are, in great measure, trace- able to our own misconduct toward them." Indeed, his position as an American provided enough intellectual distance to moderate his estimation of blame. When Europeans rationalized their conquests over the Indian subcontinent, he retorted that their own conduct on Ceylon (Sri Lanka) had "been marked by a disposition" for "treachery and cruelty." In Canton, he had learned from the Hong merchants, "when the Europeans first visited this country they were received by the Chinese with great kindness and hospitality . . . but the strangers soon began to abuse this indulgence." And, if earlier explorers had demonized the peoples of the South Sea as a savage people, Delano concluded, "it is not therefore a matter of surprise that the natives should encourage and transmit this hatred toward Europeans."[15]

When the *Endeavor* returned to Macao in March 1793, Delano was again set "adrift," this time without the influence of a Samuel Shaw to find a new berth. He had hoped to return to Boston and saw an opportunity to do so when he met up with William R. Stewart, captain and supercargo of the ship *Eliza*, fresh from a sealing voyage in the South Atlantic by way of Cape Horn, and he formed a partnership with the New Yorker. Going to Canton, however, they were immediately stymied by China's arcane customs regulations. Stewart unwisely had left the *Eliza* at Lark's Bay off of Macao and went up to Canton to "learn the state of the market" for the 18,000 sealskins aboard his sloop, a breach of Chinese commercial etiquette. The Hoppo assumed that he had done so intentionally to avoid Whampoa's extortionate port charges, ordered the house where Stewart was staying surrounded by soldiers, and demanded compensation. Fortunately, "after much difficulty and anxiety," the Dutch consul, Andreas Van Bramm, intervened and negotiated a $500 fine. For his part, Delano had learned a practical lesson about the customs of the East and used the anecdote as "a warning to other masters of vessels" to be wary of the stringent regulations of the Chinese officials.

Fortunately, too, Van Bramm was in need of a vessel to sail to the Netherlands, and the *Eliza* suited his purpose. He mistrusted Stewart's ability to navigate the vessel, however, and asked Delano, whom he considered a "regularly bred seaman," to take command to Ostend. It was a curious decision, as Stewart had acquired ample experience in the Indies Trade. He had served as supercargo of the *Experiment*, the second American vessel to sail to Canton, and on this, his third voyage to Canton, he had pioneered a route around Cape Horn and discovered the seal-rich potential of Más Afuera Island off of Chile. Landing at Île de France on 10 July 1793, the Americans encountered a political situation that was even more troublesome than anything they had experienced in Canton. France's revolution had turned the world upside down, bringing global war with the recent abrogation of the Treaty of Amiens. As soon as the *Eliza* arrived, French colonial authorities ordered her embargoed. Months of idleness and anxiety followed. Eventually, Delano and Stewart saw no recourse but to sell the ship and cargo, purchase a larger vessel, the *Hector*, and in February 1794 set a course back to Canton by way of India. In describing the troubled voyages of the *Eliza* and the *Hector* twenty years later, Delano reemphasized the harsh realities of the China Trade. Chastising armchair travelers who claimed that American ships routinely sailed directly to China and returned to the United States festooned with opulent cargoes of tea, porcelain, and spices, he wrote of "broken" voyages, ad hoc affairs in which the perils of war, weather, and glutted markets forced captains to stop at any port "eastward of Good Hope," load whatever goods were available, and carry them to some other port in India, China, or the Pacific in hopes of a favorable exchange.[16]

Delano sighted the Malabar Coast at the end of February but found that rumors of a "general" war had depressed the markets there as well and "discouraged all persons from putting property into our ship." By the time the *Hector* had anchored at Bombay, he and Stewart had begun to fear that the voyage would be a total loss. The only way out of their dilemma was to accept an exorbitant offer from a British merchant—one Dunlap—who insisted on holding a bond on the ship as collateral while they probed the markets along India's Malabar and Bengal Coasts. As Delano described it, they would "yield the golden dream" of finding their fortunes in the opulent East. True to form, he turned his disappointment into an opportunity to collect useful knowledge, and he filled the *Hector's* log with observations on the natural history and cultures of the subcontinent. At Ceylon, he found another global city and cosmopolitan population. In the capital, the "large and beautiful town" of Columbo, he encountered Europeans, Indians, Africans, and "almost every race of Asia." It must have been an astonishing sight for a young man from Duxbury, Massachusetts. Again, he noted the abundance of the East, including the "greatest delicacies in the desserts of our European tables," among them, cinnamon, pineapples, pomegranates, melons, and almonds. Here, he learned to chew betel nut "till it has produced a considerable degree of intoxication." At Calcutta, he hoped to find that business had not been affected by the war and memorized the exchange rates for cowry shells, the sole currency accepted in the bazaars there. He continued to keep an eye open for goods that could fetch a dear price in the European or American marts. One of these was jute, and he noted for future reference that the fiber served a variety of uses, although its application on ships was limited because the hemp did not adhere to pitch or tar, the essential coatings to deflect the corrosive effects of salt water.

Delano continued to compile his navigational observations as well, anticipating the notoriously violent tidal bore that made the Hooghly (Hugli) River one of the world's most dangerous channels. A violent gale had already battered his ship, and he fretted over its stability and the security of the cargo. Despite Delano's vigilance, the *Hector* became another victim of Calcutta's treacherous waters, battered by "a dangerous current in the sea of our fortunes." When they reached Calcutta, the Americans found that the combination of typhoon and tidal bore would cost them $10,000 in damages to the ship and her cargo.

The news in the local bazaars was even worse. On arriving at Calcutta, they found that here, too, the outbreak of general war had dampened most merchants' willingness to risk their capital on a voyage overseas, and trade was stagnant. Sailing on to Bombay, they struck up a correspondence with Benjamin Joy, the American consul at Calcutta. Joy offered to do what he could for them, but the downturn had compromised his own affairs, and he had no capital of his own to procure a cargo. Still worse news came soon after they arrived at Bombay, as the newspapers reported that President Washington had imposed an embargo on American trade. The stoppage would be temporary—thirty days—but the same papers brought rumors of war between Britain and the United States and predicted that East India Company officials would confiscate American property. The unscrupulous Dunlap used this turn of events as an excuse to call in his capital, taking the *Hector* as downpayment, then suing the Americans for the remainder. Joy intervened to compel Dunlap to accept a token payment for the ship, but this left the Americans virtually bankrupt. Ultimately, the voyage of the *Hector* was a financial disaster for Delano and Stewart.[17]

Delano blamed himself for these misfortunes, but the conditions he had faced would trip up many more Americans who tried their hand in the China Trade: he had attempted to manage a large enterprise over great distances with insufficient capital. The partners' "high hopes were thus disappointed," and the additional losses left both men "wounded and mortified." Delano now found himself again stranded in a strange new world, this time at Calcutta, with scant prospects, little hope, and one gold mohur, or $7.00 in East India Company currency. Only friendship and society mediated his ill fortunes, as they would time and again. He was able to secure passage to Philadelphia aboard Jeremiah Stimson's *Three Brothers*, and he made his way to Duxbury sometime in 1795.[18]

Four years in the Pacific had changed him, and he considered his return from Calcutta as the close in a chapter of his life. His cherished memories of adventure as a respected officer aboard the *Panther* and *Endeavor* were "mingled indeed with regret" of his disappointing efforts aboard the *Eliza* and *Hector*. The homeward voyage aboard the *Three Brothers* and subsequent years of manual labor left him time to brood over bad decisions and poor luck. He kept up his correspondence to distant ports, however. His contacts in Calcutta reminded him that in business timing was critical, and they reassured him that an arrival either six months earlier or later would have made him a wealthy man. He returned to Duxbury's shipyards and secured a comfortable position supervising ship construction and repair. With his expectations of fortune and fame dashed, Delano embraced "ordinary comforts, diminished activity, and the still small pleasures of a life of peace" that came with middle-class life in his home town.[19]

Delano did not return to sea for another five years. It took that long for him to recover his spirits and mend his finances. In 1799, a decade after his first voyage to China, now at the advanced age of thirty-six, Amasa mobilized the Delano family resources, particularly harnessing the sweat equity of brothers, Samuel and William, to build a new vessel designed to meet the harsh realities of the China and India Trades. Unlike the *Massachusetts*, with its cargo of ginseng and Spanish dollars and high expectations of an immediate return to Boston

filled with teas, silks, and porcelain, this vessel would sail with an empty hold to the South Sea. Delano would pack in a cargo of sealskins and follow the country trade from port to port until he had earned his *lac*. Her name—the *Perseverance*—perfectly suited her mission. This would be a voyage on his own account.

The *Perseverance* departed Boston on 10 November 1799, commencing Delano's second circumnavigation of the globe. He returned to Boston three years later, having rounded Cape Horn and touched on the coast of Chile, the Galápagos Islands, Hawai'i, Canton, and Cape Town. He was no longer a green Yankee, and when he described the peculiarity of Spanish fashion in colonial Chile, he could reflect that "to a gentleman who has been accustomed to travel, it would not be worthy of much notice." The captain continued to compile notes on navigation and trade for a China Trade guide that he seems to have been contemplating, and he filled the ship's journal with minute observations of currents, depths, and uncharted islands. He had become an avid reader as well. His *Narrative* would quote at length from Byron's *Voyage* and Wallis's journal of the *Dolphin* for 1766 and 1767, cite William Dampier, James Cook, and Jean-François de Galaup, Comte de La Pérouse to dismiss the mythological terrors of doubling Cape Horn, and incorporate George Vancouver's remarks on Valparaiso in his description of that place. He interviewed everyone who would give him a hearing, learning, for instance, from a Spanish commander who had sailed with Alessandro Malaspina's 1789–1794 expedition that he could find good harbors among the islands along the coast of Chile and, although hair seals were abundant there, "it was hazardous for a vessel to go to look for them." From these sources he learned to write in the parlance of the explorer. Readers of his *Narrative* could learn, "In running down for Owhyhee, the easternmost of the Sandwich Islands, it is best to keep in about 20° north latitude" and "a ship, sailing through the straits of Formosa, will find it most easy and plain navigation to make Formosa, in which case she should be kept in latitude 22° 00'."[20]

Delano's records served a dual purpose of discovery, locating legitimacy on terms that were both national and personal, as Samuel Shaw had written a decade and a half earlier. To this end, he forged a literary strategy he had learned under Commodore McClure, keeping notes for a travelogue that would document his contributions to natural history and, ultimately, secure him a reputation as a gentleman of the world. But he would do so as an American. He was no longer a lieutenant in the service of the Bombay Marine, his nation was no longer in thrall to the British Empire, and this condition of independence distinguished his *Narrative*, marking the author and his countrymen as new men who should be taken seriously. As the *Perseverance* sailed in the same waters that had been charted by Cook and Anson, Delano tested their observations against his experiences, verifying or correcting the charts compiled by the illustrious explorers of an earlier age. Consequently, Delano commented that the *Naval Gazetteer's* description of Coquimbo Bay was "nearly correct" and James Colnett's positioning of the island of St. Felix was consistent with his own observations of it but that explorer's description of Stephen's Bay in the Galápagos was dangerously mistaken. Years later, he would even appropriate the traditional sobriquet for maritime expeditions—"voyages round the world"—for the subtitle of his own memoir. It was the title used by virtually every renowned explorer of the seas, from William Dampier's *A New Voyage Round the World* (1679), to George Dixon's *A Voyage Round the World; but More Particularly to the North-west Coast of America* (1789), and beyond.[21]

Delano's comments came with a caveat. He advised his readers that they should not accept his observations blithely, as he had not credited those of earlier explorers. His measurements might be off a bit, and so the seasoned mariner would verify these for himself. He added that his observations of longitude were "generally correct." Yet, many bearings, such as the *Perseverance's* position in the Falkland Islands in January 1800, could not "be depended upon," and the jumble of high islands, inlets, rocks, and shoals that he found there made navigation dangerous. In framing his discoveries in this way, Delano's writing revealed a pronounced element of cultural nationalism. His was a particularly American form of exploration, one not sanctioned or supported by the government but embarked upon by an individual and for individual gain. Like *The New American Practical Navigator*, which Nathaniel Bowditch was publishing in Boston at virtually the same moment, Delano composed a testament to America's vernacular Enlightenment. In this incarnation of the Age of Reason, anyone could go out into the world, test a theory against his or her own experience, and so make a significant contribution to Western science. Consequently, the language that Delano chose for his own *Voyages Round the World* was one in which he wrote "from my own knowledge, and from what I have been credibly told by those who have visited these parts." In seeking the authority of higher learning, he used sources such as Rees's *Cyclopædia*, "except as I am satisfied from my own experience are correct."[22]

Such was the way that the Indies Trade developed for Americans. The Amasa Delanos and Samuel Shaws gathered all the information they could find, exploring islands, surveying bays and inlets, and traversing distant lands, to learn where goods could be procured and where they would sell.[23] They disseminated their global intelligence by word of mouth, or committed it to ship's logs and journals, or published it in books, essays, and newspaper accounts. A few tried to keep their discoveries secret, as did Jonathan Carnes when he located the source of the pepper trade of Sumatra in 1794, but these efforts would be frustrated. For the most part, the trade developed through cooperation and the publication of "useful knowledge." As Delano recalled of his 1802 sojourn in Canton, "The method of doing business is soon learned, as any European or American who is acquainted there, will give a stranger any information relative to the general way it is transacted in."[24]

The *Perseverance* had embarked on a sealing voyage, and Delano planned to gather pelts from islands throughout the South Atlantic and Pacific and sell them in Canton, with stopovers at Hawai'i and Cape Town for provisions. Like other prospective China traders, he had in mind the voyage of the *Columbia*. When the *Columbia* returned to Boston in August 1790, Captain Robert Gray reported on the favorable market for otter and sealskins in Canton, and his ecstatic account had primed an entrepreneurial bubble. Over the next decade, Americans learned where to search for furs and mastered the art of collecting sealskins throughout the South Sea. One of these seagoing pioneers was Delano's erstwhile partner, William Stewart, who had opened the coasts of Chile and Peru to American sealers in 1793. On his previous sojourns, Delano had learned that furs commonly sold in Canton for $1.00 per skin, with payment rendered in teas, at a time when the monthly wage for a New England mariner was about $8.00. Prices could fluctuate in unnerving rhythms, however, fetching as much as $4.00 per skin and as little as thirty-five cents. The optimistic Delano pinned his hopes on a lucky draw. By late January 1800, the *Perseverance* had made the Falkland Islands and in mid-March rounded Cape Horn. The crew collected furs at Más Afuera, following Stewart's instructions, then anchored at Juan Fernández for provisions.[25]

The *Perseverance* arrived at the Galápagos at the end of June and reached Hawai'i on 10 December 1801. The crew looked forward to the ten-day stopover, but Delano approached his visit to the Sandwich Islands warily. It was well known that Captain Cook had been surprised and killed on Kaua'i, in an attack similar to the one he had witnessed on the *Panther*, and Delano had learned on his previous visit to the islands that the crew needed to remain vigilant. He allowed only as many Hawai'ians to come on board as he could while maintaining security. He knew also that American and British expatriates inhabited the

C.E. Bensell's painting of Oahu in 1821 represented a haven for American mariners crossing the South Seas and documented the idea of the true Yankee as a citizen of the world. Courtesy of the Peabody Essex Museum.

islands, making a living by supplying provisions to visiting vessels, and they could be "very serviceable." One of those serviceable expatriates was George McClay, who had served as ship's carpenter aboard the *Eliza* in 1793 and had sailed with Delano aboard the *Hector* to Bombay. He had then joined the ranks of those American global travelers who began to populate the ports and isles of the Pacific and Indian Oceans, and he eventually made his way to Hawai'i. He was a favorite of King Kamehameha I, who assigned him the task of building ships for the islands' royal navy. Along with McClay, Delano found other acquaintances, including captains Hills, Ebbets, and Winship of Boston, and a Captain Hudson, whom he had met at Massa Fuero the year before.[26]

The new year found the *Perseverance* on a course for Canton, and on 21 January 1802 the ship passed the Ladrone Islands (part of the modern Wahshan group south of the Pearl River) in the South China Sea with a cargo of sealskins. Delano arrived during the height of the trading season (September through March) and was able to exchange the pelts for tea, sugar, and other China goods. Sailing from Whampoa on 6 April 1802, he brought the *Perseverance* to anchor in Boston harbor on 1 November 1802, "after having been absent a few days short of three years." Apparently, he made a respectable profit: the log of the *Perseverance* recorded few complaints about mutineers or sharpers during the long voyage.

Even after three years away, Delano immediately began preparations for another sealing voyage. He commissioned his brothers to build a smaller ship, rigged her as a schooner, and named her, appropriately for both his surroundings and calling, the *Pilgrim*. He found time—and the *lac*—to procure a wife, marrying Hannah Appleton, a widowed boardinghouse operator in Boston, "both then resident in Providence, and late of Boston." The forty-year-old Delano could now boast that he was principal owner of two ships, and the addition of brothers Samuel, William, and an invalid seven-year-old nephew made this endeavor a family enterprise. It would make the voyage, as well, one of gnawing anxiety for a man who had grown "less active in body and mind" and who bore the responsibility of sundering family bonds with the knowledge that, like the crew of the *Massachusetts*, most of them might never see home again. On 25 September 1803, the *Perseverance* and *Pilgrim* sailed with their crews of sixty men and eighteen cannon, "bound to the South Sea" to gather sealskins. This would be Delano's "third and last long voyage."[27]

The *Perseverance* and her "consort" set a course for Tasmania, then known as New Holland or Van Dieman's Land, named for the Dutch East Indies governor who had sent Abel Tasman on his voyage of exploration in 1642. Delano would not have known that the British had begun to plant its notorious penal colony and "female factories" there a year earlier when his ships anchored in the treacherous currents of Bass's Strait (now Bass Strait) on 20 February 1804. They remained until October, as the *Perseverance* settled in at Kent's Bay while the *Pilgrim* made two excursions among the fifty-plus islands of the straits in search of seals. In November, the ships made the Snares, off of the southwest coast of New Zealand. Delano continued to think of himself as an explorer, culling the journals of earlier European expeditions for inspiration and quotable material. George Bass and Matthew Flinders had discovered the strait just six years earlier. Of Vancouver's discovery of the Snares, Delano wrote, "I know of no other person, except him and myself, that has ever seen them." The idea that contributions to science could offer a way of legitimizing reputation for both the nation and himself had been securely planted in Delano's thoughts on his voyages on the *Panther* and *Endeavor*, and during his second and third circumnavigations it flowered.[28]

In early November, the *Perseverance* and *Pilgrim* set a course for Chile and Peru, and Delano continued to fill his journals with commentary on the natural history of the Pacific, polishing his treatment of the themes of beauty, abundance, and commercial potential. He observed that "all the bounties of nature fell to . . . the two kingdoms of Chile and Peru." For readers whose travels would never take them farther than the countinghouse or the coffeehouse, he reported that there was enough salt in the mines north of Lima to load the world's entire fleet of ships. Interspersing his poetic descriptions of the plentitude of the Eastern world and the exotic wares of India and China was an account of the guano trade of the Chincha Islands off of Peru. He extolled guano as "a great article of trade" and estimated the annual tonnage of shipping engaged in the trade at 7,000–8,000 tons, netting profits of $8,000–$10,000 per trip. Peruvian vicuna provided another opportunity to the sharp-eyed Yankee, and Delano advised, "the vicuna can be tamed and domesticated as well as llamas. Flocks gathered of these animals might open a new speculation to the cultivator, and afford great commercial benefits to the whole community."

The Pacific empire of Spain's Catholic Majesty that Delano observed in the early 1800s presented a complicated view of the world's political alignments, challenging his republican sensibilities and shaping the great theme of his later journals. As a boy, Delano had tried to run away from home to take part in a war for independence from Britain's tyranny. As a man he continued to embrace the republicanism of Washington and Jefferson that heralded the expansion of liberty in a world of Christian monarchs and Celestial emperors. His voyages "made the coast of Chili and Peru my home for five years," and he would come to regard the capital, Concepción, and its port, Callao, as icons of another decadent Pacific empire. The prisons of Spain's colonies, in particular, were hellholes in which British and American seamen might find themselves confined for years on trumped-up accusations of piracy, smuggling, or privateering, and they provided settings for Delano's extended reflections on the fortuitous alliance between liberty and commerce. There, he found "the Spaniards are ever jealous of foreigners in that part of the world . . . They are not a very sympathizing people, and feel very little for the suffering part of the community and have treated prisoners of war in general unfeelingly by keeping them confined in close, and many times unhealthy prisons." In his *Narrative* he boasted of having negotiated the release of fifty foreigners. The "true-blooded Yankee" of Delano's *Narrative* was now not only a citizen of the republic but also a liberator of the world's peoples. In this context, Delano's travels along the coasts of Chile and Peru likewise gave him the opportunity to offer commentary that distinguished a Yankee identity from the characters of other, more decadent nations. Spain's neglect even of its own subjects throughout the Pacific offered germane lessons for a republic that was still unsure of its cultural and political legitimacy, and Delano could provide object lessons of his own based on the record of history and his own hard experience. In describing the *Perseverance*'s passage off Patagonia in 1800, for instance, he would augment his description of the "rough ragged coast, indented with deep bays and coves" with the recollection, "There was once a settlement formed in these straits by the Spaniards. They sent three or four hundred people, and left them at a pleasant place, for that climate, which has since been named Port Famine. They were all left to famish and die, not having any supplies sent to them . . . the poor creatures starved to death."29

Delano's humiliating encounter with Spain's petty officialdom at Juan Fernández Island, along the Chilean coast, represented everything that his enlightened new republic opposed. The *Perseverance* had stopped there five years earlier, and his journal had contrasted Governor St. Maria's warm reception of the American captain against the callous disregard that Alexander Selkirk—Daniel Defoe's real-life Robinson Crusoe—had received from his own countrymen, including Defoe himself. By late November 1805, separated from the *Pilgrim* and with his crew suffering from scurvy, Delano hoped to purchase fresh fruits and vegetables at Juan Fernández to alleviate their discomfort and catch a few seals. But a new governor had replaced St. Maria, and this martinet proved to be less accommodating to Yankee seafarers. Circumventing the custom of receiving guests at his palace, he intercepted Delano's whaleboat at the pier, warned off the crew, and informed the captain that he would be prohibited from taking anything from the island. The official advised Delano that his predecessor "had been removed from that post on account of his lenity to the Americans" and for this now sat under arrest at the capital city of Concepción, and this man was not about to make the same mistake. The incredulous Delano reminded him of the many services he had rendered to Spain's subjects over the years, particularly his intervention on behalf of Spanish prisoners of war, all "sufficient to deserve so small a favor as I had solicited." To no avail: "He shrugged his shoulders, and said he did not remember much about it." Nor, despite an approaching gale, would he even grant permission for the boat's crew to remain on shore overnight. Delano considered all of this an outrageous breach, both of maritime etiquette and the humane principles he associated with his new nation's character. The insidious nature of Spanish tyranny was revealed particularly by the fact that the governor was actually an Ibero-Irishman—Thomas Higgins, nephew of Chilean president Ambrosio O'Higgins—and that even the liberty-loving Irish could be entangled into the arbitrary authority of Spain's corrupt throne.[30]

By the end of the month the *Perseverance* had made her way to Callao, where Delano could replenish the vessel, care for his crew, and renew old acquaintances. The extended stopover gave him an opportunity to reflect on another manifestation of global tyranny, that bête noire of Protestant America, the Roman Catholic Church, and he could easily have given in to the formulaic indictment of the Black Legend that enthralled his countrymen. The Yankee skipper certainly mistrusted the reach of such an authoritarian institution as disturbingly broad, and he fretted over the Church's deeds among the peoples of the Pacific and Indian Oceans. The global reach of the most infamous of European institutions, the Spanish Inquisition, particularly troubled him. Portuguese power, he wrote, had carried the worst of Church practices to the subcontinent, as at Goa, where the "influence of the inquisition, and of the worst forms of papal superstition, has tended much to corrupt the morals of the people." Reflecting the spirit of his imagined republic, he recalled that many other writers had ruminated on the cruelty and tyranny of the tribunals, but for an American in particular, "the mere name of it strikes the people of the protestant countries with horror." The problem, Delano found, lay in the outmoded superstitions that continued to hold sway within the Church, and he noted dismissively, "A court founded upon the principle of trying and punishing people for their religious opinions, is inconsistent with reason, and the ideas of liberty of conscience entertained at the present time." Again, he wrote from experience. Just two or three weeks before the *Perseverance* had anchored at Callao, an Inquisition court had tried and executed a Spanish woman for heresy: "She died a true martyr," he commented dryly.[31]

Delano's reflections on the Church and Iberian officialdom easily might have become a complement to the standard treatment found in British and American travelogues and political essays of the times. His observations would prove useful in distinguishing the national character of his countrymen from that of a servile and oppressed people abroad. Yet, the portrait of American identity that Delano drew described a complicated character which was urbane, cosmopolitan, and tolerant of the ways of the world. In his 1817 *Narrative*, he established his bona fides by reminding his readers that he had made several voyages to Peru and had been to the viceroy's palace in Lima more than fifty times. Observing, "The Spanish people, perhaps, have been kept more under the influence of superstition and bigotry than most others," he situated the Old World in an advanced stage of civilization marked by obsolete, decaying institutions. But this American, activated by true republican principles, could express a measure of cultural relativism and understand, if not appreciate, the cultural context even of institutions he found wanting. "It must be recollected," Delano mused, "that the people of all countries are governed more or less by some species of priest craft, and as long as society remains in its present state, there can be no doubt but those possessed of power will make use of it as the best means they can adopt to control the bad passions and propensities which a large portion of their subjects possess, and which cannot be governed by any other means."

During this voyage, one incident, in particular, stood out that complicated Delano's facile construction of the American national character. The encounter with the Spanish slave ship *Tryal*, under Captain Benito Cereno, brought to the surface fundamental contradictions between the persona of republican liberator and of the enlightened citizen of the world that Delano had attempted to fuse as equal parts of a true Yankee. The events had begun before the *Perseverance* reached the coast, on the morning of 20 February 1805, after two months of cruising the Pacific shoreline and collecting seal furs. Delano's ship was sailing in light airs when the watch sighted a ship that "acted very awkwardly." Ascertaining that she was a Spanish slave ship, the *Tryal*, and that she was in trouble, needing provisions and water, Delano went over in his ship's "large boat" to provide aid. After two hours, just as his men pushed off from the *Tryal*, the Spanish captain suddenly leapt into the American tender and cried out that the slaves had captured his ship and murdered several of his crew. Delano quickly returned to the *Perseverance*, then sent out his boats, "well manned, and well armed," to recapture the slaver. He brought the *Tryal* into Concepción six days later, having provided the Spanish crew "every possible kindness."

In retelling the tale, Delano expended a good deal of ink to complain about the subsequent "ingratitude, injustice, [and] want of compassion" on the part of Cereno, who refused to pay the costs of salvage required by maritime law. Even so, his imagined Spanish Pacific was a complicated creation. In Delano's version, the Chilean viceroy, "too great and good a man to be misled by [Cereno's] false representations," came to his rescue and pressured Cereno to pay the Yankee skipper what he was due. A naval commandant came to Delano's aid as well and spoke on his behalf, asserting that the conniving Cereno had treated "the American" with unparalleled ingratitude. Delano's tale of the *Tryal*, appearing all over the newspapers of the day, was presented through the voice of the philosophical world citizen rather than the truculent Yankee Doodle, and his readers were given an interpretation of the characters of both peoples that was nationally multifaceted and culturally nuanced. His praise for the Spanish colonial officials who aided him filled American journals from Boston to Charleston, from the Green Mountains of Vermont into the Blue Ridge of Virginia. Throughout 1806 and 1807—the story often appeared even before Delano had berthed the *Perseverance* back in Boston—readers could find versions of it, as well as letters from Delano, the Spanish consul in Boston, and the Spanish minister plenipotentiary in the *Newburyport Herald* and *Salem Gazette; Portsmouth Oracle;* the *Vermont Centinel;* New York's *Mercantile Advertiser, Public Advertiser, Republican Watch-Tower,* and *Spectator;* the *Democratic Press* and *Poulson's American Daily Advertiser* of Philadelphia; and Alexandria's *Daily Advertiser* and Richmond's *Enquirer.* The *Perseverance* and crew hailed from New England, but the journals constructed the "humane and spirited exertions of [Delano] and his brave crew . . . in the Pacific Ocean" as an American enterprise, carried out by an "American ship." For most readers, also, the Yankee values that were celebrated—the king's gift of a "Golden Medal" and "Tribute of Respect"—redounded to the credit of Yankees across the country. Delano applauded these tokens of European acceptance as well as the "kind and generous treatment" and "most sincere friendship and benevolence" he received from Spanish officials. The story resonated with an American public that cheered acts of heroism by other Americans, especially by those who operated on a global stage, and decades later, it attracted the attention of Herman Melville, who adapted Delano's account for his notable short story, "Benito Cereno."[32]

Yet in describing the American as a liberator of disadvantaged peoples and in using the Spanish Pacific as a setting, Delano was curiously indifferent to the plight of the *Tryal's* human cargo. Instead, he accepted the Spanish assessment of the mutiny as "those heinous and atrocious actions" rather than as a spirited struggle for freedom. He was not ignorant of the fate of the mutineers. Six were condemned to "the common penalty of death," and "the heads of the five first [were to] be cut off after they are dead, and be fixed on a pole, in the square of Talcahuano." Others were sentenced to ten years of hard labor. What accounts for Delano's failure to liberate the slaves of the *Tryal* or to decry harsh sentences imposed on men and women who had attempted to take back their liberty, not unlike the actions that he and his countrymen had taken twenty years earlier? Throughout the *Narrative* he would boast of rescuing British or Spanish prisoners of war. On his previous circumnavigation, he deviated from the business of the voyage to carry stranded Japanese sailors from Hawai'i to Canton, and he barely masked the self-congratulatory tone of this passage. In his earlier travels, he had encountered slavery in any number of cultures. In the Moluccas (Maluku Islands), he noted that the Dutch enslaved Malays and "a few negroes" as servants and musicians. In the Palau Islands during the summer of 1791, he observed the negotiations between Abba Thulle and two rebel chiefs while sixty women were exchanged as hostages. When the king offered the choice of women first to the Europeans, then to his *rupacks*, or counselors, and finally to his subjects, Delano registered only curiosity, describing the hostages as a picture of "cheerfulness and pleasure" and condoning the king's policies as wise and effectual. In recounting the matter of the *Tryal*, however, the global citizen who employed his pen to chastise European conquests of other peoples fell silent. In none of his previous travels did slavery seem to trouble Delano's conscience, even as he represented himself as a liberator. Like the majority of white Americans in the early nineteenth century, his concept of liberty did not extend to African or Asian peoples. It exposed a cruel paradox at work in Delano's America. His 1817 publication came at an historic moment, when working-class and middle-class white men were becoming more vocal in demanding expansion of the vote and elimination of property qualifications, even as they sought to eliminate these rights for women and African Americans. The new "ladies journals" that had begun to appear advised Yankee women to subsume their energies into the domestic sphere of childraising, and budding abolitionists could go only as far as joining colonization societies that promoted the emigration of black Americans to Africa.[33]

The affair of the *Tryal* kept Delano in Chile far longer than he wished and almost lost him the trading season at Canton. Finally, on 21 June 1806, the *Perseverance* departed the coast from Point St. Helena, set a course for the Galápagos Islands, then reached Hawai'i in September to take on much-needed provisions. The *Perseverance* arrived at Macao on 10 November 1806, the last time Delano would visit China. He had left the *Pilgrim*, under the command of his brothers, Samuel and William, at the Galápagos Islands in July, with orders to collect skins for the Canton market, and they did not arrive until September 1807. Trading in China was no longer new to him, and by 1806 several American companies had established resident offices in the factories to facilitate exchange. Consequently, it appears that Delano could enjoy the sights and observe Chinese culture more closely, and his thoughts again turned philosophical. His journals repeated themes that he had developed at the beginning of his travels. Delano was again satisfied with the treatment he received from Europeans, noting, "On going up we passed the English frigate *Phaeton*, commanded by Commodore Wood, with several other men of war under his command. We were boarded from the squadron, and treated politely, they offering us any assistance we might be in want of." Over the next two months, he made observations for a brief essay on China, and later incorporated this material into twelve pages of his *Narrative*.[34]

Much of the China Trade literature sought to demystify the East. If one were to do business "eastward of Good Hope," one had to quash its myths, understand its realities, and, in particular, render its people humane and civil. The captains and factors who carried their experiences into the public sphere made the peoples of the East compatible with the culture of commercial civility that they found in the community of Atlantic trading nations. In this vein, Delano advised his readers that Chinese laws might be harsh by Western standards but they were just and fit the temperament of the Middle Kingdom. Lurid tales of Chinese travesties were exaggerated, he insisted. It was not true, for instance, that Chinese women commonly drowned their own children, as previous writers had asserted. In describing Japan, as well, he reported an instance in which a Chinese merchant who tried to smuggle pearls out of Japan in a pumpkin was caught in the act and sliced his own throat rather than face the "dread punishments . . . of this empire." Yet the Yankee described Japanese laws as rigorous but fair.[35]

The homeward passage should have been favorable. Delano's Canton sales promised a profitable voyage and the almost forty-four-year-old captain could look forward to a modest retirement with Hannah in Boston. But something went wrong. The *Narrative* describes severe privation aboard the *Perseverance*, and the captain began to chronicle a bout of melancholy that continued well after his return to Boston. The passages that described this leg of the journey were particularly plaintive, and he wrote, "My reflections . . . and after my arrival home, were that I should rather prefer an honorable death, than to undergo such hardships and severe trials as I experienced during this passage and had frequently before endured while at sea." This cannot explain why, as late as 1810, the aging mariner decided to make a voyage to St. Bartholomew's (St. Barthélemy), carrying China goods and dried cod. Appalled, his friends urged the sailor, now forty-seven, to hire a captain to navigate the vessel. Embargoes imposed by the Republican administrations of Jefferson and Madison—notably that of 1807—and the postwar depression that followed the 1812–1815 conflict with Britain no doubt had hampered his efforts to find work. Despite Delano's "great exertions to secure a handsome living in the world," his situation had become "unfortunate at his time of life, which is now approaching to old age, and in which new adventures cannot be resorted to for riches or support." There may have been some personal disappointments as well. Again, his anonymous biographer provided some vague allusion to "recent misfortunes and embarrassments." That these were not just financial problems is suggested in the comment from "his old acquaintance" that, "if he has sometimes erred in judgment . . . he is not capable of designing to do wrong to others." Delano himself makes a vague reference to his later problems in describing the preparations for his last voyage. A man should "keep clear of being dragged into the law, harassed and wronged out of all his hard earnings." He had been "called upon to pay sums of money that he never owed . . . to people he never saw before." Now, he had been "left in his old age penniless and without a friend." And, abruptly, here Amasa Delano's personal narrative ends.[36]

Amasa Delano spent seventeen years navigating the world's seas, and it was out of these experiences that he wrote his *Narrative*. Long after he came ashore, too old and worn to roam the Indian and Pacific Oceans anymore, he turned to converting his recollections into *A Narrative of Voyages and Travels, in the Northern and Southern Hemispheres: Comprising Three Voyages Round the World; Together with a Voyage of Survey and Discovery, in the Pacific Ocean and Oriental Islands.* Through the coldest winters in memory, especially the year without a summer, that of 1816, Delano took up the pen. We know something about his motivations to write. He certainly had not been a childhood scholar, like Shaw. As his biographer has written, "Captain Delano, when very young, was averse from school and study." But his preference for action over observation reversed, and in this he appears representative of the first generation of China Trade writers, who felt an urgency to tell their stories in their later "years of reflection." After his retirement from the sea, he had time on his hands and few obligations. He and Hannah were childless. His parents had remained in Duxbury, where his sixty-eight-year-old mother died in 1811 and his seventy-five-year-old father passed away in 1814. But there are intimations that these may have been difficult times for the fifty-four-year-old world traveler.

For retired mariners like Captain Delano, the concern with profit inhered not only in overseas adventure but also in their *accounts of* their voyages. Through extensive reading, autodidacts such as Delano were quite aware that the struggle to navigate around the world and return with a profitable cargo was matched by the effort to write a book worthy of the refined literature they sought to emu-

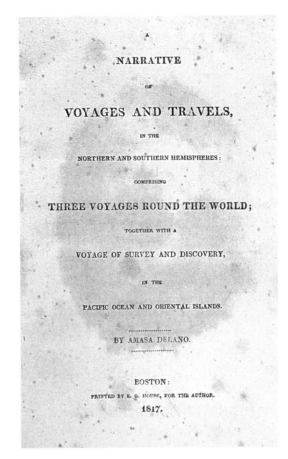

The title page of Delano's 1817 *Narrative* represented a new kind of American literature that sought to reinvent the national character as enlightened world traveler, explorer, and writer. Courtesy of the William Reese Company.

late. Throughout this period, men who came home from the sea penniless and broken—and there were many—had sought to recover their finances by selling their stories. Amasa Delano left Duxbury and sailed throughout the Pacific between 1790 and 1807 because he lacked work in the depressed economy of the Confederation's Critical Period. Similar circumstances sent Samuel Shaw, Edmund Fanning, and many others aboard ships bound for Eastern waters. There were financial incentives for writing. It was well known that John Hawkesworth had received £6,000 for his account of Cook's first voyage—against the £1,000 that Henry Fielding had received for his now-classic novel *Tom Jones.* A "huge market" had developed for sea voyage narratives by the eighteenth century, and "generic conventions" had also developed for accessing and entertaining that market. As one editor observed of Delano, "He had never earned much money, although he had earnestly sought to do so. What little he saved he lost; his book was, in part, an effort to recoup his fortunes." Delano himself alluded to other, more personal reasons for filling up his time. He had become "depressed in his spirits" and needed to occupy his mind "in a rational and profitable manner" over 1815 and 1816, "which might otherwise have been left a prey to melancholy and painful meditations." Writing was a godsend, providing "a mode of beguiling his sadness" in work that was "useful in regard to the community, and at the same time agreeable and reputable in regard to himself."[37]

We do not know how long it took to produce the 599-page text—Delano said "a number of months"—but we know something about his approach to writing. He thought he had something to offer his countrymen: "No seaman from the United States has enjoyed the same opportunity for observation and discovery in the Eastern Ocean, which was afforded to me by the voyage I made with commodore McClure. My remarks upon the navigation along the coast of New Holland, Van Dieman's Land, New Zealand, and round Cape Horn, will also be new to my readers, and I am confident, of great real value." He had kept the logs and journals of the *Perseverance* and *Pilgrim*, "made at the time minute and full upon whatever was extraordinary," and had made a lifelong habit of collecting or copying other ships' logs, including those of the *Panther* and *Endeavor.* He kept the letters and legal documents attendant to the Benito Cereno affair, and his text frequently mentioned extracts culled from logbooks. In addition, he had access to others' letters and journals, likely held at the Boston Marine Society. And, in the ten years since he retired from the sea, he had time to make up for his lack of formal education. His work was sprinkled liberally with quotes from the authoritative texts of his day, including the *Edinburgh Encyclopedia* and *Rees's Cyclœpedia*, which Samuel Bradford of Philadelphia had begun to publish between 1806 and 1822; John Malham's *Naval Gazetteer,* which Spotswood and Nancrede published in Boston in 1797; and Hawkesworth's collected *Account of Voyages.* And it appears that he had some editorial control over the final product. In describing his second voyage to the Palau Islands, Delano excused the awkward addition of materials that he tacked on at the end of the section, explaining that "something of an apology is due to the reader." He had surmised that he had incorporated enough information to bring the section to press, but friendly readers later urged the author to include important details he had left out. He was able to compare the galley proofs with "my notes, which were taken at the time" and virtually all the current reference works that were then available in Boston. All in all, he had time, materials, and incentive, and so, he observed, "The difficulties therefore were not greater in regard to me than they have been in regard to many other voyagers and travelers, who have very properly and usefully employed their pens in writing accounts."[38]

Delano published under a title that sounded distinctly like the exploration tales found in Hakluyt and Hawkesworth, and he offered readers an American version of the great European expeditions. The book was a modest financial success, which no doubt helped ease Delano's mind. A second edition of *Voyages* intended for distribution in the American South was printed in 1818. Elite readers could find in the *North American Review* for July 1817 a thirteen-page review of the *Narrative* amidst accounts of the Dey of Algiers, Ali Bey, and "Arabick Manuscripts." Further notoriety came well after his death, with the publication of Melville's short story, and Delano would no doubt have appreciated the public recognition in his own day.[39]

Delano had traveled throughout the East and wrote of it in his "character as an American." But what was this imagined place, and who was the American he had sought to describe? The full title of the *Narrative* tells us much about early Americans' understanding of their voyages "round the world." Delano's travels had carried him from the North Atlantic to the Caribbean, to the China Seas and the South Pacific, and so he wrote of "voyages round the world" in the Great South Sea and the Eastern Ocean, a phrase that recalled the chronicles of renowned navigators William Dampier, Woodes Rogers, Edward Cooke, George Dixon, and, of course, Captain James Cook. As for the national character—the true Yankee—he sought to represent, readers found throughout the *Narrative* a figure whose traits were an amalgam of folk wisdom and literary tropes. Delano's Yankee incorporated a real Jonathan who played jokes on his crew; the genteel raconteur and citizen of the world who appreciated "persons of the best character" yet felt comfortable among the harems of Java or the rajahs of Sumatra; a Yankee Doodle who rescued prisoners from Spanish jails and recounted "the daring feats of a true-blooded Yankee"; and a Poor Richard who filled his book with useful knowledge for other navigators, identifying safe harbors and provisioning ports, describing the proper way of preserving a vessel and cargo in the tropics, and warning of the need to bring spare parts on vessels voyaging East.

Delano died on 21 April 1823 in Boston. The *Independent Chronicle* and *Salem*

Gazette carried the story, and although they got particulars such as his age and the date of his death wrong, they were in agreement that he died "very suddenly" and were uniformly respectful in designating his title as "Capt. Amasa Delano." The funeral proceeded from his sister's house in the tony new Fort Hill section of Boston. His wife, Hannah, died the same year. Curiously, the newspapers did not mention Delano's *Narrative*, the book that became his legacy. As he had written during his last voyage through the Pacific, he "always had a strong desire to see all extraordinary places, and particularly this which I had heard so many wonderful stories about." In adding his own stories, he constructed both an imagined East and an imagined national identity, each a reflection of the other.[40]

"The Strangers Were Americans"

S AMUEL SHAW'S FIRST ENCOUNTERS with the peoples of the East brought the early republic a much-needed sense of national achievement, but his travels did not encompass the totality of Americans' experience in the East. Early contacts between Yankee voyagers and the Chinese mandarins, Polynesian chiefs, and Indian banyans whom they met in "voyages round the world" both introduced their countrymen to a wider world and altered their sense of national identity. The "voyages of commerce and discovery" that dispersed Americans across the globe in the early years of the new nation signaled a new phase in the development of this "true Yankee" character. Americans began to imagine themselves as "citizens of the world," in the phrase of the times, no longer provincial colonials but cosmopolitan travelers. A second, darker, and more complicated discovery was marked by the array of responses to the peoples of the Great South Sea that appeared in the accounts of these voyages, mirroring tensions within society at home over matters of race and religion. True Yankees like Delano and Fanning continued to feel concerned about national legitimacy, especially as a wave of English critics descended on the republic in the aftermath of the War of 1812. But they were not concerned in the way that some historians have suggested, nervously obsessed with acceptance by European, and especially British, observers. Instead, Shaw, Delano, and others spoke for a forceful assertion of their nation's legitimacy and their countrymen's character.[1]

Coincident with the Treaty of Paris, two migrations of Americans broke out onto the world, one across the Appalachians to the West and another across the Indian Ocean to the East. The former was driven by a hunger for land and committed to reproducing settlements in the continental interior; the latter was nurtured in a passion for trade, counted its success in voyages made, and fostered a richer global consciousness. Americans had faced east throughout the colonial era, and they continued to do so in the half century following independence. In the year of Jefferson's election as president, less than 7 percent of the population lived beyond the Appalachian Mountains. Expansion away from the coast had begun with Daniel Boone's foray that breached the Cumberland Gap into Kentucky in 1775, but well into the second decade of the new century, more than two-thirds of Americans remained within fifty miles of the Atlantic seaboard. In time, the demographics would shift. Over the course of the Old Indies Trade and into the years of the First Opium War (1840–1842), 40 percent of the population, amounting to just under seven million, settled the lands beyond the Appalachians. As they did, a different construction of the national identity further complicated the way Americans thought of themselves.[2]

The initiative for the diaspora into the East did not come from the government but from individual merchants who organized consortia like those that financed the *Empress* to China and the *United States* to India in 1784. The success of the *Empress* sparked a host of ambitious proposals for the Indies Trade, and a few merchants encouraged both Federalist and Jeffersonian administrations to establish overseas bases to support their voyages. In 1784, John Duer urged the Confederation Congress to establish an American presence on the Comoro Islands off Africa as a stepping-stone to Asia. Samuel Shaw, John Wingrove, and others touted the formation of an American East India company. The Irish American shipmaster John O'Donnell, who reached Calcutta in the *Chesapeake* in 1789, suggested to John Jay the idea of a commercial treaty with Atjeh (Aceh) in Sumatra three years earlier. But the first steps of the republican government into the world economy were hesitant and "experimental." The concerns that dominated the critical era precluded aggressive outreach beyond organizing the Northwest Territory in the Ohio Valley, and the Confederation's foreign ministers were not inclined to do more than place a few consuls in the Pacific to facilitate American trade.[3]

The flow of Americans across the Appalachians was matched by an eastward movement that made itself felt asymmetrically, exerting an influence on American consciousness and manners far greater than that of the Western pioneers despite its comparatively modest numbers. Even before independence had been secured in 1783, some 75,000 British Americans had dispersed across the globe, an estimated 60,000 white Loyalists who fled the American Revolution along with their 15,000 slaves. They were followed by thousands of mariners who sought economic independence—what they called a "competency"—in the years after. Hundreds of these "birds of passage" remained abroad, coalescing in diverse expatriate communities throughout the Indian and Pacific Oceans. During the brief period of the Old Indies Trade, the encounters of these expatriate Yankees contributed to a reformation of American life, Orientalizing their countrymen's language, dress, food, furniture, and philosophies, and by extension, helping them to understand the world and their place in it.[4]

Within a generation, it seemed, Americans were everywhere, scattered from Canton to Calcutta, and from Macao to Manila to Mauritius, carrying a bit of American life on virtually every sea and into every port, and channeling knowledge of the wider world back home. The oceans and ports of their eastern frontier differed substantially from the deserts, mountains, and plains traversed by their westward-ranging countrymen, who were carving borderland societies out of the struggle with Native Americans and the environment. The true Yankees of the Great South Sea elbowed their way into expatriate communities that had been established hundreds of years earlier by Portuguese, English, and Dutch merchants, missionaries, and colonial officials, a world already formed. Those who settled the West made the American a conqueror of native peoples and nature's forces, but those who sailed East necessarily had to conform to confident civilizations that had existed for millennia. There were, of course, some recent arrivals within the world of the East—the Qing Dynasty in China, Mughals in India, and Europeans everywhere—who came for conquest and commerce, but they had long since established themselves in the places where Americans now sought to carve a niche. Consequently, Yankee travelers were far more dependent on the goodwill of others than their countrymen on the Western frontier, and they felt their vulnerability keenly. A few cantankerous souls, like the merchant William C. Hunter in Canton, who ridiculed the Chinese regulations as "stereotyped phrases," pushed against the cultural boundaries that confined them. Others, like Harriett Low in Macao in the 1830s, poured out their frustrated dependence in caustic journals.[5]

By the time Amasa Delano sailed to Canton in the *Massachusetts* in 1790, Americans had been meeting up with each other across the globe so frequently that their reunions overseas had become a staple of American letters. On his homeward voyage from Canton, as the *Empress* berthed in Table Bay in July 1785, Samuel Shaw greeted Captain Jonathan Ingersoll, piloting the *Grand Turk* of Salem on its first voyage to the Cape of Good Hope. Twelve years later, Captain John Crowninshield wrote to his multigenerational family of merchants and mariners back in Salem that "there have been here a great many American ships" anchored in the Hooghly River, which drained Calcutta. About the same time, Richard Cleveland observed, "Most of the strangers, who then visited Batavia (Jakarta), were Americans." Anchoring off Calcutta on 6 April 1803, Captain Dudley Pickman wrote home that he "was happy to find Mr. P. T. Jackson of the ship *Pembroke* of Boston, and Messrs. Ellis and Cabot of the *Asia* of Beverly," but he expected to see "other Americans in port" as well. In 1819, John White reported at San Salvador, a stopover to the East Indies, that "the American and English residents . . . form a very agreeable society among themselves." What all described was a social phenomenon of the early republic that has been understudied by historians outside of the Indies Trade—expatriate Americans, sometimes living singly, sometimes gathered in enclaves, for extended periods across the globe. In time, Yankee travelers transformed some of these places so extensively that they became unrecognizable to earlier visitors. In 1850, returning to San Francisco after thirteen years, opium runner Captain Edward Faucon noted, "Here everything is American & I must really say that I don't know the place. Except some old undisturbed land marks, there is nothing to remind me of San Francisco as it used to be."[6]

The effects of these "voyages of commerce and discovery" on the American imagination were as electric as Benjamin Franklin's kite and reverberated as strongly as Eli Whitney's cotton engine. Reported in newspapers, filling conversations in Congress, and bandied about in taverns and coffeehouses, accounts of the "federal flag" appearing in Eastern ports reassured the country that the South Seas were filling with Yankee vessels and extending the reach of their new republic. In 1791, the *Salem Gazette* celebrated the *Columbia*'s second "voyage of observation and enterprise to the North-Western Coast of this Continent" as precedent setting. Editor Thomas C. Cushing had "no doubt but the impression made by the Capt. and his company on the tawny natives of the coast which is the object of her destination, will be favorable to the future visits of the Stars and Stripes to those regions." By the next year, the depression that had shaken the foundations of the Confederation was a memory, and the papers bragged of ports packed with American ships. The "Marine Intelligence" out of Charleston for 19 January 1792 took the measure of this resurgence, boasting, "This port is crowded with ships from England, Holland, and the United States, so as to be obliged to lie four or five a-breast at the wharves, to receive on board their cargoes. It gives pleasure to every sincere patriot to see many excellent ships carrying the American flag, arriving daily from the northward into Carolina, to waft their produce to the ports of the eastern world." Recalling those heady days of global encounter and economic recovery in his 1833 *Voyages Round the World*, Edmund Fanning cribbed the journal that he had kept aboard the *Aspasia*, anchored at Mocha Island, off of Chile, on 7 April 1800, to register, "We learned there were upwards of thirty sail of American sailing vessels on this coast, whose cargoes were destined for the China market."[7]

By the time Delano had published his own *Narrative*, Yankee travelers were touring the world in ships called *Sumatra*, *Hindu*, and *Houqua*, in search of sandalwood from Owhyhee, guano from Mocha, and birds' nests for the Asian delicacy birds' nest soup. They navigated waters now so familiar that many journals recorded that the passage through the Indian Ocean was "unattended by anything more than the usual occurrences of similar voyages" or that a vessel "had the usual winds and weather experienced in passing the Cape of Good Hope." Those who had put down roots in Hawai'i or Macao formed an arc of familiarity that welcomed their countrymen with shared language and customs, as well as providing much-desired news of friends at home and abroad. Dudley Pickman of Salem enjoyed such a reception when his *Belisarius* anchored off Calcutta in 1799 and 1800. There he found Captain Cheever of neighboring Danvers, Massachusetts, who had resided in India for nearly fifteen years: "master of a country vessel, has acquired but little property and will probably never return to America." Pickman brought word of Cheever's relations back home. Stephen Minot of Boston was there, also. Pickman had known Minot in Salem, when he resided with Nathaniel West, one of a family of Indies traders. Minot was now a denizen of the Indian Ocean, engaged in the country trade between Mauritius, Tranquebar, and Madras. He seems to have benefited particularly from the French Wars, trolling the prize auctions held on Mauritius to buy up vessels that had been captured by French privateers and then selling them at a premium in India. Perhaps the most ambitious of these global wanderers was another Salemite, Jonathan Lambert. In 1811, Lambert claimed possession of Tristan d'Acunha, the South Atlantic archipelago strategically situated along the Indies trade routes, intending to establish a supply station there to replenish the Indies fleets. Another citizen of the world was William C. Hunter, originally from New York, sent abroad at thirteen, educated at Malacca, a resident of Canton for four decades, finally settling and ending his days in Nice on the southern coast of France.[8]

When Yankee voyagers returned to New York, Philadelphia, and Boston, they carried their experiences in Asia home, introducing their landbound countrymen to the languages of the East. For Americans, the East was a new world of goods such as jute, nutmeg, sandalwood, and sherbet, of creatures like birds of paradise, boobies, cockatoos, kangaroos, and camelopards (giraffes), and of people called banyans, compradors, coolies, and mandarins. Americans imbibed a vocabulary that today we claim as our own: *atoll, bandana, bazaar, buggy, catamaran, chop, chow, hookah,* and *tank.* They festooned their homes and public buildings with symbols of Hawai'ian pineapples to offer welcome and of Chinese coins and persimmons to celebrate prosperity. They filled their cupboards with blue and white Canton porcelain, adorned their bodies with nankeen, silk, and madras, and complemented their philosophies with ideas from Buddha and the Bhagavad Gita. In seaports like Salem, it was said, one heard shopkeepers telling boys to hurry to the *bazaar* for a *chow* of *dungaree, madras,* and *bandana,* and if they ran *chop chop,* they would be rewarded with a *cum shaw* of *ginger* or *mocha.* That boy might ask for a *chop,* or permission, to sail the family's dinghy, or *hawpoo,* and if refused, complain that the parent was being a *mandarin.*[9]

On the far side of the world, in the Eastern frontier that Shaw and Delano inhabited, Americans thought they could remake both themselves and the nation. "We have laid the foundations of a new empire, which promises to enlarge itself to vast dimensions, and to give happiness to a great continent. It is now our own turn to figure on the face of the earth, and in the annals of the world." So boasted the historian of the recent Revolution, Dr. David Ramsey, in his lecture "An Oration on the Advantages of American Independence" in 1778. It was a world of possibilities but also of ambiguities. While American consumers enjoyed the material benefits of this trade, the appreciation for other peoples described in Shaw's *Journals* and Delano's *Narrative* was often lost on their countrymen. What *was* taken in were impressions of decrepitude and decline that molded the idea of race at home. Amidst the Great South Sea, Yankee travelers employed a particular kind of cultural navigation, distinguishing an imagined national character from the cultures of both "civilized" Europeans on the one hand and the "barbaric" Asians and Africans on the other, giving Americans a decidedly positive impression of Yankee values displayed among Oriental peoples. These literary mariners reported experiences that resonated with the entrepreneurial values of true Yankees—civility, hard work and disciplined order, and productivity—indeed, often in contrast to their representations of their British, Portuguese, and Spanish counterparts. It was in the genteel and polite recognition they received from Europeans, especially in comparison to the Chinese— to the "foolish prejudices" and "illiberal laws and customs" of "these bigoted people," "this eccentric people," "this singular people," "those people"—that an American identity came to fruition. As a counterpoint to Ramsey's assertion of promise, Archibald Robbins, an American sailor who spent years in another part of the Eastern world observed in 1831, "Although Africa holds the third rank in point of size among the four great continents that constitute our globe, in a moral, political, and commercial point of view, it is decidedly inferior to them all. While the continents of Europe and America have been making rapid progress in civilization, the arts and sciences, Asia may be said to have been, for the most part, stationary, and Africa retrograding."

In carrying commerce to the Pacific, then, American expatriates would have the opportunity to contribute also to a less material, but no less pressing, need. Their "discovery" of markets in the Pacific and Indian Oceans following the Revolution launched a buoyant celebration of American character. Through their tales of adventure in the "new lands" of the East, these author–sea captains created a literature of maritime discovery that contributed to the development of a nascent national character—the true Yankee.

CHAPTER THREE

Edmund Fanning's
"Voyages Round the World"
1792-1833

I N MAY 1797, thirteen years after the *Empress of China* sailed from New York, Captain Edmund Fanning stalked the wharves of the same East River, readying his ship for a sealing voyage to the South Atlantic and Pacific Oceans. Intruding into his thoughts, a curious young man accosted the commander to make a plea to sail with him into the Great South Sea. Fanning was doubtful; "as innocent as he was simple," this farm boy from Vermont offered no maritime experience, no knowledge of the sea, not the slightest acquaintance with rigging, ropes, or sails. But his enthusiasm disarmed Fanning. The twenty-seven-year-old veteran of Caribbean and Atlantic voyages liked the "tall, raw-boned, stout, good natured looking fellow" and appreciated the young man's rationale. "Folks had told him," Fanning recalled, "that my vessel was going t'other side of the world; he had never seen the salt water before, and he would now like to have a chance in her, as he wanted most nationally, to see how t'other side looked."[1]

"How t'other side looked" mattered greatly to Americans in the early days of the republic. It mattered commercially, because in 1797 Yankee merchants and mariners, their trade battered by the Quasi-War with France and disrupted by the global reach of the Napoleonic Wars, were still engaged in a desperate search for bountiful markets. And it mattered "most nationally" because even sixteen years after the Treaty of Paris, Americans were struggling to define the character of the emergent United States. Fanning was a transitional figure in the Indies Trade. His voyages began in the Federalist republic of Shaw and Delano, a world that gazed eastward, preoccupied "nationally and personally" as Shaw had phrased it, with the trappings of legitimacy and gentility, and culminated in a Jacksonian democracy that had begun to look westward toward an expansive democracy of individualism and gain. Fanning shared the defensive posture of this earlier generation but lived into another, in which national legitimacy was taken for granted and national expansion was the order of the day. His had become a society that Shaw would have found uncomfortable and to which Delano never adapted. Yet, even after age forced him from the quarterdeck, Fanning remained an ardent Hamiltonian, promoting public interest in the Great South Sea and urging the federal government to support maritime exploration of the Eastern frontier. Fanning's voyages, like those of Shaw and Delano, were not just about making one's *lac*. Encompassing themes of discovery, encounter, and cultural exchange, they embedded American national identity within a global context, even as much of the country now turned inward toward the Western frontier.

Edmund Fanning was born in Stonington, Connecticut, on 16 July 1769, to Gilbert Fanning (1733–1804) and Huldah Palmer (1737–1813), descendants of Irish Protestant emigrants. By the fifth generation, the Fannings had become an extended family of shipwrights and mariners whose reach sprawled from Long Island to Nantucket and whose graves testified to the opportunities and perils that attended overseas voyages. Like Delano, young Edmund was born into a large network of kin, one of eight brothers, all who followed the sea. And, when he penned his memoirs in 1833, he had survived his parents, brothers and one sister, wife, and two sons, preceding only one sister and a daughter, Sarah, in death.[2]

Unlike those of Shaw and Delano, Fanning's family divided over the Revolution. His father and uncle Phineas followed the pro-war Whigs; uncles Thomas and Edmund "embraced the Royal cause, and were warmly engaged in furthering the interests of his Britannic majesty." Young Fanning had been named for his Uncle Edmund, who rose to the rank of general in the British army and who would continue to play an important role in the young man's career, albeit indirectly from his seclusion as a Loyalist refugee in Nova Scotia. Father Gilbert was commissary for George Washington's army, and all of his sons followed in the patriot cause. The eldest, Nathaniel, served aboard privateers, was captured twice, and later served under John Paul Jones in the famous victory of the *Bonhomme Richard* over HMS *Serapis;* upon his death, his brothers published a journal of Nathaniel's exploits. Gilbert and Thomas were captured on the privateer *Weasel* and held aboard the notorious prison ship *Jersey.* Gilbert died in a futile effort to swim to shore. After independence, the surviving Fannings remained in the maritime trades or went to sea. Edmund himself had been deemed too young to participate in the war; yet, the struggle inculcated a pronounced patriotism that framed his worldview. When he wrote his memoir in 1833, he dedicated it "to the American People."[3]

As soon as the conflict ended, fourteen-year-old Edmund went to sea, signing onto ships out of Stonington and New London embarking for the coastal trade and the Caribbean. He proved himself able and rose from cabin boy to first mate rapidly. Fanning was ambitious, and he considered Stonington's prospects confining, so he and kinsman Asa Rossiter headed for New York, where they enlisted as seamen aboard a brig bound for Hispaniola (Haiti). Unfortunately, Captain Miller's reputation for "being the 'hardest horse' a man could sail with" and a slave trader, as well, proved true. Fanning looked about for other opportunities and, while berthed at Aux Cayes (Les Cayes) for several weeks, he made a connection that would change his life and carry him "round the world." He befriended Captain William Nexsen, whose family operated in the "Curaçao trade." Based in New York, Nexsen and his brother Elias had set up a profitable merchant house and were beginning to think about a voyage that would follow the *Columbia*'s 1787 course to the Northwest fur coast.[4]

Meanwhile, events in Europe continued to complicate America's recovery, again rendering the Atlantic a battleground and sharpening Fanning's sense of overseas cruises as nationalist missions. The execution of Louis XVI and his circle during the spring of 1793 transformed the French Revolution into a war between Europe's empires that challenged the Washington administration's efforts to maintain neutrality. For Yankee merchants, on the other hand, the broadening of the war promised extraordinary profits and offered "a sufficient inducement to a people situated as were the Americans . . . possessing all their enterprise and spirit of adventure."[5] Consequently, in June of 1793, the twenty-four-year-old Fanning found himself aboard the New York vessel *Portland* off the Scilly Islands, carrying a cargo of Pennsylvania flour for the port of Le Havre. He never arrived at his destination. A British cruiser captured the *Portland* and carried her into Falmouth, where a "hot press" swept the crew into service aboard a Royal Navy frigate. Not waiting for the captain or American emissaries to set things right, Fanning himself determined to secure the release of the crew. Boldly boarding the frigate that held his men, he insisted on, and secured, their liberty. When the US consul and various captains inquired how Fanning had achieved the feat when their own efforts had failed, the brash youth reported, "I answered, that . . . the officers . . . guessed I was a true Yankee."[6] In fact, Fanning was able to liberate his crew through the intercession of Falmouth's lord mayor, who ordered their release when he learned that the

American mate was a nephew and namesake of a famed Loyalist general. But, for Fanning, the episode represented something else, something about the nation and the national character. It became clear during an elegantly appointed dinner between the "green Yankee," as the first mate described himself, and the cosmopolitan lord mayor, that the wounds of war were healing and his country would be accepted as a legitimate partner among the community of civilized nations. And, in this episode, elements of this national identity emerged, representing the true Yankee as an American who displayed brashness, courage, and determination. As they left the Atlantic behind to pursue the Indies Trade, Fanning, Delano, and other China traders used their encounters abroad to fill in the features of this imagined national character.

The *Portland*'s cruise had burnished Fanning's reputation as an able sea hand, and the celebrity it brought resulted in his first command. He was made captain of a new schooner, the *Dolly*, with the charge to test the British blockade around the West Indies. Dozens of American vessels, including Fanning's *Portland*, had been swept up by the Royal Navy and redirected to Halifax, where ship and cargo were confiscated. Yet, when the young commander anchored his ship in the East River, the *Dolly*'s "safe arrival caused considerable surprise" on New York's mercantile exchange, "and many speculations and shrewd guesses were also advanced, to account for the same." The answer had less to do with Fanning's skill than his connections. He could not avoid capture by a British frigate operating off of Sandy Hook, but when the captain learned that Fanning was the nephew of "General Edmund Fanning, now residing in Portman-square, London," he announced that the general had been "his particular friend at court, was his godfather, and had given him much assistance in his education and advancement in life," and he released the Yankee. It was a remarkable reenactment of his capture in the *Portland*. The voyage to Curaçao proved "a most fortunate venture" as well, as Fanning's private stock included 18 cases of beaver hats and 160 kegs of butter, all of which sold at a tidy profit.[7]

Elias Nexsen's decision to test the China Trade unfolded cautiously in his South Street countinghouse, as he weighed the prospects of extraordinary profits against the uncertainties and dangers of unfamiliar seas. Even two years after Robert Gray brought the *Columbia* home to Boston from the Northwest Coast and Canton, Fanning described the proposed voyage as "experimental." Yet, the first leg of the voyage would bring them only to the Falkland Islands in the South Atlantic. By spring 1792, the *Betsey*, a modest 100-ton brig which Fanning described as "a first rate sea boat," was ready, "fitted out with every necessary article" that the crew would need. Surprisingly, in May, she remained stranded in the East River. The obstacle was finding "officers acquainted with this new business, in our then young commercial community." Fanning had signed on as first mate, but this would be his first sealing cruise. Seaman William Whetton had some experience in seal hunting and whaling in Greenland, and he was made second mate. But the command of the *Betsey* stood vacant. Finally, a Captain R. Steele presented himself to the Nexsens and "assured the owners he was acquainted with seals of every kind, as also every thing connected with the sealing business." The merchants should have been suspicious but could not afford further delay. With the ship's company complete, the brig immediately got underway.[8]

The *Betsey's* cruise was like a thousand other voyages that broke into the global economy of the early modern world. As Yankees explored the South Atlantic, Indian, and Pacific Oceans, their "want of knowledge" was exposed, often in comical episodes. On reaching the Falklands, one shipmate, an "uncommonly large and stout Irishman, named Michael, commonly called Mike," had bragged that he looked forward to facing the feared bull seal, and "with his *shilelah* he would soon kill tiers of them." Mike's bravado, however, turned into timidity at the first rookery they came upon, which contained a herd of some three hundred powerful sea lions. Now Mike asked, "Do you think these overgrown monsters are seals?" When one of the mammoth creatures yawned to reveal two rows of enormous ivory teeth, shook a "long and shaggy mane," and bellowed out his "tremendous roar," Mike turned pale and fretted for "his precious body to be devoured by the shutting of the jaws of such monstrous creatures: indeed, sir, only look; by St. Patrick!" At this point, Fanning ordered his companies to action, whereupon the herd rose as a group and charged to the sea, knocking down every one of Fanning's army of invaders. That these were sea lions, and not the fur seals they were after, became apparent only after the battle ended.[9]

More serious was the inexplicable performance of their captain. Steele was more like the hard-edged Miller and less like the capable sea masters who had commanded Fanning's earlier cruises. Even as the voyage commenced and the pilot guided the *Betsey* through New York's Narrows, questions about the captain's seamanship arose. Steele had gotten into a dispute with the pilot, and, with neither attending to the ship's progress, she grounded in low tide. Fanning's doubts were raised further on the "somewhat lengthy" cruise. As they passed Ascension Island on August 7, and with the ship's water kegs precariously low, the first mate suggested they stop to replenish. Instead, under Steele's orders, they "pressed sail" southward. Upon reaching the Falklands, it became clear that his ignorance of sealing complemented his incompetence in seamanship. Fanning confided, "We found here, to our great disappointment, that our captain, notwithstanding his declarations when he engaged with the owners, had not the least knowledge of the sealing business." Steele, in fact, could not distinguish male seals from female. Fortunately, they found other Yankee ships berthed there, and their skippers were willing to share their knowledge. Fanning made full use of their cooperation. Still, Steele proved useful for Fanning's larger purposes. The captain's inexperience exposed the novelty and experimental nature of the China Trade. And his bravado provided a useful counterpoint to the true Yankee who later formed in Fanning's *Voyages Round the World*, displaying traits that Americans should avoid.[10]

By January 1793, the crew had filled the hold of the *Betsey*, yet "Captain Steele was in no haste to return." Fanning had had enough. "This sacrifice of time was more than I felt willing to submit to," he complained, and, finding another New York ship nearby, he secured Steele's permission to leave his post. He arrived in New York in March, preceding the *Betsey* by three months. Fortunately, "that upright and liberal merchant," Elias Nexsen, made sure that Fanning received his shares from the *Betsey*'s cruise, although technically he had forfeited any reimbursement by abandoning his station. Nor did his premature departure compromise his reputation. On November 16, the *Daily Advertiser* included a notice for a voyage to Curaçao in the *Dolly* under "Edmund Fanning, Master."[11]

His second cruise in the *Dolly* again proved a success for Captain Fanning. Upon his return to New York in May 1797, he had accumulated a modest profit and augmented his reputation for clear thinking and decisive action. Merchants and captains sought him out, offering positions aboard ships destined for Europe or the Caribbean. More intriguing, however, was an offer from Captain John Whetten (1763–1845), commander of the Indiaman *Ontario*. Whetten regaled Fanning with the tales of the riches to be made in the China Trade, especially in furs, "where the article was well ascertained to be greatly in demand," and could be sold "at prices that furnished good grounds upon which to hope a very handsome profit." He proposed a joint venture. The *Ontario* would sail ahead to Canton, while Fanning would "proceed to the South Seas, there to procure a cargo of fur seal skins, and with this cargo thence to cross the Pacific for the Canton market," expecting to arrive by November. Fanning would, then, entirely bypass the *Columbia*'s Northwest Coast route and explore a new course, setting off from the Falkland Islands. Having "an ambitious and aspiring mind," "with a strong attachment to a seaman's profession," and stoked by his previous tour of the South Seas, he saw an opportunity for profit, adventure, and honor.[12]

Fanning was interested, but he would not be taken in by false promises of the untold riches of the East. After his experience with the bumbling Captain Steele in the Falklands, Whetten's active participation in the proposed enterprise was a "great inducement." "The intimate knowledge that Captain Whetten possessed of the manner of doing business with those people, and the great assistance he could afford, being conversant in all their intricate trade" proved reassuring. As Fanning expected to return to New York with a cargo of silk, Whetten's demonstrated knowledge of Asian cloth markets would prove particularly valuable. Something about Whetten's character must also have impressed Fanning, and he no doubt had made inquiries into the captain's integrity. He would have learned that in 1783, when John Jacob Astor was embarking on his voyage to the United States, Whetten advised him to take a more comfortable ship rather than his own; it was on this voyage that Astor learned of the Hudson's Bay enterprise that launched his fortune. Later, Whetten served as president of the New York Marine Society and first supervisor of Sailor's Snug Harbor, an asylum for elderly seamen. The proposed cruise would be another experimental voyage, and Fanning had learned that character, as much as experience, spelled the difference between profit or loss, and perhaps even life or death.

A voyage to Canton offered another kind of inducement, one that resonated with the working and middle classes of the early republic. Like Delano, Fanning had "perused" the journals penned by the great explorers—Drake, Byron, Anson, Bougainville, Cook—and had dreamed of pursuing their passages, both nautical and literary. The "hope of being able to add some new discoveries to the knowledge already in the possession of man relating to those seas, and the no less flattering hope of realizing a fortune" were enough to commit him to the enterprise. He could make a contribution to the "useful knowledge" that the civilized nations were accumulating and so began to think about a travelogue like that penned by the great explorers. In doing so, he would bring honor to the republic and add luster to his own reputation. Consequently, the canon of discovery and exploration became both inspiration and reference point for his own writing. It is not clear when he began to immerse himself in tales of "voyages round the world," or even how much education he had received before going to sea as an adolescent, but an aspiring young man could readily find at home and on shipboard such titles as William Dampier's *A New Voyage Round the World*

(London, 1697), William Funnell's *A Voyage Round the World* (London, 1707), Woodes Rogers's *A Cruising Voyage Round the World* (London, 1712), Edward Cooke's *A Voyage to the South Sea, and Round the World* (London, 1712), George Shevlocke's *A Voyage Round the World by Way of the Great South Sea* (London, 1726), George Betagh's *A Voyage Round the World* (London, 1728), George Anson's *Voyage Round the World* (1748), Louis Antoine Bougainville's *Voyage Autour du Monde* (Paris, 1771), John Reinhold Forster's *Observations Made During a Voyage Round the World* (London, 1778), and George Dixon's *A Voyage Round the World; but More Particularly, to the North-west Coast of America* (London, 1789). When Fanning published his own journeys in 1833, his travelogue appeared under a familiar and distinguished title—*Voyages Round the World*.

Before he could proceed, however, Fanning needed money and a ship, and for these he went back to Elias Nexsen. Nexsen offered the 100-ton *Betsey*, a vessel that Fanning knew well from his 1792 voyage, and agreed to furnish half of the investment. By the end of the day, three other merchants had promised enough capital to make the voyage possible. As the *Betsey* would not even load a cargo in New York and would sail in ballast to the sealing grounds of the Falklands, preparations moved ahead briskly, and the voyage came together in less than a month. Clearly, this was a dramatic improvement over the days of the *Empress*, when financing took nearly a year to generate, was tentative, and ended in disaster for some of the project's investors. Now all that was necessary was a crew. The experienced Fanning would command the expedition, and Caleb Brintell of New Haven, Connecticut, a "great disciplinarian," would serve as first mate. It was deemed "to be the most judicious policy" to draw from New England's rich supply of sailors and fishermen, and so in June the *Betsey* sailed to New Haven, then to Stonington. Aboard was Fanning's quintessential American, the Vermonter, Jonathan.[13]

The twenty-seven-year-old Captain Fanning commanded the *Betsey* out of Stonington harbor on 13 June 1797. At Watch Hill Point, just west of Block Island, the brig stopped to release the harbor pilot. Fanning took the occasion to call together his crew of twenty-seven men and, citing a maritime tradition for such an "experimental" voyage, offered the opportunity to "all those who were unwilling to encounter the dangers, privations, and sufferings" of a voyage around the world to disembark with the pilot. None of the Yankee crew hesitated, Fanning later boasted, "confirming the same by three hearty cheers." For Fanning this was another example of the spirit of enterprise that exemplified his fellow Americans and that would frame the meaning of the voyage. As it had been for Shaw and Delano, Fanning's journey was as much about documenting the national character as about making his *lac*.[14]

They reached the Cape Verde archipelago in July and anchored off Bonavista (Boa Vista), the easternmost island. A month of sailing had given Fanning doubts about the *Betsey*'s ability to maneuver in the conditions they would face in the South Sea. Consulting with his officers, he determined they would alter the rigging of the vessel from a two-masted brig to that of a full three-masted ship, to allow the vessel to be steered by their fourteen-year-old cabin boy, Henry, while the men collected furs on shore. This was the kind of adaptation that Fanning celebrated as exceptionally American, and he praised his crew for accomplishing the feat in just five days and "without one dollar extra expense to the owners." By July 23rd, they were on their way. At the end of August, Fanning had another opportunity to laud his Yankee crew when Henry fell overboard. Immediately, Fanning had ordered an officer to the topmast to keep an eye on the boy. Eventually, a rescue boat found Henry "laying perfectly composed." When asked if he had been frightened, the youth answered that he had not, "for as I passed by the stern, the captain told me to keep still, only to try to float, and not to be frightened, and that he would send a boat for me; so that I was not scared."[15]

Patriotic pride would not address the larger question of the nation's legitimacy, however, and the captain continued to be concerned about the treatment that Americans would receive from European officials as they ventured into the South Sea. He took care to note that in the evening of July 5th, the English frigate *Romulus* fired on the *Betsey* and sent an officer to examine the American's papers and interrogate her crew, but then "he took leave, saying, as soon as we pleased, we might sail, and wished us a fortunate voyage." At Bonavista, he was relieved to report that they were "received very politely, and throughout the *Betsey*'s stay, was treated with the most friendly attention."[16]

On October 19, the *Betsey* came to anchor in Shallop Cove along the rock-bound coasts of the Falkland Islands. Although Americans had been hunting seals in the Falklands and whaling in these waters for over a decade, this quadrant of the South Seas was still a "novel country" for them. A number of crewmen gazed incredulously upon the tussock and the vast expanse of wildlife, and Jonathan, the Vermonter, begged to be among the first to set foot on shore. Gazing upon six acres of the "feathered fraternity" of penguins and albatrosses, he burst out, "Oh! wonderful! who would ever 'a thought such sights as these were in the world!" So delighted was Jonathan that he announced to Fanning that he had been "sufficiently well paid for coming" and would happily dispense with his wages. Yet, the charm of Jonathan's naïveté at times would be lost on us today. After departing the Falklands and setting a new course off Patagonia, on 11 December, Jonathan asked Fanning about the mythical giants of Patagonia, "of whom folks talk so much about." Magellan's men had been the first Europeans to encounter them in 1520, and Portuguese chroniclers described them as eight-foot giants, dubbing them Patagonian, or "big feet." Along with several of the crew, Jonathan had concocted a childish plan to capture one of the indigenous people, carry him home to New England, and exhibit him as a freak of nature through the countryside, "making a swinging great deal of money by it."[17]

For his part, Fanning divided his time between gathering seal hides and keeping a journal. Over the course of a dozen voyages, he disciplined himself to filling his ships' logs and personal journals with detailed observations of the winds, currents, extraordinary weather, unusual sea life, and curious natural features that he encountered. He imagined himself following in the steps of those "able and celebrated European navigators" who had traversed the Great South Sea before him, and he kept their accounts on board to inspire him and to provide the benchmarks against which he could gauge what he believed were particularly American experiences. Well before Frederick Jackson Turner formalized his frontier theory before an audience at Chicago's Columbian Exposition in 1893, Fanning, Shaw, and Delano maintained that encounters with the peoples and places of the Eastern frontier shaped the national character.[18]

With an astute awareness of audience, Fanning focused on the singular and unusual, attempting to bring home to his countrymen the exotic elements of the South Seas. He had little to say about sites such as the Cape Verde Islands, because "they had become so familiar to every reader, by the frequent reports given relative to them, that any farther description in this work is thereby rendered needless." Years later, he retold harrowing tales of false anchorages and deceptive shoals. He described in vivid terms the fetid, sulfurous waters at Fogo and the eruption of its volcano, "with the burning lava pouring down on every side, accompanied by a loud roaring, as of distant thunder, [as] one of the most beautiful and awful sights ever witnessed." And he filled his journals with passages that brought out the danger and excitement of reaching the shore of a newly discovered island.[19]

The Falklands in mid-October presented the *Betsey*'s crew with a stunning panorama of the South Atlantic in its springtime guise: a raw, storm-swept domain of blue-green sea broken only by the rock-strewn archipelago and the majesty of its teeming wildlife. Anchoring at Shallop Cove, he and his crew stood dumbstruck over a six-acre plain so filled with seals, penguins, albatrosses, and rock shags that the creatures appeared to blanket the entire expanse. Assuming the role of amateur naturalist, Fanning took pains to record the minutiae of king, jackass, john, and macaroni penguins. He found the macaroni especially amusing, sixteen inches high, sporting brightly colored plumes on each side of its head, and overall presenting "a very consequential and proud appearance." Ever self-conscious of his paltry formal education, Fanning employed a stylistic strategy that generations of practical mariners had found successful in reaching the reading public. To complement his observations, the captain consulted the small library that he kept aboard the *Betsey*, which included "various accounts" of the "able and celebrated European navigators."[20]

Tattered volumes of voyages round the world crammed the modest bookshelf in the *Betsey*'s great cabin, and in their mottled pages Fanning found that Cook, Bougainville, and others had catalogued the vast varieties of flora and fauna that populated the new worlds they encountered in the Great South Sea. In this, they followed the form developed by promoters of the great sixteenth- and seventeenth-century colonial projects like the Virginia Company and Dorchester Company, with their exhaustive lists of "strauberries," "turkies," sea rams, and sheepheads amidst a "howling wilderness," to lure England's wealthy aristocrats to invest and its impoverished, wandering poor to settle. The travelogues that inspired Fanning aimed at something grander than primitive marketing pamphlets, however. The book that he wanted to write expressed the romanticized and mysticized sense of nature that was beginning to emerge by the beginning of the eighteenth century in the music of Beethoven, the poetry of Tennyson, and the painting of the Hudson River School. His *Voyages Round the World* would carry his readers to a Great South Sea whose grandeur would inspire, whose beauty would delight, and whose bounty would awe. His readers would experience vicariously a volcanic eruption in the Cape Verdes. They would gaze across the verdant valleys of Brava Island, where the "fragrance of these green valleys, brought off to us by flaws of wind at intervals, was truly delicious, and a person that has at no time enjoyed it, can scarcely be able to conceive with what delight we received it, after having been for a length of time at sea; it actually seems to take hold upon the feelings in such a manner as to reanimate the whole system." His readers would join him on a South Atlantic shore as he sat for hours at a time "to observe sea lions' manner of approaching the shore, after a spell of feeding in the sea." And they would feel the "gratification derived from beholding" a rookery of macaroni penguins, that "noble bird."[21]

Fanning's vision of the *Betsey*'s cruise as a "voyage of commerce and discovery," incorporating elements of both commercial enterprise and national destiny, demanded more than a compilation of desultory observations of rookeries and penguins. Following Franklin's archetypical self-fashioned gentleman, Indies traders like Fanning hoped to leverage his experiences at sea into a reputation for erudite distinction. He fancied himself an amateur naturalist whose observations of nautical features and ecological conditions contributed useful knowledge toward the great project of expanding the horizons of human understanding. Fanning enjoyed dabbling in homemade experiments and was particularly keen on developing new methods for improving shipboard life. In the Falklands, he provided directions for preserving penguins' eggs for a length of time (immersing them in seal oil, alternating layers of sand and eggs). Not all of these trials succeeded, and some ended with comical results. Since dried kelp had made a useful fuel in the Falklands, Fanning had a store carried aboard the *Betsey* "but found, to our sad disappointment, after being a few days at sea, that it became moist and soft, and when in this state, would not burn to any advantage." Success was not the measure of his efforts, however. It was the spirit of inquiry that he hoped would establish his reputation as a man of letters.[22]

Like many Indies traders who hailed from working-class backgrounds, Fanning had trained himself to be an astute mariner, and his jottings followed the style that characterized the seaman's guides that filled his own sea chest, identifying safe routes, sheltered anchorages, reliable sources of water and provisions, and the like. As the *Betsey* probed the South Seas, he confirmed "the recent experience of commanders of our South Sea sealing vessels" in finding a safe course around Cape Horn. In an entry for 6 January 1798, off the west coast of Cape Horn, he advised, "The sea water was this day observed to be highly colored." A few days later, taking advantage of a calm sea, he "made trial with the boat to ascertain whether there was any current, but found none." On the 24th, having been favored with smooth seas for several hours, the captain ordered a boat lowered away, "for the purpose of ascertaining the current, which was found to be setting to the north-east, at the rate of three quarters of a mile per hour." The tone of Fanning's observations melded two themes of the early republic. "Useful knowledge" contributed to humankind's understanding of nature, and, at a time when men and women were less insulated from the hazards of storm, flood, and drought, to their ability to control, or at least anticipate, danger. But, in the early republic, contributions to science were couched in a particularly nationalist guise as well. Four years later, Nathaniel Bowditch of Salem captured the ideal in his *New American Practical Navigator.* Improving upon European theory-based approaches to celestial navigation, Bowditch offered an American alternative that reduced mathematical calculations to a simple chart that even an unlettered Jack Tar could understand and apply. Underlying the tables and star maps was a democratic notion of the new nation that put science at the disposal of the common man and education at the center of the political system. That such guides enhanced the reputation for genteel erudition of an up-and-comer like Fanning or Bowditch did not detract from the enterprise.[23]

In composing his own account of "commerce and discovery," there were times when Fanning's attention to the natural world clashed with the financial purpose of the cruise, and this undercurrent of tension emerged at the end of December. Over the course of his career, he commanded voyages that killed tens of thousands of seals. Yet, in the winter of 1797, the cruise was becoming a commercial disappointment. The Falklands were barren of fur seals. Fortune often shined on the captain from Stonington, however, as it had not on Shaw and Delano, and he chanced to encounter the Nantucket whale ship *Olive Branch,* which had put in for water and provisions. From Captain Obed Paddock he learned that he could find plenty of fur seals on the other side of Cape Horn, on the island of Massafero (Isla Más Afuera, now Alejandro Selkirk Island). Fanning faced a dilemma. Paddock's advice "was in direct opposition to my previous advices." Yet, when the Nantucket whaleman spoke of his experience in the eastern Pacific, having landed at Massafero many times, his advice confirmed the tales that Fanning gleaned at other anchorages, and the *Betsey's* captain grew "confident that the utmost dependence could be placed upon his word." Consequently, he ordered his crew to stow the *Betsey* with fresh water, ample geese, and fifty-six barrels of penguin eggs, and on December 8 set sail in company with the *Olive Branch* to round Tierra del Fuego. The passage around Cape Horn was intermittently squally, and although it was midsummer, they fell into a gale that covered the crew with a "wet jacket" of snow and sleet, "the usual salute in doubling Cape Horn."[24]

By 19 January 1798, the *Betsey's* watch sighted the Juan Fernández archipelago, off of Chile's Valparaiso region. The westernmost of the group, the mountainous Massafero, occupied a mythical place in sailors' lore as the site where Alexander Selkirk had been marooned for four years and became the inspiration for Daniel Defoe's pirated 1719 account, *Robinson Crusoe.* The shipboard view brought good news: "near its northern shore, on which, with the assistance of the glass, numbers of seal were seen." In fact, Fanning estimated

300,000–400,000 fur seals had "presented themselves" along the shore and predicted that the island held between 500,000 and 700,000 of the creatures, along with thousands of goats that would keep his crew well provisioned through the long autumn stretch. After a nearly disastrous landing, in which one of their boats was dashed to pieces, Fanning and his crew spent the next ten weeks on the island, collecting pelts. By April 2, Fanning's "skinners" had filled virtually every inch of the *Betsey*, and the captain could boast, "Even after the hold was stowed so as not to have room for any more, then the cabin, and finally the forecastle, were filled, leaving just space enough for the accommodation of the ship's company." Four thousand skins remained stacked on shore, and Fanning left a small party of volunteers on the island to continue the work, promising to send to New York to dispatch another ship for them. Meanwhile, the *Betsey* would continue on to Canton, where Fanning would exchange the furs for China goods "suitable for the home market."

The extended stay at Massafero gave Fanning an opportunity to add to his journal. He described havens where a ship could find water and fresh fish as well as how to locate the safest anchorages along the east and northwest sides of the island. He even provided a handy point of recognition: at a distance, as the island sank below the horizon, its mountains appeared to resemble a shoe. He offered little commentary on the ecological devastation he had wrought on Massafero and its two to three million fur seals. In time, he later estimated, one million of the creatures were slaughtered. But, in a nineteenth-century cast of mind, such slaughter was cause for celebration of national accomplishment. "Such an amount from this isolated spot, is one evidence in the many of the important advantage American enterprise, in this fishery and commercial trade of the Pacific, has heretofore been to the nation," Fanning boasted. The *Betsey*'s voyage injected hundreds of thousands of dollars into the national treasury as well. In consequence, the government, he asserted, had an obligation to "exploring, to discover new places and sources for its continued support." He was forming a theory of economic cooperation between government and private enterprise that departed from Adam Smith's system of laissez-faire, and, years later, he frequently petitioned Congress to fund expeditions whose discoveries would sustain the country's overseas commerce.[25]

Departing Massafero on April 5, Fanning registered the clear skies and gentle trade winds that had inspired Magellan to label this sea the "Pacific" two centuries earlier. As the *Betsey* plunged deeper into the southern swells, and coursed farther from American shores, Fanning's nationalism grew grander. He extolled the *Betsey*'s twenty-seven mariners as trustees of an American identity whose ingenuity, initiative, determination, and resourcefulness were truly "exceptional." Occasions to delineate the character of these "new men" came with remarkable frequency as the *Betsey* sailed the waters of the Eastern frontier. Rather than follow the well-laid track of the Manila galleons, a traditional route that had guided merchant ships throughout the previous three centuries, the *Betsey* would pioneer an alternative course. New seas brought fresh dangers, however. Fanning nervously anticipated the China Sea and its devastating typhoons, described in terrifying detail in the travelogues he consulted. For this experiment, then, the crew would have to rig a new suit of sails, although Fanning took pains to note that Elias Nexsen had outfitted the ship with fresh gear before it left New York. It would be a tricky operation at sea, but they had "hit upon the expedient of stripping one mast at a time," a strategy that Fanning styled, "an American precedent."[26] Even the pioneering navigators of history whose accounts he had studied with such care had to put into port to repair their sails, and "nothing of the kind had ever been performed."[27]

Nearly every task his crew took on offered Fanning an opportunity to illustrate his nascent idea of American exceptionalism. They used their free time in staging the new rigging, and Fanning saw in this a remarkable measure of initiative. When preparing to depart the Falklands, they piled every foot of the *Betsey* with pelts, and "by perseverance and industry, was our little ship completely laden to cross the Pacific to Canton, for a market." Off Sumatra, the ship's carpenter fashioned the false wooden guns that they styled "quakers," and these "were such good imitations of iron cannon, as to require a close inspection to detect the deception." Consequently, he lauded the "ingenuity and perseverance" of these "first-rate workmen." When the crew came under attack from Sumatran pirates, the captain boasted of their courage and discipline under fire. Crewmen who gave their all, like Jonathan, came in for particular praise, and even the cooper, "although entirely ignorant of the business for which he shipped," was valued as "a good natured fellow, and being willing to learn," he mastered his craft.[28]

By 19 May 1798, the Pacific trade winds had carried the *Betsey* to the Marquesas Islands, in Polynesia, nine degrees below the equator and some four thousand miles off the coast of Chile, one of the most remote stopovers on the track to China. The passage through the Pacific frequently carried American ships into contact with peoples they had not encountered previously and of whom many of the crew had never heard. Fanning's shipboard archives revealed that Álvaro de Mendaña de Neira had located part of the archipelago and named the group for his patron in 1595. His maps identified the group by their Spanish names—St. Pedrie, St. Dominique, and La Christiana (Santa Christina). And he knew that the *Betsey* was not the first American vessel to happen upon them. In April 1791, on a passage to the Northwest Coast, Joseph Ingraham of Boston had encountered an outlying group of isles, dubbing them the Washington Islands. Ingraham shared Fanning's nationalist spirit and named individual islands for heroes of the Revolution: Washington, Adams, Franklin, Knox, and Lincoln (for General Benjamin Lincoln), as well as Federal Island.

Fanning described his initial encounters with the Marquesan people as positive, and he found much to appreciate in the islands and people. Upon entering the first agreeable inlet, a double-hulled canoe brought eleven Marquesans to the ship, and although they clambered up to the railing, they were too shy to step on deck. At St. Pedrie, he confirmed earlier accounts that declared, the "island is said to be inhabited by the handsomest built race of people of all the South Pacific Islands." The only sour note—a curiosity, as Fanning described it—was the surprising dearth of fresh provisions that the natives could offer in trade. Against valleys brimming with breadfruit and cocoanut trees and waters teeming with blackfish, whales, and seabirds, the Marquesans offered only a few eels and squid in trade. This disappointing development seemed to belie the near-mythological impressions of the Great South Sea as a cornucopia of abundance that the captain had acquired in the pages of Anson and Cook, and it raised doubts about continuing the voyage.[29]

La Christiana confirmed Fanning's initial sense of the Marquesas Islands as a peaceful paradise inhabited by a timid, beautiful people of "a friendly bearing." Here he learned that the Marquesans were reluctant to board the ship because they feared the *Betsey*'s carriage guns, and Fanning ordered the weaponry drawn back. Over the next two days, the trade became brisk, with Fanning exchanging iron hoops and nails for the cocoanuts, breadfruit, and fish that would make the final leg of the voyage possible. More villagers canoed to the ship, including two chiefs, who were paddled out in impressive double-hulled war canoes, each bow festooned with human skulls. When the natives asked for gunpowder and axes, Fanning demurred, in part from caution and in part to induce the Marquesans to part with a few of their succulent hogs. They replied by urging the captain to bring the *Betsey* closer in to shore, further stoking the captain's suspicions.[30]

Fanning's impressions of the Marquesas as an idyllic paradise were dashed late on the afternoon of May 22. The trading day ended abruptly when a rain-squall drove the Marquesan dugouts back to shore. Fearing the onset of a gale, Fanning had ordered the *Betsey* into deeper water when the lookout spied a small canoe hastening toward them. His curiosity piqued by "so singular a circumstance," Fanning ordered the ship about to ascertain the identity of the visitors. To his dismay, a voice called out, "Sir, I am an Englishman, and now call upon, as I have come to you, to preserve my life." The refugee was a British missionary, the Reverend William Pascoe Crook. Once aboard the *Betsey*, Crook slumped into a chair, and after taking some moments to compose his emotions, breathlessly recounted a convoluted tale of greed and betrayal. Some months before, he revealed, an "insinuating" Italian had deserted the ship that had brought the missionary to Polynesia and had inserted himself, along with a single "invincible" musket, into tribal politics. Befriending two renegade chiefs—the two who now beckoned the *Betsey* toward their village—he had instigated a bloody civil war, "with all the savageness and barbarity peculiar to their form of war," against the other tribes.[31]

The reverend carried a harrowing warning; the *Betsey* would be in "utmost danger" if Fanning drew her into the harbor, as the villagers were urging. The "villainous scheme" hatched between the Italian and the chiefs was to lure the *Betsey* close to shore, storm her rails, massacre the crew, and plunder the iron she carried. Now it became clear why the Marquesans had produced so few trade goods and why they had so stridently coaxed Fanning to bring his ship toward land.[32]

The wiser course was now to locate another site for procuring water, and Crook suggested Ingraham's Washington Islands to the northwest. The isolated group of ancient volcanic cones included Nuku Hiva, later made famous in Melville's novel *Typee* (1846). Crook believed the local dialects were similar enough that he could act as interpreter. They reached the Washington group the next day in a heavy squall, and at the southernmost island, Wepoo, were immediately met by a flotilla of canoes. These dugouts resembled the double-hulled war boats of La Christiana, and were likewise ornamented with human skulls, and stashed with spears, war clubs, and throwing stones. Fanning sensed that he was encountering a more primitive people than those to the southeast. "It did not appear that these people had ever seen, or been visited, by a civilized being before," he noted in his journal. They showed no interest in the iron that had been a staple of trade elsewhere, preferring bits of broken crockery instead. Finding no water, with dangerous swells nudging the *Betsey* toward a reef, and threatening signs from the people, the captain elected to leave Wepoo behind, keeping his crew safe and his ship intact.[33]

By May 25, the enervating heat of the tropics was taking a toll on the *Betsey*'s crew, now nearly desperate for fresh drinking water. Fanning stood the ship in for the shore of Nuku Hiva, Ingraham's Madison Island. As before, the indigenous people displayed an excess of caution, refusing to come aboard or to trade, and Crook could ascertain the location of neither a deep harbor nor a fresh spring. Yet, the "Nuggohevans" were at least sociable, and they engaged in lively conversation. Fanning attributed their timidity to their "uncivilized" state. Even so, he was sensitive to the inherent challenges of communicating across cultures.[34]

That afternoon, a lookout spotted a spacious bay where the *Betsey* might anchor. But Fanning's patience had worn thin. When a canoe bearing an elderly chief approached, Fanning decided to trick the old man into coming aboard. In his journal, he rationalized his deceit with the explanation that American deception was less cruel than the outright slaughter that had characterized European expeditions. When the old chief, Tearoroo, prostrated himself at the captain's feet, Fanning lifted him up, reassuring him that "this was not the manner of salutation when friends meet friends in my country." Seeing Tearoroo aboard the *Betsey* as she glided into Paypayachee bay, the villagers now showed themselves "very friendly." A plentitude of gifts now lubricated the wheels of commerce, as Tearoroo called for hogs and breadfruit to be ferried to the ship and guides to lead a landing party from the *Betsey* to a watering place.[35]

The warm introduction on Nuku Hiva, so different from the reception on La Christiana or Wepoo, established a few protocols of engagement between these very different peoples. Tearoroo and the captain exchanged names, saying, "Now we are true friends." Surprisingly, the Nuku Hivan king even refused to accept any gifts, asserting he had already accumulated an abundance of Western trade goods. Fanning thought he had now reached "the most perfect understanding" with the tribal leaders.

On the 26th, so many canoes gathered for trade that they entirely surrounded the *Betsey*. Fanning was cautious, but under Crook's urging agreed to allow the native traders aboard, sequestering them to one side of the ship until the *Betsey* tipped on a "rank heel" under the weight. In exchange for figs, fowls, breadfruit, cocoanuts, yams, taro root, and sugarcane, the Nuku Hivans now avidly sought "bits and scraps of old iron" and discarded wine bottles.

Tearoroo begged "chief" Fanning to visit their king, who remained ashore, and again Crook advised the captain to comply as a gesture of goodwill. As always, the captain had difficulty justifying the time away from his main responsibilities, "sacrificing my owners' time and interest" and "gadding or roving about the country." The security of the ship was paramount. Rather than feel threatened, Crook reassured Fanning that the Nuku Hivans were "a generous and open hearted tribe." So confident was he that Crook now advised Fanning that he was inclined to accept their invitation to stay among them. Consequently, Fanning could find no reason to avoid a visit to the young king ashore.[36]

The Nuku Hivan rainforest presented a picture that contrasted dramatically with Stonington's manicured meadows, fields, and commons, its neat, modest farms, and its well-laid paths. The Yankee travelers might well have recalled the subtle fragrance of apple blossom and the bloom of chestnut and hurtleberry that would have marked May in Connecticut as they began their trek into the steamy Polynesian jungles. Against the looming cone of the island's cloud-washed Tekao volcano and a panorama of lush valleys of breadfruit, cocoanut, and hibiscus rainforest unfolding in the distance, a procession of chiefs led Fanning and his steward the mile inland to the king's timber-framed palace. The men of the *Betsey* now discovered a society so unlike their own Federalist New England as to tax their imaginations. The hour-long walk through thick swaths of staghorn fern, shrubs, and grass frustrated the Americans' patience, as their pace was periodically punctuated by speeches from one petty chief or another. More disconcerting still was a Marquesan welcoming rite. As the party approached a stream, pairs of strapping native men locked arms around the Westerners to ferry them across. The first time that he was swept up in a human palanquin, Fanning's steward assumed he was being assaulted and roared out a scream of terror, only to be embarrassed when the crowd burst into laughter.

Among the bewildering displays that the Yankees beheld were the traditional adornment sported by the peoples of the South Seas. Nuku Hivan men cropped their hair close to the scalp in the middle, leaving on each side a long lock, which was either left hanging loosely down or bound up in a bunch. In contrast, women wore their hair "negligently," with those connected to the royal family letting their hair flow loosely down the back, or partly over the shoulders in front and also down the back, while the lower class always coiffed theirs in short bangs. Both men and women draped a simple covering about the waist. The men were "well formed" and extremely active, while Marquesan women were winsome, although Fanning thought their beauty was marred by the copper tint of their skin. Western observers commonly associated nakedness with a "savage" depravity, but Fanning held back judgment, reasoning, "The mildness of their climate [did not require] much clothing."[37]

The *Betsey's* crew were amused and repulsed by the traditional greeting of pressing noses, "a most uncourtly sort of ceremony," Fanning complained. The cloying aroma of cocoanut oil, applied liberally by Marquesan women, repelled even sailors who had not seen a female in months. The practice of tattooing, the suspicion of cannibalism, and the loose bounds of property rights likewise dismayed the newcomers. Yet, reflecting the relatively tolerant spirit of the 1790s, in the waning days of the Age of Reason, Fanning's judgments were muted or couched in apologetic context. There was ample opportunity for miscommunication, but in this, too, the men from Connecticut attributed confusion to cultural and linguistic differences. The Americans had been confused when they inquired into a deep anchorage, and the Nuku Hivans led them to shallow coves of sandy beaches. When Fanning realized that the islanders "considered every place where their canoes could be hauled on shore as a harbor," his conclusion pointed not to native ignorance or stupidity but mutual misunderstanding: "Our not sufficiently understanding each other, was the cause of our getting into that difficulty, and not any intentional misleading on their part." And, they observed a few cultural differences that were improvements on the routines they remembered in their Yankee villages. When a troop of women from the Nuku Hivan royal family boarded the *Betsey*, they arrived exactly on time, "a rare thing at home."[38]

Inevitably, Marquesan political practices disturbed the Americans' republican ideals. When Fanning complained that the villagers were interfering with his crew's access to the stream, one chief encouraged the captain to just "knock them on the head" if any of his people got in the way. For his part, the king issued a *taboo*, banning the Nuku Hivans' use of the stream from dawn to dusk. Fanning was appalled to learn that this traditional prerogative allowed the king a monopoly on favorite streams, beaches, and even particular stands of cocoanut or breadfruit trees. The *taboo* was inclusive, prohibiting the villagers from even swimming and canoeing in the bay. The regent also conscripted his people to work for the foreigners, promising "to furnish a sufficient number of good swimmers to take the water casks to the shore, and after they were full, to re-take them through the surf to the boat." The bearers received a nail for each leg of the route they completed. Fanning registered no complaints about the compensation, although his journal entries suggest some discomfort with the aristocratic structure of Marquesan politics.

Despite the repeated demonstrations of amity shown by the Polynesians, the captain took occasion to demonstrate Western power whenever the opportunity presented itself. He made sure to bring along his fowling musket to his parley with the king. After one Marquesan pilfered an azimuth compass from his cabin and fled by leaping into the bay, Fanning ordered a cannon blast, the noise and flash rendering the natives "the very pictures of fear and terror." But this was as far as he was prepared to go. The chiefs conducted their own search and returned the instrument, although it had been shattered in the plunge from the ship. Fanning took the chiefs' hands, reassured them that he was pleased at their efforts, and "expressed a hope that now our friendship and confidence in each other" would be strengthened. When asked if he wanted the culprit executed for his crime, the captain declined, asking that the thief be punished only if found again aboard ship and nothing "more according to my own notion." Sill, Fanning had read too many accounts of surprise assaults on unsuspecting vessels to let down his guard. At sunset, he ordered the crew to rig nets around the ship and to load the cannon with grapeshot. As an officer and four crewmen stood watch throughout the night, the call of "All's well" broke the evening stillness every half hour.[39]

Yet, friendship was the order of the day. Ironically, the cordial relations between these two very different peoples contributed further to Fanning's construction of Yankee exceptionalism. Like many Yankees who sailed to the far side of the world during these years, Fanning used his journals and ships' logs to document the disruption that Western contact brought to the cultures of the Pacific. And, like that of his countrymen, the captain distanced his encounters from those of the earlier European conquerors. Álvaro de Mendaña de Neira's 1595 expedition provided an apt illustration. Over a two-week period, Mendaña's men killed 200 Marquesans with wanton cruelty. Historians have estimated that 100,000 people inhabited the archipelago at the time of the Spanish visit; by the time Ingraham and Fanning arrived there, it is thought, Western diseases had left perhaps 30,000–40,000 remnants. Subsequent societal disruption created religious and political instability and contributed to ongoing tribal wars. It seems that the "Kind Providence" that again and again intervened to save the *Betsey* left the Marquesans bereft.

None of this history, however, clouded the harmony between the American visitors and their Marquesan hosts. The next day, all hands loaded enough water aboard to carry the ship to Canton, and at dusk Fanning notified the king of their impending departure. On the morning of May 29, Fanning ordered the anchor raised from Paypayachee harbor. The captain touched noses with Tearoroo and bade goodbye to Crook. He thought that most of the Marquesans were reluctant to see them depart, especially the king, who begged they stay for at least another month and was disconsolate when he saw the *Betsey*'s sails unfurl. For his part, Fanning recalled, he "could feel nothing less than the strongest attachment" to the Marquesans.[40]

The *Betsey*'s brief sojourn in the Marquesas marked an early phase in the gradual Western domination of the South Seas. In 1813, amidst another war with Great Britain, Captain David Porter brought the USS *Essex* to anchor off Nuku Hiva to replenish his provisions. Within a span of two months, Porter claimed the archipelago for the United States, embroiled his country in tribal wars, bombarded one village, and launched assaults on others. Congress was appalled, however, and rejected any colonial pretensions to the islands. Not so the European powers. In 1842, Louis-Philippe's government claimed the islands, and, by the end of the century, France had incorporated them into its Pacific empire as part of French Polynesia.

Well after Delano and Fanning had plied the waters of the Great South Sea, an erstwhile whale hunter from New York fashioned a tale that would become the dominant narrative of the American experience in the Pacific. In his youth, Herman Melville had chased whales in the Pacific and women in the Marquesas, and in *Moby Dick*, his 1851 tale of a sea captain obsessed with killing the white whale that took off his leg in a pitched battle, the aging mariner established the idea that Americans had sailed beyond the Cape of Good Hope to pursue marine leviathans. In fact, most of the men who trekked the South Seas were fixated on more mundane matters. Like Delano and a host of other Indies traders, Fanning became obsessed, too, but the goals that consumed them were exploration, discovery, and the potential for making their reputations as gentlemen. Yet, even this pedestrian pursuit of adventure and fame could end in catastrophe, as the men of the *Betsey* learned in the summer of 1798.

In May, Fanning ordered his ship off the well-established route of the Manila galleons, seeking adventure and hoping to don the glorious reputation of a world explorer. As the trade winds continued to push the *Betsey* toward her destination, the crew lived sumptuously off of Marquesas hogs, now complemented with a favorite maritime delicacy, the fat meat of flying fish. On 31 May

1798, the *Betsey's* lookout spotted two islands that did not appear on the nautical charts, although an abundance of small fires lighting the night sky indicated that these were inhabited. Fanning designated them New York and Nexsen Islands (now Hatutu and Nexsen). On June 7, the *Betsey* tacked across the equator again, in search of unmarked atolls, impervious to the dangers that lay beneath the sea. At 3:00 a.m. on the 11th, panicked voices shattered the stillness of the night, as the watch spotted "one continued sheet of white foam" breaking over the reefs of yet another uncharted group. When daylight came, the captain's glass revealed that they had come perilously close to shipwreck, and Fanning named the spot Cape Brintell, after the ship's "meritorious" first officer. This was the sort of discovery that Fanning had sought. He marked the three as Fanning's Islands and reported a "smooth and easy roadstead" along with ample water, fish, and sea turtles. Coasting the triangle-shaped archipelago in the ship's cutter, he carefully recorded depths and marked "the most spacious bay" formed by the three islands. He found a sandy beachhead, and the cutter came ashore on another new world. As the men stood in three feet of cocoanuts, tossing as many as they could into the launch, Fanning contented himself with spearing a bass-like fish, tiring after tossing fifty of the five- to twelve-pound creatures into the boat. Among the bounty were uncountable numbers of tropical birds—boobies and knoddies—"so fearless and gentle, as to be easily taken by the hand." He described "a most beautiful and lovely bird, with its brilliant and richly variegated plumage." Yet, Fanning again was reminded of the danger lurking beneath: "We were much chagrined, while observing these, to see a man-of-war hawk flying by with one in his mouth, apparently having just caught it."[41]

On June 12th, the *Betsey* came across yet another uncharted island, this one standing even higher than Fanning's archipelago and, "moreover, covered with plants or grass, presenting to our eyes a beautiful, green, and flourishing appearance." The captain again called his men together for a nationalist rite: "With the unanimous approbation of every individual on board, both officers and seamen, and with feelings of pride for our country, we named this, Washington Island, after President Washington, the father of his country." Like Fanning's Island, this, too, was deserted despite the ample store of cocoanuts and a plentitude of fish and denizens of the "feathered race." These were heady days for the *Betsey's* crew, so different from the voyages of the famed Iberian explorers three centuries earlier, which had been marked by apprehension, starvation, thirst, mutiny, and even cannibalism. Fanning wrote that "it seemed more like a sailing excursion, or party of pleasure." But he was playing a dangerous game. He had set a course off the reliable trade routes, and again his crew and command might pay the price of his ambition.[42]

In the dark hours of June 14, the *Betsey* nearly ran aground on another sunken reef, again unmarked on Fanning's charts. He registered the discovery on his map, thanked Providence for another narrow escape, and resolved to put the ship on a safer course. Fanning's journal shows that he had become sensible of the dangers his obsession was creating, and he now determined it was "too hazardous to continue any farther in a route so entirely new and untraversed." He ordered the ship's course corrected, turning her northward to verge with the well-traveled and secure track fixed by Spain's Manila galleons. Steering for Tinian Island, Fanning regretted that he and his crew "were not in any probability likely to make any farther discoveries while on this passage," but his sense of duty to the investors and crew now superseded personal ambition. By the end of the month, they had found the westward current and could celebrate the national holiday on July 4 by roasting their last Nuku Hiva hog, singing "Hail Columbia," and having "a pretty jovial time of it."[43]

On the afternoon of the 14th, the *Betsey*'s lookout spotted Tinian. As the ship was "opening the bay," a shocking site appeared, a disturbing reminder of the dangers that lay in this "great expanse." Stranded athwart a coral reef was a shattered Indiaman, three to four times the size of the *Betsey*, beaten to pieces by the ferocity of the waves. Fanning ordered "the American colors" set. He sent men in the cutter to search for survivors, and they found an assortment of English and Malays stranded on the isle. They learned that the battered hulk had been the British East India Company's annual supply ship from Macao to Sydney, Australia, pummeled by storms off the China Sea and forced to beach in this remote corner over a year earlier. The captain had perished and now in command was the first mate, a Nantucket mariner named Swain. Thirty-three survivors remained, including the captain's widow, infant daughter and servant, three officers and seven British seamen, nine Lascars and eleven Malays. Fanning was dumbfounded to hear the survivors politely inquire if he would be willing to provide aid: "To this I could but reply, that . . . it was the bounden duty of every man to render all the assistance in his power, to his fellow-creatures." Three days later, the Westerners and Lascars were taken aboard the *Betsey*, leaving behind the Indiaman's cargo, her Malay crewmen, and ample provisions. There, the Malays would wait with the cargo for Swain to return with a salvage vessel.[44]

The *Betsey* coursed through the Babuyane Islands, north of Luzon in the Spanish Philippines, then basked in five days of pleasant weather across the

China Sea. Reaching Grand Ladrone Island late one evening, the ship picked up a Chinese pilot to guide them through the unfamiliar channel. Almost immediately, events tumbled out of control. Fanning found the bay so choked with junks and sampans of all kinds that avoiding them became a navigational challenge. The *Betsey*'s anchor cable became entwined in a sampan's fishing seine, and a tense standoff ensued. Enveloped in darkness, the frightened fishermen refused to answer repeated calls from the strange vessel that loomed above them. Fearing the worst, the pilot shrieked out a warning that pirates were attacking the ship: they would try to cut the cable and tow the ship ashore, the *Betsey* would be pillaged and the crew massacred. Fanning knew this was a warning to be taken seriously. The various East Indies navigational guides he had consulted advised extreme caution in these waters, as the pirates of the Ladrone Islands had earned a reputation for cunning and cruelty. Furthermore, the Americans could not have avoided the lurid tales of massacre and butchery that filled the taverns of every Eastern seaport. The captain ordered his men to the cannon, but he also wisely exercised restraint, "unwilling, through mistake, to injure any subject of the Chinese emperor." By dawn, all could see the misadventure had been a matter of inconvenience rather than real danger. Still, it would be necessary to cut the net from the *Betsey*'s cable. The fishermen wailed in complaint, lamented that the *fan quai* would cost them their livelihood and they could no longer procure a *chow chow*. Fanning employed his best pidgin dialect to negotiate a resolution, offering a *cum shaw* of rice and sugar and a Spanish dollar to each of the children. Happily, the *Betsey* could now continue into the Pei-ho River to chants of "*Chin Chin Josh*."[45]

Another misunderstanding awaited. On August 13, the *Betsey* finally anchored in Lark's Bay, off of Macao. Fanning assumed that he could discharge his English passengers here or perhaps upriver at Canton. Instead, the Chinese customs officials insisted, "It no have China custom; how can, do." The labyrinth of imperial regulations that had frustrated Shaw and Delano now caught Fanning up in an "unexpected difficulty, and one that at first was like to have caused a vast deal of trouble before it was removed." The Hoppo's men refused to provide the necessary *chop*, or permit, insisting that women could neither disembark at Macao nor travel upriver, and consequently, no one could leave the ship. Fanning was unimpressed with the mandarins' "sublime reasoning." It was well known that *fan quai* women had long been allowed to reside in Macao, and there were, no doubt, Western women in the Portuguese colony even then. The Yankee skipper was outraged, and he complained that the Hoppo's position

The Macao visited by Fanning in 1798 was a global city circumscribed by a web of Chinese and Portuguese regulations. Author's collection.

violated the standard practices of common decency that any civilized nation was required to honor.

"Nothing was sufficient to induce these officers to vary or make any allowance for a case (as this) not contemplated by their laws," Fanning lamented. The standoff had dragged on for five days when the president of the British East India Company Council arrived from Canton. Mr. Richard Hall posted bond and offered "the mandarin a handsome *cum shaw*"; in return, the Hoppo issued the *chop* that would allow Fanning to disembark his passengers. Yet, Fanning's travails were not over. Hall asked that the Americans convey another passenger upriver. A British merchant named McKenzie had contracted fever at Batavia and desperately needed the attention of the British East India Company surgeons at Canton. Two British captains and one from Philadelphia had already refused to take on the task. Perhaps motivated by opportunism, or humanitarian concern, or a bit of both, Fanning agreed, bringing aboard the invalid along with an Armenian and a Persian merchant. The *Betsey* flew the federal flag, but she had become a ship of the world.[46]

Still more obstacles hampered the passage up the Pei-ho River. At the Bocca

Tigris forts, the Hoppo's agents again stopped the *Betsey*, demanding payment for another *chop*, one that would allow her up the next leg of the passage. But now, Fanning's earlier generosity was rewarded, as his Armenian passenger arranged for the *fan quai* captain to view the imperious Chinese fortifications. The self-styled chronicler of exotic lands could not refuse his first real opportunity to record his observations of the world's oldest civilization. But, if Fanning's preparatory reading had led him to expect imperial grandeur or majesty, he was disappointed. Everything he saw disturbed both his anticipation of a fabulous East and his republican values. His guide advised that "the mandarin in command" would allow them to tour a fortress, but only "in consideration of the small sum, or *cum shaw* of a Spanish dollar." For this compensation, the commander "not only gave permission to take our walk, but also directed the officer to show us to the fort." The notable absence of civic virtue was matched by the disorder that the astonished visitors saw about them. The fortress was dilapidated, its great guns impotent. Fanning recorded: "In it fourteen handsome brass nine pound canon, but all very uncouthly mounted; it was besides difficult to depress or elevate these pieces many degrees." The few soldiers he spotted presented a similar image of disarray, lolling about, napping, or gambling. "Their military discipline, so far as we were able to judge by the specimens shown, was very far from being the best in the world," he wrote. The empire's naval defenses were no more daunting. In 1784, during the affair involving the unfortunate gunner of the *Lady Hughes*, Samuel Shaw had described the Chinese navy as "not very formidable," and the army outfitted with swords, bows and arrows, and matchlock muskets. Yet, China was clearly not an impoverished country, and the contrast between the dilapidated fort and the sweep of flourishing rice fields across a stunningly verdant landscape attested to the dysfunctions that plagued the Middle Kingdom. Fanning recorded: "We strolled as far as the top of a hill near by, from which a considerable view of the country was had; this appeared, especially the rich and extensive padda grounds in the valleys, to be pouring forth its productions in great abundance, and promising an ample harvest to its owners." The tour had been instructive, and Fanning's disbelief abated as the *Betsey* continued her journey upriver. Only "after a series of tedious and vexatious examinations at five chop houses on the way up, I arrived in three hours time."[47]

The *Betsey* anchored at Whampoa on August 23, amidst the proud pennants of Europe's East India companies and, her commander was pleased to observe, several displays of the Stars and Stripes among them. Fanning found that his hu-

This painting, *"Henry Tuke," American Ship at Anchor at Whampoa*, portrayed by an unknown artist (c. 1835), suggests Fanning's *Betsey* some thirty years earlier. Courtesy of the Peabody Essex Museum.

manitarian efforts would again pay dividends. Even before the crew had reefed the *Betsey*'s sails, a British East India Company dispatch boat hailed the Yankee ship. It had come to fetch the ailing McKenzie and to offer compliments from the commodore of the Company's fleet. This was the kind of greeting, "couched in the most polite and friendly terms," that Samuel Shaw would have appreciated a decade earlier. Fanning was welcomed aboard the Company's flagship, where the British commander introduced him to his officers and offered "any friendly assistance in his power." The contrast between the reception by former enemies and the treatment Fanning received from the mandarins was striking, as the captain registered in his journal.[48]

His arrival at the factories in Canton in August 1798 was disconcerting, however. The success of the voyage now rested on a commander who had made but one prior voyage to China, who had misjudged the sealing grounds at the Falklands, and who confessed he was "entirely unacquainted" with the Canton trade. New acquaintances again came to the American's rescue. Throughout the fall, Fanning followed a daily routine that took him to the New English factory, where he sounded McKenzie and others for advice on making contact with Chinese merchants, determining the value of his cargo, ascertaining the quality of teas and silks, calculating exchange rates, and a host of other commercial matters. He found the British merchants especially generous with letters of introduction to other *fan quai*, the essential lubricant for conducting business in the East. The furious 1798 tea season had begun in September, and the willingness of the Company merchants to aid an American—and a potential competitor—reveals the remarkable degree of cooperation that bound the expatriates. Fanning settled comfortably into the factory community, befriending especially the recovering McKenzie and immersing himself in the frenetic whirl of expatriate life.[49] His world became at once both confined and enlarged, reduced to the quarter mile of Canton's "golden ghetto" and expanded into the brimming *godown*s of the factories and the cramped shops of Old China Street and Hog Lane. The search for a profitable cargo consumed the bulk of his time there, selling skins and selecting the teas, silk, nankeens, and porcelain that he hoped would fetch good prices in New York's auction houses. To this end, he studied the differences between Bohea, Souchong, and Hyson teas and learned to distinguish first chop from second chop goods.

The harried pace of the tea season left Fanning little time for his journal, and he left few jottings to describe life along the Pei-ho. The captain's apparent indifference is surprising, because an account of the Chinese customs would have added much to his planned book, bringing him greater notoriety and enhancing his reputation as an erudite man of the world. His countrymen, moreover, were hungry for accounts that described American encounters with other peoples, and they would have appreciated passages on China that complemented his more amplified portrayal of Polynesia. Fanning had indeed read much in preparation for his voyage, but he was always more interested in recording the discoveries and observing the natural history that he found in new lands, and the bare effort that he made in describing other peoples was far less ambitious than that of Amasa Delano and other Indies voyagers. Consequently, he came to Canton with as little understanding of Chinese life as he had of the China Trade, and he seems to have left the country even less enlightened, if possible, than before. In the two months that he sojourned at Canton, he ventured outside the Western compound once, visiting the Haichuang temple on marshy Honam (or Honan) Island, across the Pearl River from the New English factory. He went in company with his linguist, but the Chinese guides commonly provided little

The site depicted in Thomas Allom's (c. 1843) *Landing Place and Entrance to the Temple of Honan, Canton* is likely that visited by Fanning in 1798. Author's collection.

enlightenment into the traditions of the Middle Kingdom. Imperial law prohibited native Chinese from learning Western languages, and Western travelers frequently complained that their translators understood little English, instead relying upon a dialect used for business matters, which they called "pidgin" English. As one American lamented, "Their small knowledge of English rendered it impossible to obtain an exact, in fact a very little insight into the principles of their religion" or anything else.[50]

Fanning's burlesque impressions of the Haichuang temple were strikingly similar to those of Sullivan Dorr, a merchant from Providence and Boston who resided at the American factory shortly after Fanning departed Canton. Hovering over the entrance of the structure was a statue both described as "a very fat and portly personage" embossed in gilt, attended on each side by two chimerical figures. Western visitors identified this being as Josh, Joss, or Jos, a corruption of the Portuguese term for god, *deus*, and they equated it loosely with their own Jehovah. Fanning thought that Joss's companions were ridiculous figures. Their upper bodies resembled enormous African men, "grinning most hideously," and their lower extremities were more alligator than men. He thought it humorous when the linguist explained that the deities were present to protect the "very

Thomas Allom's (c. 1843) representation of Haichuang temple may have been the site at which Fanning described a "very fat and portly" gilt Buddha in 1798. Author's collection.

corpulent man" from vandals. The central plaza of the interior was a spacious room that held a large solitary image of Josh against the back wall, "no devils being necessary for his defense where the priests are." Before Josh were situated the altar and an offering table, on which believers set out an abundance of delicacies. Adjacent to this room were the priests' quarters, connected by a secret passageway, and to these rooms the offerings were "appropriated for their especial benefit." A gate separated the assembly of worshippers, who stood outside the temple gates to watch their priests perform arcane rites. Fanning thought that Chinese ritual consisted in the priests marching around the perimeter of the main hall, chanting and stopping occasionally to "kiss the dust." The apparent passivity of the worshippers violated his Congregationalist views, and he lamented that the people did not participate in the rituals of worship but were separated from the altar by iron railings. The pleasant aroma of burning sandalwood, he wrote derisively, was "esteemed by the people as sacred."[51]

The disparaging language of American visitors like Fanning and Dorr reflected the views of skeptics who had little interest in learning the underlying meanings of the practices they observed. Neither man recognized the figure of "Josh" as Buddha nor explained the rituals as Buddhist rites. Nor did they remark on the exquisite craftsmanship worked into the three towering Buddhist figures that graced the temple's hall. Instead, they wedged their wayward impressions into a rigid taxonomy of republican virtues. Fanning believed that an unvarnished corruption by the priests and an unreflective habit on the part of the people permeated the practices he observed. And so he wrote that the priests found it easy to take advantage of the people's "stupidity" and dupe worshippers into believing that Josh had enjoyed their offerings. He lamented that a "foreigner, by a present of one or two pieces of silver to the head priest, can obtain every information concerning their mode of worship, living, &c., which he desires."

Fanning made a pretense of bringing knowledge of the East to the "civilized" world. The vague sketch of his visit to the Haichuang site constituted the sum of his account of China, and his assertion that he learned "every information" about Chinese religion only underscored a posture of ignorance and disinterest. By 1833, however, this would have satisfied the American reading public's appetite for the foreign. The book he published in that year, *Voyages Round the World*, produced from the notes of his 1798 visit to Canton, reflected the attitudes of a Jacksonian America that could easily imagine the world divided between civilized nations and less civilized peoples. Americans could imagine, too, their culture as superior to all others.[52]

With the help of President Hall, Fanning was able to dispose of his cargo of pelts quickly. By October 23, the *Betsey*'s hold was packed with chests of Bohea and Hyson teas, picules (133 and one-third pounds by Fanning's measure) of silk, and bales of nankeen. Boxes of porcelain lined the bottom, providing ballast to steady the hull. The ship and its crew were ready to sail for home, but Fanning wisely chose to delay his departure. A second American ship, bound for Philadelphia, would soon be ready to sail, and her master suggested their passage through the pirate-infested waters of the South China Sea would be more secure if they sailed as "consorts." Meanwhile, John Whetten's *Ontario* had arrived, and this gave the partners an opportunity to confer. It was not until October 30 that the *Betsey* passed Macao, the delay justified by the arrival of the northeast monsoon.[53]

By December 6, thirty-seven days out of the Pearl River, the Yankee consorts made their passage through the Bay of Sunda off the Sumatran coast, their course set south for Java. Fanning had reason to hope that the voyage to China would establish his place in the commercial world of New York. He would return to the South Street docks with the spring thaw and feed the markets hungry for exotic goods from the East. He would bring back tales, too, of adventures in exotic lands, of sounds and sights beyond belief—volcanoes exploding against the night skies of Patagonia, icebergs that cracked like "the discharge of thousands of cannon at once, and . . . shake the earth to its very foundation," of blood-red seas, mysterious temples, and exquisite pagodas. Glory awaited, as well. If she reached her homeport, the *Betsey* would have the honor of being the first vessel to carry the Stars and Stripes of the new nation, "officered and manned wholly by native born citizens," from New York around the globe.[54]

Now, 10,000 miles from the frosty wharves of South Street, straddling the equator, her crew could spy tropical jungle and, barely twenty miles from the sea, the great breathtaking blue pepper mountains of Sumatra. Their attention focused on more immediate matters, however. These were shoal waters, festooned with reefs that lurked just below the waterline, while befuddling calms and treacherous currents could carry a drifting vessel backward into the jagged coral. At other times, typhoons and waterspouts burst in with little warning to capsize a ship and strand her crew. More ominous still, the Sunda Strait was home to the most dreaded pirates in the world.[55]

These buccaneers were Malays, feared throughout the South Seas for their treachery and cruelty. By custom, they fished the rich currents or collected *bêche-de-mer* and birds' nests—the sea worms and woven baskets that were delicacies in the China market. Always, however, their watchmen lurked "among the shoals . . . watching to take advantage of vessels which pass through" where, "embarrassed by the numerous reefs, and frequently striking on them, they become an easy prey to these barbarians, who, on these occasions, assemble together in great numbers." The sight of their *proa*s, or galleys—packed with a hundred warriors to heave the two banks of oars—froze the nerve of experienced sailors. The Malay pirates were infamous for their proficiency with a curved scimitar and the short sword known as the *cruse*, often dipped in poison. They were equally reviled for "their savage cruelty to their prisoners, massacring immediately all the Lascars, or native sailors on board the captured vessels, and putting to death, with the most lingering and agonizing tortures, all the Europeans or whites."[56]

In the uncertain passage through the strait, the *Betsey* was fortunate to sail in company should she encounter a rogue *proa*. Her consort was a larger presence than the little 100-ton brig, a modest affair by European standards, and so tiny alongside the hulking 1,000-ton and even 1,200-ton Indiamen of the great

British, French, and Dutch East India companies that Chinese observers mistook her for the tender of a greater vessel. The larger sails of the Philadelphia ship made her faster "on a wind" than the brig, but her companionship offered much-needed security. Fanning and his crew could feel a wary assurance. But this was the East, and the *Betsey* was sailing in dangerous seas.[57]

With her consort half a mile to windward, the *Betsey* rounded the southern tip of the island, when an incredulous lookout spotted the ominous triangular shapes that indicated the lateen sails of great, oared war canoes. In the approaching bay lay not just one or two, but "a fleet of piratical *proas*"—twenty-nine, Captain Fanning counted—"drawn up to meet us." Frantic crewmen immediately raised boarding nets, ran for muskets, and manned cannon. They may have been dismayed somewhat when the Philadelphia ship suddenly "hauled on a wind for the Java shore," ignoring the *Betsey*'s distress signals and leaving the smaller ship to her fate. Emboldened, the pirates gave chase with sail and oars, quickly catching up to the slow-moving brig. As the *proas* drew in, her crew saw "a set of some of the most hideous animals that ever the light of the sun shone upon," filling the air with their screams. Worse still, Fanning's notes recorded, "at this moment the wind began to abate, and finally failed us all together." Fanning further recounted, "The little preparation we could, was made to give them a warm and hearty reception . . . we waited the approach of these marauders." As his crew attended to their cannon—eight 4-pounders and two 6-pounders—the twenty-nine-year-old captain offered his "encouragement": "There was now no resource left but to defend the ship to the last, yet if every man was firm and undaunted, obeying orders and doing his duty as a freeman, there was at least a glimmering of hope that we should come off with flying colors; but should there, on the contrary, be any flinching, death by the scimitar or poisoned cruse, as usually dealt out by these villains, was certainly in store for us."[58]

The men watched helplessly as the buccaneer fleet maneuvered into three squadrons. One group pulled directly under the *Betsey*'s stern, as the other two advanced on either side of her bow, positioned for a coordinated assault. Captain Fanning had anticipated their strategy and, rather than permit the pirates to execute the plan, he determined "to beat them in detail." Abruptly, he "clapped the helm a weather, hauled up the courses, and the ship, quickly wearing off, brought her broadside as handsomely as mortal could wish, to bear directly on the *proas*." In effect, then, the *Betsey* had slowed, changed course, and turned on her pursuers. The squadron that had been stalking in her wake now stared into the muzzles of their quarry's broadside. The little brig's cannon tore through the mast of the largest vessel and disabled two others, the maneuver so shocking the Malays that they hesitated long enough for Fanning to reposition his ship and, "the better to assist their meditations, gave them another broadside with a suitable proportion of musketry." The Malay fleet then wheeled about in a mass retreat, leaving the dismasted *proa* drifting in the current as the *Betsey* gave chase, her guns "playing on the enemy so long as one could be seen to reach, for by this time their fleet were clearing out as fast as they could."[59]

An even more remarkable encounter now ensued. As Fanning guided his ship toward the lamed Malay galley, the *Betsey*'s crew grappled her alongside, and a boarding officer and men jumped aboard to do battle. Instead, they found the decks cleared and the pirates quavering in the hold. Eventually, "its commander came up, and kneeling, laid his head down, at the same time placing the officer's foot on his neck, in token of submission." The American, versed in the ways of the East, set the point of his sword on deck, "and taking this submissive enemy by the hand, raised him up, then drawing the cruse from its scabbard at the pirate's waist, gave him to understand that all his men must come up and deliver their arms also, to him." One by one, each man came on deck in answer to his commander's call, setting down scimitar and *cruse*. With this, Captain Fanning gave the vessel and crew their liberty, "an unexpected favor, and one which they acknowledged with many signs of thankfulness." Thirty-five years later, Fanning described the events of December 6 in *Voyage Round the World*, framing his behavior as a uniquely Yankee experience. The "new people" acted in ways that were glaringly at odds with the ways of the world, either in Europe or out there. In fact, the Dutch commander at Krakatoa chastened the *Betsey*'s men for their generosity, condemning the Malays as "a bad race of fellows, and . . . far from deserving such liberal treatment." The confluence of three peoples, situating Americans between Asians and Europeans, presented Fanning with another opportunity to praise his idea of American exceptionalism. The Dutchman, he wrote, "appeared to be sadly disappointed when informed that their liberty had been given to them again."[60]

On 30 January 1799, the *Betsey* rounded the Cape of Good Hope and a month later passed St. Helena by, Fanning electing to press on. It was the kind of decision for which he had criticized Captain Steele, when the latter pushed past Ascension Island, bypassing the opportunity to collect drinking water. By the time the lookout sighted Long Island on April 18, virtually everyone had scurvy, with three men confined to their hammocks. With a gale brewing and the ship shorthanded, Fanning wisely chose to sail eastward around Long Island and by evening anchored the *Betsey* in Stonington harbor. He kept the brig there only long enough to procure a pilot and refreshment for his ill crew, then proceeded for New York. They berthed in the East River on April 26, a passage of 178 days from Canton, far longer than Fanning had calculated. He attributed the lengthy voyage to the *Betsey's* wooden hull, now covered in seaweed and algae and penetrated by foot-long sea worms. In the future, the captain promised himself, he would make sure that his vessels were hulled in copper plate.[61]

Indies voyagers commonly poured out their deepest emotions "on obtaining sight of one's native land again." In the week before reaching New York, Fanning recorded "the utmost anxiety" for family, friends, and country. Who would he find still among the living? Who would have "gone on the long voyage of eternity"? And, a particular reflection of life in the early republic, "what shall we find the situation of our beloved country to be?"[62]

At least Fanning and his partners had reason to be pleased with the profits from the voyage. They had tied up their investments for a voyage of nearly two years but realized a handsome profit of $52,300. Within the week, Nexsen posted advertisements in the *New York Gazette and General Advertiser* for sale "at the wharf adjoining the Ferry-stairs," fifty half chests and fifty quarter chests of Bohea, a hundred chests of Hyson, ninety boxes of porcelain, and a thousand pieces of nankeen cloth. Storms had damaged some of the tea, but most could be salvaged and sold at premium prices. By June, over half of the Bohea and virtually all of the Hyson and porcelain had been sold. Additional profits came from the sale of the ship itself, and she was turned over to Leonard Bleeker for auction at the Tontine coffeehouse on May 7.

Of equal consequence for Fanning, the *Betsey's* return was a moment of national celebration, much like the return of the *Empress* fourteen years earlier. Fanning boasted that the *Betsey* had completed the first circumnavigation by a ship out of New York and manned entirely by an American crew. Despite typhoons, pirates, near shipwreck, and native attacks, not a man was lost. Even the federal duties that the Nexsens paid could be construed as a blessing. In a marked departure from today's corporate culture, Fanning *boasted* that the venture paid three times more into "the national treasury as duties on our China cargo" than the cost of the *Betsey*. Although the depression of the 1780s was now a memory, Fanning thought of the voyage as a contribution to the country's prosperity. It was, in the captain's view, a national achievement, and he attributed the *Betsey's* success to "the blessings of a kind superintending Providence."[63]

Edmund Fanning did not die young, as Samuel Shaw, or in obscurity, as

Amasa Delano. He passed away on 23 April 1841, at seventy-two years of age, four days after the death of his wife, Sarah, in the port from which he had launched so many voyages. Fanning had come to call both New York City and Stonington home, confounding the term "Yankee" as a regional identity. Born into a colonial province that had been ruled by King George III, he died in a self-governing republic during the administration of the tenth American president, John Tyler.

Like most Indies traders, Fanning never accrued the wealth or trappings that adorned the estates of more famous China men such as Robert Bennet Forbes, Phillip Ammidon, or William C. Hunter. In October 1813, he petitioned the Connecticut assembly for relief from debtors, due to "various inevitable misfortunes." But he did become an influential figure, achieving the celebrity of which Shaw and Delano had dreamed. He had organized nearly seventy expeditions, either as sea master or owner and investor. He had visited China, Australia, South Georgia, and countless Pacific isles. He had discovered a number of sites, including Fanning's (Palmyra) Island. In 1829, as agent of the South Sea Company, he helped to organize an expedition of "commerce and discovery" to the Antarctic under the command of Captain Benjamin Pendleton and kinsman Nathaniel Brown Palmer. No doubt he was satisfied to read in the *New York Courier* and the *Baltimore Patriot* that his role in planning the expedition all but ensured the success of "those daring adventurers." He was a booster, pushing further exploration of the Eastern frontier. He presented a number of memorials to Congress that advocated government support of exploration, using his own oceanic voyages as evidence of the benefits that the country would gain. The culmination came on 18 May 1836, when Congress authorized the United States Exploring Expedition, to be commanded by Commodore Charles Wilkes.[64]

Fanning became something of a recognized authority on marine natural history. He was cited in the *Medical Repository* (1813) as "an experienced and intelligent ship-master," and in the *Ladies' Weekly Museum*. He contributed specimens of marine animals to the New York Philosophical Society. In 1833 he took the step that would solidify his claim to gentility, publishing *Voyages Round the World; with Selected Sketches of Voyages to the South Seas, North and South Pacific Oceans, China, etc., Performed under the Command and Agency of the Author. Also, Information Relating to Important Late Discoveries; between the Years 1792 and 1832, Together with the Report of the Commander of the First American Exploring Expedition, Patronised by the United States Government, in the brigs Seraph and Annawan, to the Southern Hemisphere.* The book went through multiple editions, first in New York, and the following year in London and Paris. The *American Monthly Review* touted Fanning's tome in its June 1833 issue, and the *Journal of Belles Lettres* followed in July 1834. The book's success achieved Fanning's goal, recognized within the acclaimed canon as *Voyages Round the World.* In 1838, he followed up his success with *Voyages to the South Seas, Indian and Pacific Oceans.*

Less permanent, but nonetheless significant in its time, was the contribution to an emergent national identity. Within a few decades, this character would be eclipsed by traits associated with the westward movement. But, during the period in which the old China Trade coincided with the birth of the nation, the global encounters of Shaw, Delano, and Fanning changed the idea of the American from a provincial subject to an independent citizen of the world.

"How T'other Side Looked"

IKE AMASA DELANO, Edmund Fanning was never a resident of an expatriate community. Nor were the majority of men who trafficked in the Indies Trade. They did not sojourn for extended periods in one place, as Samuel Shaw and Thomas Randall did in Canton. The transient captain or peripatetic supercargo rarely remained in port long enough to set down firm roots, form friendships, or feel himself a member of a foreign quarter. They were more alien to any place in the Indies than even the settled *fan quai* in Canton, the *ferengi* in Bombay, the *kafirs* in North Africa, the *yabanci* in Constantinople, or the *papalangi* in Polynesia. Yet, "voyages of commerce and discovery" that crossed the globe and kept a mariner at sea for months or years at a time brought their own kinds of fulfillment. The mariner who opened new markets overseas had made his mark in the coffeehouses and on the wharves where men of commerce gathered. There were personal benchmarks as well, marking a man as a cosmopolitan citizen of the world and catapulting him into the ranks of respectability. Exploration and discovery, especially when published, established a man's educational bona fides. When Amasa Delano or Edmund Fanning charted unknown reefs, named new islands, marked hidden shoals, and mapped dangerous currents, they earned respect for their contributions to Western science along with the profits of commerce. Melding Patrick O'Brian's characters from the far side of the world, the transient Indies seafarer was part Jack Aubrey, part Stephen Maturin. Like Delano, as well, Fanning was interested not only in enterprise and civility; he imagined himself as an explorer in a new era of discovery. Torn between contradictory goals of commerce and erudition, their observations were often superficial. But, their efforts were significant as self-conscious attempts to shape the national character through their writings and to introduce their idea of the true Yankee as an erudite explorer and careful observer of natural history—a kind of American Captain Cook.[1]

When that legendary English navigator set forth into the Pacific Ocean in 1768, just as British troops descended on Boston to stifle the burgeoning resistance to the British Empire's Navigation Acts, he inaugurated a second great age of discovery. His three voyages reopened the Pacific world to Europe after a lengthy hiatus, introducing the West to Hawai'i, Australia, and America's Northwest Coast. Over the next sixty years, Cook's countrymen sent out twenty-eight more expeditions of exploration and discovery into the Pacific, France dispatched seventeen, and another thirteen carried the flags of the Netherlands, Russia, and Spain. The nascent United States sent out one, in 1838, under Lieutenant Charles Wilkes, with the nationalist title the United States Exploring Expedition. Yet, hundreds of Yankee vessels carried out their own, independent voyages of exploration, under the banner of private enterprise and primarily for the purpose of fostering overseas trade. It was said that between 1795 and 1831, some four hundred American voyages were made to the pepper coast of Sumatra alone, most of these hailing from Salem and Boston. It is a fallacy, as some historians assert, that their "logs were routinely destroyed when they returned home" to keep their routes secret. In reality, the journals of Shaw, the published books of Delano and Fanning, and the hundreds of travelogues that filled the archives of the early republic's marine societies testified to a remarkable spirit of cooperation and a desire to share useful knowledge, so consonant with the civic culture of the new nation. This experience added a dimension to the emerging national identity as powerful as the rugged individualism and self-reliant resourcefulness that later historians imagined characterized the Western frontier.[2]

Ironically, the most famous early American expedition that we recall today (and that crowds the pages of history textbooks), Lewis and Clark's overland journey to the Pacific, met with scant attention in its own day. The "voyage of discovery," as its patron Thomas Jefferson told Congress, was initiated "for the purpose of extending the external commerce of the United States" to the Pacific. But, when Nicholas Biddle eventually published an authorized record of the Corps of Discovery in 1814, the volumes gathered dust on the shelves of Philadelphia's bookstores.[3]

In the early republic, it appears, maritime exploration attracted greater national interest than expeditions into the interior, and Americans imagined overseas discovery as an indicator of national progress. The voyages of men in the "skinning trade" like Fanning, pelt hunters like Joseph Ingraham, and tea traders like Delano made the important discoveries in natural history and geography that vaulted the republic into Europe's academies of science. Newspapers and journals regularly carried glowing announcements of their first visits to the East. When the *Grand Turk* returned to Salem, the populace was excited to learn that she had anchored off Mocha, that "the natives had never heard of America," and "the strange vessel was a 'nine days' wonder'" in this port on the southwestern coast of Arabia. Many papers carried the June 1789 notice of the arrival of a Philadelphia ship from Bengal, boasting, "The *Chesapeake* was the first American vessel allowed to hoist the colours of the U. States in the river Ganges, and to trade there." In these years of the establishment of the new nation, East Indies traders made contact with Japan, India, and China, with Manila, Guam, Sumatra, and Constantinople. Fanning took particular note of his first visits and understood how these defined the American as an enterprising explorer and his nation as one among the community of civilized nations. When the *Betsey* reached its home port after three years away, he took pains to record, "Thus successfully terminated the author's first voyage around the world, performed under the blessings of a kind superintending Providence, without the loss of a man; and this he believes to be the first American vessel, officered and manned wholly by native born citizens, that ever sailed round the world from the port of New York." And, when he reached Pernambuco, Brazil, in 1800, he was pleased to report, in a style reminiscent of Shaw's letter to Foreign Minister Jay, "The governor expressed himself much pleased with the visit, it being by the first vessel of war of our nation ever at their port." He noted that his was the first vessel to pass through Australia's Bass Strait and to reach Sydney, and the first to discover the isle that he dubbed Fanning's, now Palmyra Island.[4]

The scientific spirit displayed by ordinary seamen like Delano and Fanning represented what one historian has called a "vernacular Enlightenment." Accounts of discovery brought legitimacy to upwardly mobile, middle-class men, who used their education-through-experience to acquire the trappings of gentility, just as they sought to give their nation the trappings of legitimacy. This they shared with other nations' expatriate communities, filled with young men on the make like themselves, and the project bound them in the ideal of a global community of self-educated, cosmopolitan citizens of the world. One of these communities was taking root in India, where the British East India Company's governor Warren Hastings had laid the groundwork for a group of scholar-administrators who sought to increase their understanding of India's customs and languages and where learned men such as Chief Justice William Jones had established the Asiatick Society. Affluent readers from Boston to Savannah found their countrymen's travels described in high-toned journals such as the *North American Review*, where one writer commented that every new book on the East whet his countrymen's appetite for more and "make us open every new description of them with avidity." Those of more modest means made their vicarious discoveries in a myriad of newspapers, public lectures, and chapbooks that were becoming available in the republic, where a reader learned of the wider world through *Robinson Crusoe* or a "Concise History of the Algerines."[5]

America's East Indies traders did not carry out the most famous Pacific explorations of that age, however. These were expeditions of the US Navy, and the men who led them, as Commodore David Porter expressed it, went "in search of glory." The voyages of the *Essex* in 1813 and the US Exploring Expedition in 1838 were daring, successful, and controversial. Like the voyages of Delano and Fanning, they recorded dramatic changes in the national character that had developed since Shaw's day, establishing a direction away from the Enlightenment's appreciation for exotic cultures.

The cruise of the *Essex* into the Pacific under David Porter was an accidental voyage, driven by the winds of war rather than the currents of commerce. In 1812, the administration of James Madison goaded Congress into declaring war on Britain, ostensibly over "free trade and sailors' rights," issues for which the Virginian had shown little regard up to that point. It was an ill-considered decision. Although British forces were preoccupied with the French Wars on the continent and in India, America's military establishment was unprepared to take on a battle-tested enemy. By the end of the first year of the war, the Royal Navy had established a suffocating blockade of the Eastern Seaboard that even confined US warships. Porter wanted to risk running the blockade and thought he might have better luck as a commerce raider than taking on the Royal Navy. Anticipating the German submarine tactics of the twentieth century, he planned to cruise the South Atlantic, and even the Pacific, waging war on British whalers. In February 1813, Porter tacked the *Essex* around Cape Horn, reaching Valparaiso, Chile, in May, where he celebrated the first appearance of a US warship in the Pacific. Over the next year, the *Essex* captured twelve whale ships, 360 prisoners, and a treasury in currency and whale oil. By October, Porter withdrew to the Marquesas Islands, a thousand miles west of Chile, and over the next four months repaired and reprovisioned his fleet.

David Porter was more than an ambitious naval officer in the service of a nascent nation; like Delano and Fanning, he fashioned himself a South Seas explorer whose discoveries aided mankind. In Porter's mind, the *Essex*'s turn into the Pacific was something more than a daring mission against an enemy's shipping. In fact, his publications foreshadowed and inspired much of the later Indies Trade writing. The accounts he published in 1815, and reissued in 1822 and 1823, *A Journal of a Cruise Made to the Pacific Ocean* and the sequel, *A Voyage in the South Seas,* crafted the *Essex*'s journey in the literary tradition established by William Dampier and Sir Walter Raleigh, as a voyage of plunder and discovery. This was a venture for nation and science, Porter asserted, and it made a significant contribution to mankind's understanding of the natural and social world. Framing himself as the idealized sailor-scholar, Porter employed the conventional themes that had made the literature of "voyages round the world" a favorite genre among popular audiences. In the vein of vernacular Enlightenment writing, the commodore introduced his readers to the empirical method, reminding them that in exploring the natural world of the Great South Sea observation and evidence had primacy over conventional wisdom and tradition. Rounding Cape Horn, for instance, he endeavored to measure longitude using a chronometer, an instrument that few mariners could afford. When the severe cold of the cape passage damaged the instrument, he wondered how earlier voyagers could have determined their position at sea. Still, he took the "opportunity of offering some hints to those who may succeed me in attempting the passage around Cape Horn." In making the Marquesas, and reaching a warmer clime, he identified in his *Journal* the precise latitude and longitude, using the now functioning chronometer.

Porter's South Seas writing did not discount history, however, and both *Journal of a Cruise* and *Voyage in the South Seas* incorporated another favorite trope found in the genre. The *Essex*'s captain frequently drew on the accounts of previous expeditions to situate himself within an exalted lineage of heroic navigators. In describing the passage around Tierra del Fuego, for instance, Porter compared his experience to the voyages of Anson in the 1740s, Cook in the 1770s, and La Pérouse in the 1780s. But, for Porter, personal and national imperatives required that he challenge the findings of the European explorers who preceded him. At times, his own experiences beguiled him, and he unreflectively recorded these results as well. His description of doubling Cape Horn began by ridiculing La Pérouse's harrowing passage, only to find his ship besieged and his crew terrified by its treacherous waters. Undeterred, he kept to his literary style in his approach to the Marquesas archipelago, in the middle of the Pacific Ocean, where he continued to critique his European predecessors.

The texts he consulted identified the first isle they spied as Hood's Island, "discovered by lord Hood, while a midshipman with captain Cook." Ever the empiricist, he tested this piece of conventional wisdom against his own observations, noting, "The description given of this island by the historian of that voyage, answers so little to Hood's Island, as seen by us, that I should have had my doubts as to its identity." Porter followed this flourish with a detailed history of European and American exploration of the islands, culminating in a triumphant correction of the French error of conferring French names on them. Irony was often lost on Porter, however, who lamented the hubris of European explorers, "arising from national prejudice," while asserting "the justice of the discovery" made by his countryman, Joseph Ingraham of Boston in 1791. Ingraham had named the islands Washington's Islands. Porter did not consider the merit of maintaining the names that the indigenous peoples had favored, but in this, he was in keeping with the spirit of voyages of commerce and *discovery*, as the West imagined them. Nor did his nationalist assertions complicate his sense of scientific objectivity or commitment to the accumulation of useful knowledge. Approaching Nuku Hiva, which he rechristened Madison's Island, he offered a navigational guide, identifying a bay that was "very safe and commodious," minor bays that offered good landing points, and a cove that he particularly favored and that his readers could identify "by the small, rocky island shaped like a sugar loaf." In writing of the *Essex*'s cruise in this way, then, Porter's true Yankee was an admixture of patriot, amateur scientist, and practical seaman.[6]

The one truly national effort at Pacific Ocean exploration, organized by the navy and funded by congressional appropriation, came in response to years of pleas, petitions, editorials, speeches, and committee findings voiced by the maritime community. Despite the accumulated wisdom that seafarers had amassed in nautical archives like the Salem East India Marine Society, antiquated British charts, primitive sextants, and inaccurate geographies continued to serve as guides throughout the early nineteenth century. A Delano or Fanning was sure to fill his cabin with a modest library of natural history titles, but uncorrected maps were of little use and chronometers that located longitude were expensive and often faulty. Consequently, merchants, seamen, whalers, sealers, and the like had long complained that faulty charts and error-plagued maps had caused the wreck of more than one vessel on some isolated coral atoll. Then there were the eccentrics, such as the indomitable J. N. Reynolds, a proponent of the hollow earth theory, who was convinced that great caverns opened at the North and South Poles, allowing passage to the planet's center. Reynolds called upon Congress to fund expeditions through the frozen oceans to locate these strategically significant natural wonders. Edmund Fanning became another vocal booster of maritime exploration. In numerous petitions to Congress, the Stonington commander testified eloquently on the dangers of a Pacific voyage, recalling how he had narrowly escaped shipwreck on uncharted shoals and hidden reefs on too many occasions. He, too, joined the chorus of complaint that urged Congress to support ongoing exploration of the dangers lurking beneath the immense and unpredictable Great South Sea.

In the climate of Jeffersonian parsimony that strained Congress's early sessions, a decade of debate ensued before the national legislature finally appropriated funds for oceanic exploration, and it took another ten years to organize the enterprise. Finally, in August 1838, the six ships of the United States Exploring Expedition, or South Seas Expedition, as most Americans knew it, sailed out of Norfolk, Virginia. In command of the fleet was the "exceedingly vain and conceited" Lieutenant Charles Wilkes, a by-the-book officer whose naval experience had been largely confined to a desk and whose personal insecurities escalated into paranoia and nearly scuttled the expedition. His Ahab-like character was said to inspire Melville's 1851 tale of an obsessed captain in search of a mythical white whale.

Somehow, Wilkes overcame the myriad administrative obstacles that brought endless delays for the mission's departure. Perhaps his own obsessive personality worked to the expedition's advantage here, for, in the end, the commodore's minute planning enabled the squadron to accomplish its goals to a remarkable extent, rivaling the contributions to natural science and ethnography that the Corps of Discovery had made a generation earlier. Wilkes organized the shore parties into two groups. Under his direct command were the naval officers, who conducted nautical surveys and recorded observations of currents, winds, and weather, charted islands, and mapped coastlines. Augmenting the naval detachments was a second, "scientific corps," incorporating some of the country's most renowned natural historians. Filling the ranks of the "scientificks" were ethnographer and linguist Horatio Hale, naturalists Charles Pickering and Titian Peale, conchologist J. P. Couthouy, mineralogist James Dana, botanists William Rich and William Brackenridge, and artists Alfred Agate and Joseph Drayton. Ever the naval officer, and always a martinet, Wilkes gave priority to the nautical survey parties, quarantining the civilians aboard ship at each stopover until the depth charts were completed to his satisfaction.

In the end, the South Seas Expedition gave the country something to crow about, at a time when Americans desperately needed reassurance that their republican experiment was secure. The Panic of 1837, a wrenching depression brought about by Andrew Jackson's ill-conceived plan to scuttle the Bank of the United States, shuttered business firms large and small across the nation. Amidst the morbid accounts of bankruptcies and suicides that filled the newspapers, Americans took comfort in reading Wilkes's frequent reports of the squadron's accomplishments across the globe. In 1839, as the fleet approached Tahiti, the editor of the *United States Democratic Review*, John O'Sullivan, had boldly predicted, "Our country is destined to be the great nation of futurity." As newspaper readers across the United States could trace the fleet's progress in regular accounts from Wilkes and the foreign press, they found strong evidence that O'Sullivan was right, and their navy was making the world American. One could read in the *Wisconsin Enquirer* for 29 July 1840, alongside the reports of protests in England against the Opium War and gifts sent to President Van Buren from Muscat and Morocco, a bulletin drawn from Australia's *Sydney Herald* that lauded the expedition's discovery of Antarctica, a "noble commencement in the cause of science." The *New Orleans Times Picayune* sneered that a French expedition had approached the frozen continent at virtually the same moment, but the Europeans timidly turned back in fear of the crushing ice floes and "the Yankees were ahead of them." The *Richmond Enquirer* joined in, praising Wilkes's achievement as a national effort that "will crown the American flag with honor."[7]

Cruising through 87,000 miles of ocean, the expedition's surveyors drew 180 charts that plotted navigational routes around 280 Pacific atolls and archipelagoes, located hazardous reefs and shoals, marked depths, and identified previously unknown islands. Wilkes and his men explored 800 miles along the Northwest Coast, filling in the map of what would become the states of Oregon and Washington, adding detail to the work of Cook in the 1770s and Vancouver in the 1790s. They did not, in fact, discover Antarctica, as Wilkes claimed; American John Davis's *Huron* had reached the coast of the icebound continent in 1821. But they could not know this in 1839, as Davis's log had not been published by then, and so their visit appeared to confirm both the existence of the terra incognita and its American discovery, adding another 1,500 miles of coastline to the world's maritime cartography. Yankee scientists contributed to the library of botanical knowledge by collecting two thousand specimens of flora and fauna previously unrecorded in European academies. The forty tons of ethnographic specimens and artifacts they collected told Americans much about the peoples of the world. Although the newspapers at home described their discoveries in breathless prose, little of this was surprising to the officers and crew; they had expected to perform great things. In October 1838, midshipman William Reynolds celebrated: "And behold! Now a nation which a short time ago was a discovery itself . . . is taking its place among the enlightened of the world and endeavoring to contribute its mite in the cause of knowledge and research. For this seems the age in which all men's minds are bent to learn all about the secrets of the world which they inhabit."[8]

Americans recognized the significance of their navy's two major Pacific explorations and appreciated the regard that these cruises would garner in Europe's salons and science academies. Overall, however, the record accumulated by hundreds of Delanos and Fannings who recorded their discoveries in a host of private logs, journals, and publications left a more lasting impression on American consciousness than the scientific notes of the Porter and Wilkes expeditions. American readers found adventures like those described in Frederick Bennett's *A Whaling Voyage Round the Globe*, which "would excite the jealousy of the hunter of the red deer in the Highlands, or of tigers in the jungles of Hindeostan," a more visceral, compelling introduction to the world than the sedate reports of the navy men.[9]

The naval cruises did reveal one kind of discovery that frequently lay obscured in the accounts of the Indies traders. Even as the Porter and Wilkes forays into the Pacific confirmed their country's place among the civilized nations, they charted dramatic redirections in its national identity. Where Delano and Fanning had imagined the true Yankee as a dispassionate observer of other peoples, tolerant of exotic customs and religions and even praising native chiefs such as Abba Thulle, Porter and Wilkes exhibited the bravado of a more arrogant, more racist American. This divergent undercurrent had lurked within the corpus of early Indies Trade writing, but in the nation's antebellum period this writing took on a judgmental tone that was both louder and brasher. American readers encountered this more bellicose Yankee in the voyages of second-generation Eastern travelers like Harriett Low. Rather than celebrating American encounters in exotic lands, this reluctant expatriate presented the Yankee traveler as someone who had been forced to abandon the warm embrace of hearth and home for the nomadic journeys through strange lands and among forbidding peoples. Low's once prosperous family had made their money in the South American pharmaceutical trade, but had fallen on hard times in the 1820s. Sending Harriett to China as a nurse for her ailing aunt was a solution to the problem of a large household and scant resources. Representing a new cohort of American travelers, she brought this matured, hardened sense of the East, and of the true Yankee, home.

The Second
Generation

CHAPTER FOUR

Harriett Low in Manila and Macao

1829-1834

IT WAS A RAINY MONDAY, 7 September 1829, when the American Indiaman *Sumatra* dropped anchor in the great anchorage at Cavite, the bustling port for Manila and the eastern terminus of Spain's sprawling empire. The southwest monsoon had lashed the Philippines for weeks, and a tense, electric atmosphere framed the apprehensions of a twenty-year-old passenger, Harriett Low, of Salem, Massachusetts. "I cannot believe it," she wrote to her older sister, Mary Ann. "The Cavita on one side, Manilla on the other." Scanning the bay, she could discern whole families of Filipinos who filled the *caseos*, or dugout canoes, that plied Cavite's waters. Beneath the bamboo awnings, Low saw things that would make Mary Ann cringe. As one canoe passed, Harriett wrote acidly, "The wife was rowing. I should not have known it to be a woman at first, she had on nothing but trousers, the men are merely covered about their middle. I did not like the looks of them so well as I did the Malays. Their faces are not so intelligent." Low was a world traveler, but she was no citizen of the world. She could carry on light conversations within the sheltered drawing rooms of European diplomats and merchants but lacked the intellectual curiosity, the cultural sophistication of an Amasa Delano or Edmund Fanning to grasp the cultural frame of the peoples whom she encountered and judged. In many ways, Low represented the closing of the American mind as a second generation of her countrymen poured into the East.[1]

Salem's most famous female voyager was neither merchant, sea captain, nor missionary. Nor did Harriett Low ever adapt to her surroundings in the East. During her five-year stint at Macao, Manila, and Cape Town, between 1829 and 1834, Low's disdain for anything foreign remained acutely caustic. Despite her exposure to other cultures, her views remained paradoxically parochial; belying

The effervescent Harriett Low (1809–1877), at about age twenty-four, captured by British expatriate George Chinnery, Macao, May 1833. Courtesy of the Peabody Essex Museum.

her religious commitment, her journals and letters revealed entrenched prejudices; regardless of her contacts with a diverse range of peoples, her thoughts continued along a narrow course. In this unyielding constancy, she was typical of the second generation of American travelers to the East, the sedentary residents who formed an extended expatriate community of Yankees abroad. Like others of this cohort, her views did not soften or grow more enlightened or more tolerant. Rather, they gelled into rigid categories of race, nationality, and gender, reflecting the changing national character constructed by her countrymen at home.[2]

Harriett Low was born in Salem in 1809, the second child of Seth (1782–1853) and Mary Porter (1786–1872) Low, into a family of twelve siblings, all but one surviving past their first birthdays. Both parents traced their lineage back to the founders who had settled Massachusetts Bay Colony in the Puritan exodus from England. Their beloved First Church had split amicably in the Unitarian surge that came to Salem about the time of Harriett's birth, as their liberal reverend John Prince graciously presided over the formation of three other parishes, including the East Church of the renowned literatus William Bentley. It appears that the Lows remained staunch Congregationalists, immune to the innovating fashions that swept past them and clinging to the parochial, intolerant New England Way of their ancestors. Yet, the sprawling clan were world travelers, sending out members beyond the Cape of Good Hope throughout the nineteenth century. For his part, Seth remained a homebound jobber, importing medicinals from South America and the Far East. In time, however, Salem's harbor had begun to silt up, preventing deep-draft ships from entering the port, and as New York superseded Salem and Boston, he followed the New England migration that had carried Samuel Shaw and Edmund Fanning to the East River. In 1829, Seth uprooted his family to Brooklyn and reestablished his shop there. While the new home was under construction, he and son Abbot, who was then eighteen, had gone ahead to oversee operations, even as Harriett departed for Macao. In September the rest of the family moved down to New York, but maintained their Salem contacts, returning to visit relatives and friends for years after.[3]

For Harriett Low's generation, the desperate struggle to establish the nation's legitimacy was a thing of the past. And, although the ideal of a virtuous republic that had been so potent for the generation of Samuel Shaw and Edmund Fanning continued to influence the expatriate community of Harriett's day, it did so in an attenuated form. After 1815 and a "second war for independence," most Americans believed that any questions about their national character had been settled once and for all. The next rising generation, more assertive and more confident, was also more concerned with flaunting their brick mansions, silk brocades, and elegant carriages before the world. In Low's Salem, this was the generation that commercialized the commons, relocating the poorhouse and grazing cattle to the salt marshes on the edge of town, and replacing the public meadow and ponds with poplar-lined gravel walks. Ironically, townsmen renamed the new commercial park Washington Square and hired famed architect Samuel McIntire to carve an image of the Revolution's symbol of civic virtue into the arched portal.[4] The credo of progress and improvement that this cohort embraced was a cornerstone on which manifest destiny would be built, and Americans saw peoples who did not embrace their true religion, republican government, and commercialized farms as obstacles to civilization. Such was the rationale for the eviction of the Cherokee, Choctaws, Chickasaws, and Creeks from their farms in Georgia, banishing them from their prosperous farms to barren prairies west of the Mississippi. During the years that Low resided in Macao, Congress had passed the Indian Removal Act, and President Andrew Jackson defended the policy in his 1831 State of the Union address as an act of "Philanthropy."

Nigh her twentieth birthday, 24 May 1829, Harriett Low boarded the India-man *Sumatra* to depart Salem for China. Leaving behind family, friends, and all that was familiar and comfortable, she fought back her tears, recording in her journal a week later only that she "behaved like a heroine." She had approached the voyage to Macao with foreboding. Prior to this journey, she had rarely traveled beyond Salem and, like many of her townspeople, had been offshore only once before, for a "water party." A few months earlier, nineteen-year-old Harriett had written to her "dear father" to lament, "We have not heard of anything but shipwrecks and piracies lately. It has cooled my courage somewhat. I dread nothing so much as those merciless demons, and that is too good a title for them." Her fear of the exotic framed a mindset that would judge the East according to the parochial standards of middle-class, Unitarian Salem. A week before the *Sumatra* sailed, her father wrote from New York. His counsel consisted entirely of a warning to guard her faith "among a heathenish or idolatrous people."[5]

The decision that led to Harriett's voyage had come about earlier in the year, precipitated by events on the other side of the world. After twenty years in China, Samuel Russell, founder of Russell & Company, the dominant American firm in the East, was planning the succession that would follow his retirement. Russell had been impressed with Harriett's uncle, William Henry Low, when the young man established himself at the American factory at Canton years earlier. The great man invited the thirty-five-year-old William Henry to return to China and lead the concern through the next five years. Low agreed, but his plans were complicated by the condition of his ailing wife, Abigail Knapp Low. The couple decided that she should accompany him, but Abigail wanted a companion for the journey, and their eyes set on their niece, Harriett. William Henry provided a significant inducement, promising his brother Seth that he would assume full responsibility for Harriett's financial future.

The Lows went to the East, then, for the same reasons that most Americans did during the Old China Trade—to make their *lac*. A few, such as Fanning's "raw-boned" innocent from the Green Mountains, Jonathan, were drawn to the

East by curiosity and their hunger for adventure. Others, like Richard Henry Dana, went to sea for their health. The majority, however, confided to their journals and letters the need for work and an ardent desire to return to "Yankeeland" as soon as they could. These were not the European fops who took the Grand Tour of the continent to put a worldly polish on their aristocratic cast. The effects were similar, perhaps, in refashioning one's character as a citizen of the world, but the original intent for most Americans was both more practical and more pedestrian.[6]

To bide her time, a week after departure—"It then appeared like a month"— Low began a journal, addressed to her best friend and "dear sister," Mary Ann. She intended it as a "private" or "regular" journal, yet there was a curious formality underlying the manuscript. Her thoughts were intended for an intimate circle rather than the public sphere, with Mary Ann acting as gatekeeper, deciding which passages to share and which to keep to herself. Harriett guarded the book carefully aboard the *Sumatra*, and when young Phillip Ammidon tore the journal from her hands, she feared it was "in great danger" and she was "quite alarmed."[7]

Moments of astonishing beauty defied Low's capacity for description on the *Sumatra*'s four-month outbound passage. The "splendid rainbows, the lunar bows, the meteors, the moonlight nights" and vast ocean, "tossed in fury and smooth as glass," stunned her senses. She wrote to Mary Ann in July that although she had seen several "glorious" sunsets before this, they could not compare to one in the Indian Ocean and were "worth the whole voyage." She delighted in leaning over the taffrail on languid nights to gaze at the brilliant phosphorescence of saltwater algae, which she described as the "most brilliant spectacle" that she could imagine, making the water appear as "a sea of diamonds."

By August, however, as the *Sumatra* left Salem farther and farther behind, homesickness overcame Low's appreciation for the aesthetic splendors of the East. Now, every dazzling sight only made her miss Salem more. "Home never is rightly estimated till we see it at a distance. Absence loads it with charms that it in reality possesses," she complained. The journal became a repository of poignant loss, as Harriett confided to Mary Ann, "Dream about you all every night, which is very pleasant" and, "Do not forget you Saturday nights." Every sight made her want to share the moment with family. "Dear Father" would have enjoyed the stunning verdure of the Indian Ocean. To Mary Ann she lamented, "A most glorious sunset to night. O that you were only here to see it too." The duration of the voyage wore down Low's psychological defenses. "I stood at the stern thinking of home and all associated with that sweet place till I wished that I was there and not condemned in foreign climes." She was even impatient with the "tolerably pleasant" weather that brought "not wind enough" to speed the *Sumatra* to her destination. At the end of August, she grieved, "Here we are still beating about the Indian Ocean. An immense waste of water . . . Every day calculating how many more days shall we see land, which you cannot wonder at, after being 13 weeks without seeing that precious sight."[8]

The tedium of the passage was punctuated by the cry "Sail O," alerting passengers and crew to the sighting of a distant vessel and calling all to the upper deck. The ensuing stampede elicited a confusing amalgam of feelings—"A fear that it may be a pirate, though joy and hope predominate. A hope that she may be bound home. And a hope that she may have some of our friends in her," as Low described in June. Too often, the result was disappointing, the distant ship sailing past, and the *Sumatra*'s passengers unable to "speak" her, in the nautical parlance of the times. As the *Sumatra* carried Harriett eastward and away from the warm embrace of hearth and home in her beloved Cragie Street, she recorded her exhilaration, then regret in hearing of a ship on the horizon. She recalled, "I immediately ran to the deck to see what I could see . . . I as soon ran to the cabin and wrote a letter fervently in hopes that she was bound towards our dear native land."[9]

In August, almost three months into the voyage, with the *Sumatra* steadily approaching Java, the weather was pleasant, but Low's mood grew darker. She was becoming preoccupied with the thought that she had come "so many thousand miles from home." Each passing mile left her feeling more and more powerless. She confided to her journal, "For almost 3 months now we have been floating on—from wave to wave we are driven." Harriett had read more than most travelers about her destinations, but despite ample book knowledge, she fretted for "my prospects of happiness all lying in the future—which is hidden."[10]

Low compensated for her growing sense of helplessness with a reaction against anything foreign. When passing ships hoisted an English or Spanish pennant, she fell into bitter complaint. In June she wrote of spying a vessel on the horizon, "But when she came near enough she hoisted a detestable Spanish flag. We spoke her, but there was no prospect there. Such a miserable looking set I never saw." The next month, as she perused a review of Bishop Reginald Heber's travelogue of India in the *Quarterly Review,* Low descended into a blanket dismissal of India's most popular religion. She vented to her journal, "But the superstition of the Hindoos is beyond all account. I suspect it will be many years before the Christian religion, with all its strength, will have any effect upon that bigoted and degraded race." For the Americans on board, rarely was the loss of contact with their countrymen even abated through encounters with other Westerners. When the *Sumatra* "spoke to an English ship" on July 26, Low wrote home, "It was a great sight for us, I'll assure you . . . but we all wished it had been a Yankee. We have not seen an American since we left."[11]

They bypassed Cape Town, and after three months at sea, the *Sumatra* touched at Christmas Island and Java, the notorious graveyard where tropical fevers decimated Western travelers and where Low caught her first glimpse of Asian people. The sight of Malay fishermen in their *proa*—a "little nutshell," she called it—and the sound of their chattering "amused" Low. The Malays were shorter than Americans, their teeth blackened from chewing betel nut, and, most offensive to her idea of modesty, naked. Although she concurred with Bishop Heber "in thinking their color serves as a covering," all in all, she wrote to Mary Ann, "they seem like a different race of beings."[12]

Two days later, they reached Java Head and passed though the Sunda Strait. Despite Harriett's assertion that "we all enjoyed the sail," it is unlikely that Captain Charles Roundy and the crew shared her experience of "a delightful day." Attacks by Malaysian and Sumatran pirates such as the assault Fanning had survived aboard the *Betsey* in 1798, were still a threat. Just two years after Harriett's passage through the Strait, pirates captured the *Friendship* out of Salem and massacred her crew off of the Sumatran town of Quallah Battoo (Kuala Batu).[13]

The *Sumatra* arrived at Cavite, the great, bustling port for Manila, on a stormy Monday, 7 September 1829. The southwest monsoon brought more pleasant weather for the three weeks Low remained in the Philippines. Most of her sojourn there was spent aboard ship, but the Lows did make occasional forays into Manila to visit the factory of Russell & Company, and these visits brought Harriett into contact with Spanish creoles and indigenous Filipinos. To her eyes, the sights were incredulous, and no written descriptions that she had read had captured the look and texture of Manila. The torrid, muggy climate had blackened the town's single-story, whitewashed houses, and their tiled roofs and pearl-shell windows bore no resemblance to the brick or frame-and-stave architecture of Salem. Making the city appear even more alien, Manila was a Catholic fortress, the "forts, convents, and churches taking up a large part of the place." Still, American travelers often described the colonial capital as an attractive city, and they bided their time in elegant, spacious rooms, "very high, and immensely large," where they dined "delightfully" and enjoyed sunset *pas-*

*seggiata*s (evening strolls) on the Calzada. Harriett got into the spirit of Manila's expatriate community, promenading along the boulevard and riding horses without a bonnet, "in the Spanish style."[14]

Like the Sumatrans, the Filipinos appeared to Low as a different category of humanity. A great many lived on the *caseos* that filled Manila Bay. She was surprised to see so many women engaged in physical labor and, again, she was astonished to see the public display of naked bodies. As she rode through the town, she complained of the "disgusting sights" that confronted her. The people were "such wretched looking objects" that she was surprised they could be happy. Judging from their faces alone, they seemed less intelligent than the Malaysians she had seen at Christmas Island, and she presumed that their behavior corresponded to their intelligence. "They are the most thoughtless people!" she complained, "they never remember a thing a fortnight."[15]

As for Manila's Spanish colonizers, many of their customs were equally intriguing. The ladies rode horseback on "curious" chair-like saddles and donned "singular" red gowns. Their Catholicism, especially, stood out for criticism. Harriett had come from a society whose traditions were ardently Protestant and vehemently anti-Catholic. Her colonial ancestors had defined their identity— imperial before the Revolution and national after it—in terms of their struggle against insidious papism, and later generations clung to the idea of a corrupt and despotic Church. The Reverend William Bentley had welcomed Catholicism to Salem, but his acceptance was a minority opinion. In August 1834, as Low was making her way back to the United States, in Charlestown (now Somerville), Massachusetts, just fifteen miles south of Salem, a thousand Protestant laborers gathered before a convent holding a dozen Ursuline nuns and fifty Protestant students, and over the course of the night burned the building to the ground.[16]

Low's observations of Philippine Catholicism foreshadowed a central theme of the years she would spend in China, as she compiled a rich catalogue of the failings of the "papists," who could be found in expatriate communities from Cape Town to Goa to Manila. She embraced a long-standing Protestant idea that the Catholic priests employed bizarre rituals and ostentatious display to mystify and mislead their flocks. Catholic customs were strange and chaotic to Low, and in the language of her day, "singular." Five days after the *Sumatra* had anchored off Manila, during a brief sojourn in the city, she observed a Catholic funeral and complained that no proper coffin veiled the corpse; instead, the remains were carried through the streets on a board and covered only in a purple cloth. There was "no order in the procession." Likewise, Manila's great cathedral, St. Domingo, was "a pretty church, rather gaudy in its ornaments however."[17]

Low lambasted the hypocrisy that she attributed to Manila's Catholics, claiming, "Their Sunday seems no more like Sunday than this day. It is true they all go to Mass in the morning and confess, but they spend the rest of the day in frolicking." Earlier generations of Lows and Porters had practiced a rigorous observation of the Sabbath, marked by fasting, religious exercises within the family, and attendance at prolonged sermons in drafty meetinghouses. They forbade sports, entertainment, and unnecessary labor. But, in Manila, Harriett complained, one could not tell which day was the Sabbath, "every body at work and noise as usual." She could not even find a Bible in her villa. Low was trained to doubt the sincerity of the Church's leaders and priests, but in Manila, where she first saw crowds of Catholic worshippers parading through the streets, she extended her ridicule to those who followed the faith. Their convictions seemed inauthentic, so unlike her own "true" religion, and even the Catholic practice of confession reflected this emphasis on exhibition. Observing several women leaving the confessional, she dismissed their sincerity with the comment, "They go away happy, thinking they are absolved from all sin and ready to begin a new list." In contrast to the elegance of St. Domingo, the dozens of convents that held hundreds of women were "extremely somber in their appearance," perhaps made more so by the intermittently dreary weather of that monsoon season. They seemed to Low to resemble prisons rather than places of worship. Of particular concern, she confided, the Church professed that its God was universal, but Spanish regulations prohibited foreign burials in Manila's Catholic cemeteries. For Low, only the strangeness of the Philippines was universal. It all made her long for home more fervently, and she lamented, "Everything we see makes us value more our own country and privileges." She had no misgivings when the *Sumatra* raised anchor on September 24.[18]

The southwest monsoon carried the *Sumatra* to Macao in just five days, to a society as exotic in its appeal and outlandish in its strangeness as Manila. Unlike any enclave she had ever seen, Macao was a global city. Three generations before the founding of her Salem, in 1556 or 1557, the Ming emperor Shizong had allowed Portuguese officials to set up a colony on the peninsula as compensation for the *fan quai*'s success in fighting piracy in the South China Sea. In time, Macao became the central link in Portugal's colonial network, a way station linking the tiny European principality to Goa on India's Malabar Coast, from there to the Malay peninsula, eventually extending its precarious grasp

Low's journal represented Macao as a tawdry, run-down place. Her encounters with indigenous Chinese and Portuguese Catholics here did little to alleviate her jaundiced view of other peoples. Author's collection.

to Nagasaki, Japan. By the time Harriett arrived in September 1829, Portuguese residents had fanned out into Macao's windswept hills, while Japanese, Indian, Malay, and Chinese expatriates, as well as Bantu slaves, squatted along the steamy coast below.

Low could find little in common with Macao's motley assemblage of peoples and little to appreciate in this East Asian Babylon. During the four years she spent there, she immersed herself in Unitarian doctrine but never reached out to the disadvantaged people around her, never tried to teach Christianity, and never took pains to learn anything about the Asian religious practices that she found so repellent. Most disturbing to her sensibilities, as in Manila, were the "wretched" Catholics, both the Portuguese priests and their Chinese followers. Jesuit and Dominican missionaries had come to Macao to spread the Gospel immediately following the colony's founding, and by 1610 their orders claimed 150,000 Catholics throughout China. As early as the 1630s, they were building the magnificent St. Paul's Church. When it was completed, the cathedral featured an elaborate granite façade, topped with the carving of a ship watched over by the Virgin Mary. The magnificent rococo architecture did not impress Macao's Protestant expatriates, however. Even the eminent British artist

Veranda of Nathan Kinsman's Residence in Macau, by Lam Qua, c. 1843, a view similar to the one from Harriett Low's Macao villa. Courtesy of Martyn Gregory Gallery.

George Chinnery sketched the site as a tawdry, run-down place, populated by Chinese gamblers, and Low herself had little to say for it.

Populated by sophisticated merchants and worldly diplomats, Macao could have been an alluring place for the Salem ingénue. She wrote home of the irresistible beauty and awe-inspiring sights, often shared with other American expatriates and even old friends from Salem whose travels had brought them to China. But the Salem that she had left behind would not release its hold over her, and she clung to a romanticized world of adolescent intrigue, the familiarity of "hot Orthodox Sermons," and the comforting blanket of family. "Every day seems to attach me more to my dear Mother and brothers and sisters," she lamented. Macao came to represent her lost years of exile, and the restrictions imposed by Portugal's colonial apparatus left her feeling that she occupied a ghetto. If Macao was a ghetto, it was a rather affluent one, a "golden ghetto," as one historian has styled it. Low settled comfortably into the expatriate community, and the rhythms of her life followed an endless round of parties, recitals, plays, games, tours, and dress-up in lavish gowns, Indian-style turbans, and elegant shawls. She boasted that an early morning rising was an event notable for "its rare occurrence." In April 1833, the family traveled to the studio of the renowned British artist George Chinnery to have their portraits painted.[19]

Shaw's generation had appreciated the social order of the Celestial Empire, particularly for the authority that its mandarins had imposed over its sprawling and often unruly millions. Harriett Low's cohort, in contrast, expressed only trenchant disapproval of the Middle Kingdom's political apparatus. When imperial regulations inconvenienced the expatriates, they condemned the imperial bureaucracy as tyrannical. Harriett's observations never evolved into the kind of mature analysis that Shaw and Delano recorded or that she found in the travelogues she so avidly consumed. Instead, her perceptions hardened into blanket condemnations of the "impositions" that inconvenienced American expatriates. She indicted the mandarins' officious ignorance, their unreasonableness, and their cruel application of the law. Yet, her closest encounter with imperial tyranny was a contrived affair. In the year that she and her Aunt Abigail had spent at Macao, Low had watched a stream of British women, mainly the wives of Company officials, ascend the Pei-ho to take residence in Canton's Hongs. It began on 16 February 1830, when Julia Baynes, wife of William Baynes (1789–1866), current president of the Company's Select Committee in Canton, brought her children up to the New English factory. The imperial authorities fumed at the *fan quai*'s blatant violation of the Eight Regulations, but in Low's immature view, "the Chinese are making a great fuss about us poor harmless Fanquis (foreign devils)." Her journal incorporated Americans into an imagined community of civilized nations, an indication of how far her generation had come in erasing the concerns of the country's first travelers. Western camaraderie could not easily erase China's claim to sovereignty, however. The Ming mandarins would not yield before English petticoats, and they set about finding a way to extract the ladies from their lairs in the English Hong without provoking a diplomatic crisis. Regardless, by October 1830, the Low women decided they should not be denied the same opportunity as their British counterparts. Surprisingly, they did so with the connivance of William Henry and the ordinarily conservative merchants who carefully stewarded America's Asian export trade.[20]

On the evening of November 5, disguising themselves as young tars, or midshipmen, Harriett and Abigail secreted themselves in the hold of a fast boat, which carried them up to Jackass Point, the quay that opened up to the Western factories. The often-repeated tale that they were immediately discovered when they disembarked, as Harriett forgot herself and extended her supple white hands to accept an escort from the boat, is, of course, a fabrication. Yet, the mandarins had inserted their spies everywhere, and the ladies' presence was reported soon after they landed on the morning of November 6. Later that

The Factories of Canton, attributed to Lam Qua, shows the spot where Harriett and Abigail Low likely arrived at Canton. Courtesy of the Peabody Essex Museum.

day she noted that "the Hong merchants were making a row, and it is doubtful whether we remain long." Within the week, the mandarins had "disturbed" the Low women's visit by issuing a *chop* warning "that trade would be stopped if one Low did not immediately remove his family to Macao." Still, on November 17 they were still in Canton. It appears that the mandarins, "good-for-nothing creatures that they are," were in fact exerting remarkable patience and were waiting for William Henry to announce the departure. Harriett observed, in the event that she and Aunt Abigail were not ready to return to Macao, the Chinese officials would be willing to "putty off a little," in her mimicking language.[21]

In fact, the Lows' sojourn lasted three weeks, long enough for Harriett and Aunt Abigail to incite further commotion. On November 27, taking advantage of "a delightful moonshiny night," a party of Americans strolled through the Hong compound. They drew little attention as they walked in front of the factories, then up and down the byways from Old China Street on the west to New China Street on the east. But the entourage pressed their luck too far, "were discovered to be Fanquis there; and lights were called for, that the Chinamen might look at us." Soon, a large but well-behaved crowd formed, stoking lanterns to examine the Western women closely. When the Americans reached the entrances of the factories again, a squad of "gallant tars" on shore leave from Whampoa who filled the promenade chased away the mob, and the party returned to William Henry's domicile. For Harriett, the escapade had been a lark, and she described it in the customarily breezy tone that had come to characterize her thoughts about China. Her depiction of Canton's populace revealed the ambivalence that American travelers felt toward the peoples of the East. One entry in her journal described the onlookers who had formed a gaping "rabble" around the Americans' strolling party as a step below the civilized men and women of her own country. Yet, in a later entry, Low showed a more philosophical side. The Chinese crowd had been "perfectly civil," she mused, and their curiosity was no different from what one would expect from the pedestrians of Salem. In fact, the wonder that she saw in the eyes of the Chinese was a trait "of which they have a share in common with their fellow-creatures of more enlightened parts."[22]

Why had the "sober" merchants of Russell & Company, customarily so cautious and deliberative, permitted such a frolic? Certainly, they were aware of the mandarins' irritation with the British in bringing their women up to Canton, as well as the limits of Chinese justice. Why would they risk the company's season, and perhaps the entirety of American trade, on such a lark? For one thing, by the 1820s, the expatriate community no longer respected the authority of the imperial government or feared China's might. A young member of the company establishment, William C. Hunter, derided the imperial directives as "stereotyped phrases," and boasted, "We pursued the evil tenor of our way with supreme indifference." It appears that the Americans were not only indifferent to the demands of local custom and law, they were prepared to stake their season on this gamble. In fact, the initiative for the visit may have come from the boardroom of Russell & Company itself. "Every one advised Uncle to make the experiment of taking us up" to Canton, Harriett recorded in January 1831. Low's visit, a rather pedestrian affair on the surface, signaled a sea change that had been long underway in the nature of American encounters abroad. It may be that William Henry had reason to test whether the Americans were on an equal footing with the British. Under Executive Committee president William Baynes, relations between the commercial houses had deteriorated, and the Americans felt that they had suffered indignities from Canton's English community. By January, Baynes and his staff would be replaced and cordial relations restored. But, in the interim, the American house sought to advance its claim to legitimacy in the global arena beyond acceptance to preferential treatment.

Russell & Company wanted the same privileges that the British had claimed and sought the same recognition as the British East India Company. The presence of the Low women in Macao offered an opportunity to force the issue before both the Europeans and the "Celestials."[23]

Curiously, Low did not direct her ire at the English, and she even described Mrs. Baynes as "a heroine" and "a pattern for all wives." Rather, she and her countrymen targeted the mandarins and their backward, uncivilized, and corrupt "impositions" as the source of their annoyance. Writing to Mary Ann early in 1831, Harriett summarized her reasons for going to Canton: "I could not bear to let the Chinese know they could do anything with the Americans." Ironically, the Low family's modest invasion of Canton reprised and revised a central theme of Americans' earlier China Trade writing. In the years immediately following the Treaty of Paris, Shaw, Delano, and Fanning might well have written that they "could not bear to let the *English* know they could do anything with the Americans." Forty years later, the Lows represented a generation of Yankees who believed that they had been accepted into the community of civilized nations and could now look out upon the world from a position of privilege. Consequently, the hubris that they had not long before experienced at the hands of English writers, they now embraced and directed toward the peoples of the East. The Yankee critique of Asian peoples did not yet take the form of the full-bloom racism that they applied to Native and African Americans, or even the scorn that they would soon direct toward German and Irish immigrants. But the seeds had been sown and would ripen in Harriett Low's lifetime.[24]

The standard that Yankee globetrotters like Harriett Low applied to both the East and Europe was a favorite theory among the intellectuals of the new nation. The men and women who took on the task of envisioning the early republic feared that the historic transformation of humankind, from barbaric hunter-gatherers to effete courtiers, necessarily ended in the decline of civilization. Over the millennia, in every society, they believed, the people had abandoned the virtues of civil society—the connective tissue that bound men and women in a common endeavor and held republics together—to surrender to the temptations of luxury, dissolving attachments to the nation and responsibility to the civic life of the larger community. Harriett's thought was inconsistent in where she situated the Chinese on this scale of social development. At times she placed the world's oldest civilization in "the decrepitude of age." Describing religious feeling among the Celestials for her sister Mary Ann in Brooklyn, Harriett predicted, "Think of the time when all Europe was in the same state, but as the

Harriett Low's excursions beyond the walls of her Macao villa brought her into the vernacular world of ordinary Chinese people but did nothing to broaden her disparaging appraisal of them. Courtesy of the Martyn Gregory Gallery.

world becomes enlightened, this bigotry and superstition will be done away. The mighty fabric is gradually decaying—the foundation will soon be undermined and a new one will be erected."[25]

Regardless, she felt "no sympathy" for the Chinese. More frequently, and paradoxically, she often condemned the Celestial Empire as less civilized than her own. "They certainly do not possess the sensibility and feelings of other nations," she wrote smugly back to Brooklyn. Anticipating Charles Lyell's idea of "missing links"—he first used the term in 1851 in *Elements of Geology*—she confided to her journal, "They appear to me to be a connecting link between man and beast, but certainly not equal with civilized man." Against the stagnation of the Middle Kingdom, she situated her own country, asking rhetorically, "Ought we not to be thankful that we are so much farther advanced in civilization?" Like other expatriates, Low believed in a golden mean of republican simplicity, civic responsibility, and creative energy, and, above all, virtue. Progress certainly produced its own constellation of evils, yet, she insisted, "they are of a more refined and civilized kind." On her homeward voyage in January 1834, reaching Cape Town aboard the *Waterloo*, she reflected on her residence in China and concluded, "For my own part my desire of travelling would lead me to civilized countries."[26]

Yankee travelers like Low believed that the Celestial Empire failed the test of civilization, and they located the wellsprings of its decline in the capricious and often cruel ways in which mandarins applied the law, creating a society distinguished by disorder. Their arbitrary application of the law was an injustice that American observers found galling, especially in the wake of their recent history against the tyrannies of the Sugar, Stamp, and Intolerable Acts. Seventy years before, Low's forbears in the seaports of Essex County had protested "every Outrage committed, and every Refinement of Despotism practiced by a Wicked and corrupt Administration . . . for the Purpose of extorting a Revenue" from them. They had resisted "pernicious innovation" and the conspiracy to "involve a free and loyal People in the ignominious Gulph of Slavery and servile Subjection." And they rebelled against "the numerous Obstacles that have been thrown in their way by the Great Enemies of the Liberties of Mankind." The rhetoric of revolution continued to resonate in the consciousness of antebellum America and to promote the sense that China's imperial apparatus likewise displayed the signature traits of tyranny. What Low found so "provoking"—ironic for one who herself enjoyed the role of cultural provocateur—was the liberty that the mandarins gave the "Company ladies." The women of the British East India Company were allowed to remain in Canton "because they are a body and can bully them, are permitted to stay, and we, poor creatures, must go." Low lambasted "the knavery of these fellows," the mandarins and Hong merchants. She was furious with Mowqua, the Canton merchant who had the temerity to admit that he had lied to the viceroy, claiming that Baynes and Turner had fallen ill and required the immediate attention of their wives, "which was false." Mowqua had claimed that Mrs. Turner was Baynes's cousin, " 'and he so sick he wanchy too much to see her.' Now, he says, that we have come, 'O no can alky sick any more. Now I know not what talky.' " As for Governor Le, she was happy to learn that he had "lost face" by allowing the English ladies to remain while sending the Americans down to Macao, and she hoped that all of them "will get paid for it one of these days." The emperor, however, now distracted by an insurrection in distant provinces, would never learn of the episode, and so justice would never come. The Chinese had succeeded in prying the American women from their perch through a clever ruse, threatening to stop the trade of Russell & Company while permitting the other firms to carry on business. "They were very shrewd, and knew just the tender point to touch," Low observed. "So we were obliged to give in." This was the reasoning of an arbitrary and corrupt administration, and it infuriated Low. "There is no reason in it," she complained. Two years later, in October 1832, when Low heard a rumor that "an order issued to take from foreigners all China women, they are generally wet nurses," she evinced no interest in how this change in policy would affect the "China women" who provided mothers' milk for Western infants. Instead, she raged over the "very dreadful" inconvenience the shift in policy would bring to the doyens of the expatriate community. "Oh these mandarins are too barbarous," she complained.[27]

Regardless, by November 17 the Lows could no longer put off their inevitable eviction from the factory. The ladies looked forward, at least, to a "very pleasant" return, still oblivious to the diplomatic imbroglio they had instigated. Harriett's feelings toward the frolic were curiously complicated, however. On November 27, she asserted indignantly, "We should have been very happy here for three months if they would have let us stay, but they will not." Yet, by January of the new year, she claimed that she had not wished to remain in Canton any longer than her uncle required, that she and Abigail had both fallen ill during their stay, and that they had had to tolerate endless visits from a constant train of visitors in whom she had no interest. "Three weeks answered my purpose very well," she concluded. By early December, they were back in Macao.

On 25 January 1831, reflecting back on the escapade from the comfort of her spacious Macao bedroom, she admitted in a letter to her sister, "I daresay you will think we were wrong to attempt it, thereby breaking the laws of even the Chinese." Again, she defended her violation of "even" China's laws by drawing comparisons between "civilized" peoples and the backward Celestials. Then, contradicting herself, Low claimed that she could find "no comparison to be drawn between the Chinese and any other nation in the world." And, in the circuitous path of her thought, she introduced a second criticism of the Celestial Empire—what she saw as the country's attachment to tradition and its refusal to modernize. In her indictment, Low followed earlier Yankee travelers whose writing explored interwoven themes of Oriental decadence and Yankee virtue and for whom "the stubborn and unfeeling mandarins, governed as they were by illiberal laws and customs," came in for particular mention. "They will not allow any innovation upon 'old custom,'" she complained. Indeed, Canton's mandarins themselves acknowledged that "they 'cannot talky reason,' and must be 'bullied.'" Low imagined a time in the distant future when the cycle of history would swing full circle, and the impositions and tyrannies of the mandarins' rule would give way to a rebirth of enterprise, virtue, and liberty. Two months later, a passage in her journal on the tortured practice of foot binding, which custom required of aristocratic women, predicted, "We shall, or others will see these

Chinese exalted in the scale, their turn must come I think—the barriers must be broken down, ignorance must give place to knowledge, and slavery to freedom. Females will then be exalted; what a state they are in now, poor degraded beings, mere toys for the idle hours of their oppressive masters—crippled, tortured, merely to please them."[28]

The stagnation that irritated American expatriates like Harriett Low was exceeded by another retrograde quality of the Celestial Empire—the corruption they found in trade and government. As Low lamented, the mandarins and merchants would not alter a jot of their ancient traditions or law "and will ding those words into your ears forever if it is not for their interest to violate it, when it is quite a different thing." She followed Shaw, Delano, and Fanning in depicting China as a venal, not heavenly, empire and in claiming that their own voyages of "commerce elevated and expanded the human mind." Americans were confounded by what they perceived as a culture of corruption, and Low was no exception. Not long after she settled into her residence in Macao, Low wrote, "The Chinese are a most singular people . . . They will impose greatly upon foreigners if not closely watched." She characterized the mandarins as "these despicable Chinese, who are not worth our notice" and condemned "the knavery of these fellows." Her views hardened, and by early 1831 she was complaining, "The Chinese are very cunning, and know very well what they are about." She believed that the rationale that underlay the policy of precluding Cantonese women from nursing Western infants was pecuniary as well: "The moment they see a fellow creature making money they begin to squeeze them as it is termed. No doubt this is to extort money from them." Well after Low left Macao, she continued to consider Chinese customs to be the benchmark for "impositions" that Americans could expect to find overseas. At St. Helena in May 1834, she was outraged to be charged seven shillings for a bath, writing that the Chinese were even "excelled by the Europeans," at least in this regard.[29]

The republican thought embraced by the generation of Shaw, Delano, and Fanning assumed that government, in its various forms, influenced the formation of a people's character. Many Indies writers attributed the backwardness and poverty they saw among the peoples of the East to the oppression of cruel and greedy rulers. Low's sweeping condemnations of China rested on a different foundation, and she seldom distinguished between its government and its people. Throughout her Macao residence, she indicted mandarins and servants alike as "these creatures" whose "brutal customs" condemned all to an existence that fell below the scales of humanity. Her vaunted self-education brought no deep insight into the conditions of environment or economy that had fortuitously elevated her and destined so many others to lives of grinding poverty. In her journal, she vilified the assemblage of servants who attended the Low villa as brutes who could barely comprehend the simplest of commands. In letters, she complained to Mary Ann, "Such a sight you never saw." And, everywhere, she represented the Chinese as "having none of the delicate ideas of more refined people . . . They sit on their feet, and are dirty and ugly . . . and as to morals, I will not say . . . I often wish to ask what they think, or if they think at all."[30]

"On our return to Macao it seemed more enchanting than ever. The lovely weather and the quiet were really delightful; and since my return I have employed my time much to my own satisfaction, which is very comforting." Only one challenge soured the return downriver. For Harriett, the myriad duties of managing a household required regular interaction with a dozen or so Chinese servants, and she found these encounters tedious. Her depictions of the villa's staff were jaundiced, and we might imagine her journal's disparagement of "these people" as signs of a particularly ugly racism. Some caution is warranted in reading her thoughts, however. The disdain toward the Chinese that taints her entries reads like the derision that middle-class Americans commonly employed in writing about their own servants in the nineteenth century. Low herself was no aristocrat, but as a particularly pampered favorite within her uncle's household, she imagined herself among the elite, and she considered everyone beneath her as "the canaille" (or riffraff). She derided sailors, laborers, clerks, and especially the European and American servants, whom she could not avoid in Macao's expatriate enclave, including her own maid, Nancy. In describing the Chinese who filled her world, Low revealed the traces of a racist sentiment that diverged from the writing of many first-generation travelers. She echoed the emerging conventional wisdom of her times, however, and reflected the development of the true Yankee in a new guise.

At times, Low reflected on her callous disregard for the Chinese, but she found it difficult to account for. On 23 February 1833, the last year of her residence in China, events caused her to consider again the source of her attitude. William Henry had taken a fast boat up to Canton to aid in rescuing the crew of a junk who were "very near perishing." For her part, however, Harriett wrote to Mary Ann that she could "hardly account for the indifference we feel regarding these creatures." Their stoic resistance before grinding poverty, floods, hunger, conflagration, and a host of other misfortunes made little impression on her, and she confessed that she could not muster the same sympathy for them that she would feel for Americans or Europeans. In one entry in her journal Low did admit that, were the masses of the Celestial Empire given the opportunity to develop democratic institutions, they would become a remarkable people. Yet, more common were slights like "these horrible-looking Chinese," and she ridiculed the queues worn by her Chinese servants, telling her sister, "I should like to show you some of the long-tailed *species*." Her description of a Chinese village on 11 October 1832 was typical. Leading a tour of Macao for two visiting American merchants, Low "undertook to pilot them through the village." She derided the "crowds of huts with legions of squalling children . . . Dirty, filthy creatures I saw no escape from it either, but after some time we made our exit." She could not imagine that the Chinese had the same sensibilities as she and noted that "gallantry and kindness are not understood by the Chinese in general." And she lambasted the Celestials as superstitious and ignorant people. When, in December 1829, she learned that a raging conflagration had consumed two hundred houses in Canton, she was disdainful, observing, "The Chinese will not put out a fire. They say it is 'Joss pigeon (God's business), and no can.' They are a most remarkable people!" Her use of the terms "remarkable" and "singular," in this case, was not complimentary.[31]

Although Low could not account for the indifference that she felt for the Chinese, her disapproval of Europeans was equally acerbic. Insisting, "I will not judge," from the beginning of her residence at Macao, she proceeded to condemn the rest of China's expatriate community with as much venom as she directed toward the peoples of Asia. Even as the *Sumatra* slipped into its berth in Macao Roads on 29 September 1829, gazing upon one of the world's truly cosmopolitan cities, Low was no more content to find herself under Portuguese authority than under Spanish. Her thoughts remained anchored to Salem, a place that, despite the hundreds of global crossings made by her townsmen, was for her immune to the benefits of contact with others. She remained a citizen of Salem, in the world but not of it. Within a month, her alienation complete, she wrote, "I saw a ship passing up to Canton from our door this morning. I watched it for a long time, hoping that I should see the stars and stripes, but could not make any thing of it but an English signal." She had come to associate home with her nation, and her personal identity had merged with her national identity. Exiled to the edge of the world, she turned her gaze toward the elements that offended her American character.[32]

Throughout the nine volumes of Low's journal, Salem emerges as the haven that had drawn her Puritan ancestors out of the corruption infesting Europe's spiritual communities. It was the sanctuary of true religion, "where they worship [God] in a more Christian way, at least in a place where every person knows what they worship and where I hope is more heartfelt than I think it here." Equally indifferent to the cares of the indigenous Chinese or the colonial populace, Low directed her antipathy not at the Spanish or Portuguese themselves but toward the institution that represented to her all that was spiritually corrupt and morally abandoned—Macao's Roman Catholic Church. And, while she condemned what little she understood of the Church's teachings, it was Catholic practice, with its rituals, processions, and festivals, that she pilloried in the letters and journal entries she sent home. Consequently, her correspondents found in the Catholic religion—"if we can call it so"—none of the simplicity and authenticity that characterized Americans. Gathered around the hearthside, her family no doubt nodded in agreement to passages such as, "There is none of that holy stillness here which pervades the air at home."[33]

For Miss Low, as she would have been called, the years spent in Asia brought her closer and closer to a decayed old tyrant, whose tired grip held tenuously but tightly the throats of its subjects. The bawdy funeral scenes that she had witnessed in Manila presented themselves in Macao in March 1833. Raucous processions wove through Macao's streets, assaulting once again Low's sense of social order. She described the scandalous exhibition of the corpse as she had in Manila: "The manner seems to us very shocking. The body is exposed in the coffin through the streets." It all lacked the attention to decorum that the Lows expected—"every thing we see makes us value more our own country and privileges."[34]

Roman Catholic ritual offended the Protestant sensibilities of many Americans, particularly those who traced their heritage back to the pietistic or Puritan traditions of their European forbears. Rejecting this reformist impulse, the early Spanish and Portuguese explorers had wrapped their voyages in Catholic ritual, and such rites remained entrenched tradition throughout the East when Americans like Harriett Low encountered them. The Lows were staunch New England Unitarians, but their emphasis on reading, particularly of religious tracts, and embracing the women as well as the males of the family, harkened back to their Puritan ancestors, who had privileged communal literacy and study of the Word of God as centerpieces of their practices. Harriett bridled at the superstitions, rites, and rituals she found in the Portuguese outpost. In a journal entry for 8 April 1830, she observed, "Mr. Otadue says he went to the misericordia today, and Mr. Parraira was performing the office of our Saviour washing his disciples' feet, twelve old men for the disciples. I cannot bear the idea. It appears to me sacrilegious." The next day, a typical Good Friday in Portuguese Macao, she was further repulsed to see another procession forming, and she documented it acidly: "I cannot bring my mind to think it right to perform this ceremony; it appears to me too solemn to be made a farce of, but I suppose they think it right. But it seems horrid to me to see an image made to represent so divine a person."[35]

A particularly damning charge that Protestants in colonial America had leveled against the Church lay in the hypocrisy, falseness, and "mockery" that its priests practiced to defile the Christian message. The Indies Trade literature redirected this traditional assault to the new nation's twin projects of establishing its legitimacy and constructing a national identity. The republic's eastern travelers identified examples of false faith within every feature of Church practice they encountered in Macao, Manila, and elsewhere.

"Their Sunday seems no more like Sunday than this day," Low had observed in Manila. It was no different in Macao, where an entry for 28 February 1830 revealed, "I have just returned from seeing a procession of this wretched people, the *Catholics;* if I could discover any signs of devotion in their hearts, I could tolerate them, but to see such mockery is beyond every thing." Low's revulsion at such exhibitions of false faith further confirmed her commitment both to Protestantism and to her republican homeland. Consigned to her journal, Low's impressions of a retrograde East, corrupted by indigenous rulers and despotic colonizers, contributed to the hardening of the national consciousness. Those who read and those who heard the hundreds of journals, diaries, and ships' logs that issued from voyages of commerce and discovery or from Americans' sojourns in the East confirmed their own sense of the true Yankee as republican, Protestant, and superior. In a journal entry for 28 February 1830, Low reflected another Catholic procession and commented, "When I see these things I thank my God that I was born where they worship him in a more Christian way, at least in a place where every person knows what they worship and where I hope is more heartfelt than I think it here."[36] The extensive reading in Unitarian literature that filled her empty hours and gave her solace also confirmed her prejudices. Andrew Bigelow's *Travels in Sicily and Malta* and Heber's Indian travelogue helped to guide her gaze toward those Church practices that continued to offend American readers in Harriett's generation. She agreed that confession, absolution, and holy day processions, which could be found around the globe, did nothing to check the "wicked propensities" of its congregants. Low disdained even the Church's liberal acceptance of orphans, who could be left in a basket at a church door. It was, she wrote in August 1833, another example of the "melancholy" state of morals in all Catholic countries.[37]

The most serious complaint that Yankees like Low leveled at the Catholic missions, and what most offended their national sensibilities, was the subtle oppression and real terrors that the Church inflicted on its congregants to keep them steeped in ignorance and subservience. The pantheon of America's revolutionary thinkers, from Adams to Jefferson, had indicted the monarchies of their day for inculcating superstition, dependence, and blind subordination in their peoples to shore up their hold over a populace. Indies voyagers such as Delano, Fanning, Cleveland, and others poured their harshest criticism upon regimes, Western and Eastern, that withheld knowledge and education to keep their peoples in subjection. Low and the travelers of her times continued this theme in their critiques of the Church in Manila and Macao. Harriett registered a disappointing encounter in Macao on 23 January 1830, when she "went into the Cathedral this afternoon. Were not edified." Public education was a central plank in the republican platform of the early republic, and reformers continued to push for wider school participation throughout the antebellum era. Class, race, and gender biases kept many out of the schools, but these obstacles could not close off educational opportunities entirely in a country in which self-learners like Delano and Fanning found books readily available. Reading communities of all ages and both genders engaged in constant exchange of books, diaries, journals, and newspapers. Overseas, however, American travelers portrayed a different relationship between power and education, and they implicated the Church as a chief offender. They frequently described a carefully cultivated maintenance of ignorance, among both congregations and priests, as the modus operandi of tyrants and their oppressive institutions. From Macao, Low sent to her journal readers in Brooklyn disturbing anecdotes of the Church's efforts to control knowledge and freethinking. "They have great power over the minds of these poor ignorant creatures," she wrote on 17 March 1833, "and from all accounts many of them are very unworthy of their charge." When a parishioner dared to break the Church's monopoly on knowledge, the institution responded with force rather than reason. At times, the tyranny was direct and cruel, pitting the strength of the world's largest institution against a weak individual. Harriett was outraged to hear of an incident in which a Portuguese woman had been tormented by her priest for the sin of praising some English residents who had eased her poverty. Guilt had "preyed so upon her mind that she actually went mad." Low's confidant and physician, Dr. Thomas Colledge, thought that she would not survive the anguish. "Is it not horrid?" Low asked. "Many such instances of oppression occur and it seems dreadful that such creatures should have such power."[38]

During her Macao years, Low did not confine her parochial gaze to Catholics and coolies. The English residents of the Pearl River became the unfortunate targets of her jottings as well. Low was predisposed to dislike the English, both by birth and breeding. Her birthplace had been a patriot stronghold during the Revolution, sending out fleets of privateers—the *Yankee Rebel, Yankee Lass, Yankee American*—to harass British shipping, support the American cause, and, coincidentally, augment the wealth of her family and neighbors. Low's education only reinforced her prejudices. On her voyage out to Macao over the summer of 1829, the "traveling spinster's" reading list included Captain Basil Hall's *Travels in the United States,* which she found, on "another cloudy foggy unpleasant morning . . . I do not think he does the Americans justice, nor do I believe any Englishman ever will." Resisting the temptation to toss the book overboard, Low complained, "He in some places makes the Americans appear quite ridiculous."[39]

Actual encounters brought her in touch with people whom she found were "however very polite." Encountering the *Roxbury Castle* from the deck of the *Sumatra* on 26 July 1829, she "again altered my opinion of the English . . . All the English that I have seen are quite as cordial in their manners and even more so than the Americans." When a group of English officers came aboard, she anticipated some tension between John Bull and Brother Jonathan, but instead she reported, "They and we however were very civil, and after taking a glass of wine and begging a pack of cards, inviting us to dine, offering any thing they had on board, asking and answering many questions, they bid us good morning." At Macao, her disposition toward the British continued to mellow. Following a visit from Lady Claridge in October 1829, she pronounced, "I have altered my opinion of the English entirely. We have found none stiff, as we anticipated; on the contrary, affable, polite, and pleasant."[40]

Even so, Low continued to find the English a useful foil for the Americans. On Christmas Day, she was invited to dine at the British East India Company's lodgings in Macao, where the "time passed very pleasantly, and there was nothing stiff about it." Still, she was used to a simpler and less secular celebration, and when the group was invited to join in the English custom of snapdragon, in which the table was set with blue lights and guests "were all to put our hands

176 The Second Generation

into these blue flames, and pull out the raisins beneath," her fortitude melted into apprehension. "I thought I was in the infernal regions, and I never shall forget the frightful visages of some of the gentlemen as they held the plates up near their faces." This diffidence Low shared with other members of the American expatriate community. When English guests were absent, Yankee socials were often marked by moments in which "we got much engaged talking about the manners and customs of England and the impositions of that place." When John Bull did make an appearance, the atmosphere could be one of friendly rivalry.[41]

Such jousting continued throughout the period of the Indies Trade. On a warm afternoon, 1 February 1833, Low engaged in another verbal skirmish between a John Bull and a party of Jonathans. She had played battledoor, an early form of badminton, in the morning, then "had some rational conversation" with the English physician, Dr. Colledge. Colledge was all too representative of the national character of his countrymen: "thoroughly English, somewhat aristocratic, and fond of old customs. The English resemble the Chinese in this respect. Even though their reason tells them they are wrong, they stick to old habits . . . prejudiced like all others, not at all knowing what they do profess." Although she admired the charming, young physician—"so frank in his manners that you cannot help liking him"—he could not think beyond the national conventions he had imbibed. When Colledge chastised Harriett and her American guests for their impertinence in rebelling against their sovereign and predicted that they would "before many years have to *indent* for a *king* for America," the Yankees "all opposed with a true republican Spirit." In the face of English ridicule, however, it became important not just to promise future greatness but also to show the world what Americans had accomplished.[42]

Low faulted Macao's English residents for their "odd expressions" and their "odd prejudices." She doubted that she could ever really trust Englishmen. Their servants were "deceitful creatures," although she later admitted this was a fault they shared with the Lows' own Nancy. Their attitudes toward marriage were disturbingly lax, and she found "English people are different from what we know of Americans; they don't seem to think it any harm to have a *small flirtation* with married ladies. Never mind—no treason here." Chief among their "odd prejudices," was the penchant of English expatriates to boast of the virtues of their nation. Just nine months after her arrival in Macao, she recorded a fresh wave of British travelers, including "Mrs. Crocket who is said to be a very nice person or rather a 'clever' [one] which expresses every thing good with the English." Low dismissed the annoying "display of *patriotism*" that marked their conversation and their books, asserting that she did "not like people's praising their own country and drawing comparisons at all times," oblivious to her own habit of doing so. She warned her countrymen against the English practice of ridiculing anything that did not originate from their own nation. Her criticism continued up through the end of her residence in Macao. On 16 November 1833, she described for Mary Ann a "horrid row" at Cap Sing Moon and explained, "the English are at fault." The incident began when a local Chinese man stole a small article, but it escalated dramatically into an international fracas, with East India Company ships bombarding the man's village. Low frequently castigated her Chinese servants whenever something in her own villa went missing, but now she blamed the English for overreacting and allowing things to develop into a "very bad business."[43]

After four years Harriett Low had had enough of China and its expatriate community, and her life's desire was to get home. Uncle William Henry's health now determined the family's course. On 9 September 1833, he showed up in Macao unexpectedly, troubled with boils, fighting fever, and "looking like death." It was now the height of the trading season, but his colleagues in the Canton factory had determined that his condition did not permit lingering. Dr. Colledge advised that the Macao air would restore him to health and he should remain downriver. William Henry was caught in a common expatriate bind: he could not abandon his responsibilities with Russell & Company, and he could not return to America without securing his *lac*. Ultimately, he had to face the inevitable. As Harriett phrased it, "What will it avail with ruined health?" In fact, it appears that the thirty-eight-year-old Low had contracted tuberculosis, virtually a death sentence in the early nineteenth century. Just months before, he had been the handsome director of Russell & Company and his considerable charm lit up a parlor; suddenly, a withered body, ashen complexion, and nagging cough confined him to a sick room.[44]

On the same day that William Henry turned up at the Low villa, Harriett had reason to contemplate death on a more extensive scale, and she showed far less empathy. The autumn monsoons had brought flooding to the Pearl River, deluging the rice paddies around Canton and driving villagers from their homes. Harriett heard that thousands of Chinese farmers had died. She recorded in her journal that autumn, "All these things are right," and in a Malthusian sense observed that populations in all countries must be "thinned out." She was only twenty-four but had become as world-weary a soul as any old China hand, and even those things that had sustained her throughout the early period of her sojourn—religion and nation—had lost some of their sparkle. In early November, as a round of guests visited the Low household to make their farewells, she complained about her countrymen, "These Yankees do make such unconscionable morning visits that they quite wear one's patience."[45]

As William Henry's health continued to decline, the Lows booked passage on the next departing vessel, the East India Company ship *Waterloo*. By November 14th, amidst the packed crates that held their belongings, Harriett was in disbelief that she would finally be "one of the departing ones" and leave China "for ever, and so soon to be steering westward 'to the land of our love!' Happy thought!" Five days later, the Lows boarded the ship and soon left Macao, "after a little squeeze by the mandarins." She was now one of the "birds of passage," as she described those unsettled travelers in the expatriate community who seemed constantly on the move. She would write from Cape Town that "all are *strangers* and every *thing* strange, with an *uncertainty* how long we shall be here." Harriett kept up her reading regimen, and in early December began Oliver Goldsmith's *Citizen of the World*. She was "much delighted," but the satire about a Chinese philosopher in England would not penetrate her hardened prejudices. Instead, she tested her "Americanisms" on the British passengers and officers and enjoyed the frolics of the tars, who dressed up as donkeys and cavorted with their sixty monkeys.[46]

By the time they had passed through the Sunda Strait and anchored off Anjer (Anuer), along the northwestern coast of Java, in mid-December, William Henry realized that he was dying and asked the *Waterloo*'s captain to make an unanticipated stop at Cape Town. Here, he and Abigail planned to disembark, but they encouraged Harriett to continue on to St. Helena or London to await the homeward voyage of cousin James Low. True to her family, she refused to leave them.

The *Waterloo* reached Table Bay on 12 January 1834, after a passage of seven weeks and three days. Harriett liked the Dutch and enjoyed Cape Town, all but the subtropical African dust blown in by the southeast monsoon. A tawny grit flew everywhere and kept her feeling constantly dirty. Even so, the word that filled her journals and letters throughout her three-month South African sojourn was "delightful." Venturing out into town, she found the music of the Highland Guards band delightful, although she was disappointed to discover that they wore trousers rather than kilts. She strolled through gardens and animal parks, where the gnu, the springbok, and the ostrich fascinated her, and the fragrant gardens filled with oleander and heliotrope offered solace. In contrast to Macao, much in Cape Town reminded her of Salem and felt "homish." The cooler air of southern Africa offered a refreshing reprieve from the oppressive humidity of Macao, reminding her of summers "in America," and "it actually seemed as though I was breathing my own native air." The Anglican services recalled those of Reverend Prince's congregation in the First Church at home. Here, too, "the town was as still as Salem of a Sunday—in Macao it was the same as any other day." She especially liked the Dutch residents, who in many ways reminded her of Americans and who seemed immune to "the formality and stiffness that you find in John Bull wherever he is." The Lows found lodging at a boardinghouse run by the widow Cruywagen and her two daughters, where "everyone was kind and attentive," and where they found a measure of solace in the difficult days ahead.[47]

Harriett's attachment to home and her frequent references to family and friends continued to fill her journals. These entries went beyond an affinity for the familiar ways of Salem. Rather, they formed a signal element in her sense of national identity. When Low compared time in Cape Town to "our Sunday evenings in Salem in America," she did so as a drifting transient, grasping at some association that would make her feel complete. Salem and Macao had become the anchor points of her young life, one representing her romanticized past, the other marking an errant passage into a world that would remain strange and alien. Sailing through the Sunda Strait three weeks earlier, she had described Anjer and Krakatoa as sites of remarkable beauty, so unlike Macao, and consequently "quite enchanting to our eyes." The Cape people knew as little of Macao as the citizens of Salem, and their ignorance endeared them further to Harriett, fostering a satisfying distance from China, as if she had put the place and its people behind her. They asked her about it, which she did not mind, as "I had much rather talk of it than be there." Here, they had few visitors, "just the reverse of what we had been accustomed," and mostly women—it pleased her.[48]

The indigenous people were another matter. "The variety of faces, the African, the Hottentot, and the Caffres, all ugly enough in their way," that filled the streets of Cape Town reminded Low of Manila and Macao and offended her sense of social order. She likely had few actual encounters with the native Kaffir and Hottentot people, except in their roles as servants, but this did not prevent her from making sweeping denunciations. She described the Kaffirs as so primitive that it was preferable that the "poor creatures" should live as slaves, serving under the tutelage of the "civilized" Boer colonizers. Unlike Delano and Fanning, she approved of the Moravian and Methodist missionaries there,

who "teach the natives the arts of life first, teach them to be industrious, provide them with tools and land, and give them instruction and gradually instruct
them in the religion they profess." Indeed, under Boer and British slavery, she
insisted, they lived lives that were remarkably entitled. Treated more like pampered children, "they will never be so comfortable and well off as they are now."
For this, they gave little in return. They were "miserable servants" and could not
be trusted, traits they shared with Europeans and Americans. But her denuncia-
tion of native South Africans, like that of the Chinese, carried a decidedly racist
tone reminiscent of the original seal of her native Massachusetts. Her Puritan
ancestors had inscribed onto the colony imprimatur an image of a Massachusetts Indian, speaking the words, "Come over and help us." The idea that other
peoples required the civilizing influence of the West transcended generations.[49]

Yet, emancipation would come to Cape Town, a result of the Slavery Abolition Act passed by Parliament the previous August, and the American visitor
disapproved. The first news that greeted the Lows on reaching South Africa
was of revolutionary proportions—the dissolution of the East India Company's
charter and the abolition of slavery in the West Indies. Yet, Harriett's sole comment was, "Where is the English government to get 20,000,000£ Sterling for
the emancipation of her slaves?" When the new governor landed on the morning of January 16, she ridiculed the slaves who desperately sought a glimpse
of their emancipator: "They all fancy they are to be liberated at once. Poor
creatures, they will never be so comfortable and well off as they are now in my
opinion." Instead, the masters would be the beneficiaries, liberated, ironically,
from these "great torments." As for the emancipated slaves, they would engorge
the avenues of Cape Town and reduce the seaport to a haven for beggars and
paupers.[50]

Over the two months that he lingered at Cape Town, William Henry received the best medical care that was available in that part of the world. It was
primitive. Dr. John Murray, inspector-general of British troops at the port, ex-
amined Low as soon as he came ashore but prescribed no medicine. Instead,
he recommended that the invalid "eat every thing good" and begin a regimen
of "building up." Medical practices had not advanced greatly from the days
of Washington, whose passing a generation earlier had been quickened by the
application of leeches to bleed illness from his body. In March 1834, one could
read the notice from Mr. Threadgold in the *South African Commercial Advertiser* that he had just received "a considerable supply of vastly superior India
Leeches, which are now for sale at his Dispensary, No. 93 Long-street." Still,

William Henry's condition seemed to improve day by day. By now, however, the tuberculosis was not remedied, and he coughed incessantly. At the end of January, the Lows moved inland to take advantage of the bracing mountain air of Kirstenbosch at the estate of Dirk Gysbert Eksteen. William Henry seemed to improve at times, and Harriett could happily report that he kept her busy as his private secretary. At other times, his condition worsened. In mid-March, the family met with Dr. Murray, who had concluded that "Uncle's lungs are diseased" and there was no chance of recovery. Suddenly, in mid-March, William Henry entered into a state of decline. By the 18th, he confided to Harriett that he knew he was dying and that "it was the will of heaven that he should leave us in this strange land." He succumbed in the evening of March 22, at age thirty-eight and was buried two days later, the first to be interred in the new Episcopal cemetery overlooking the waters of Good Hope. Like Shaw and so many other American expatriates, he had come out to the East to make his *lac*, but his health failed in the enervating climate of East Asia. His story was representative of the Yankees who sailed the South Seas in the early years of the new nation—born in Salem, he conducted business in China, died in South Africa, and was buried in a cemetery recently consecrated by an English bishop on his way to Calcutta.[51]

Abigail and Harriett returned to Cape Town on the 26th of March, to "change the scene" and to begin preparations for their departure. Their timing was inauspicious, however, as this was the season for European expatriates to make the journey home from the East. The Low women, widow and orphan, watched from the Cruywagens' bustling boardinghouse as heavy-hearted travelers headed homeward. Now, everything seemed to be going through passages—the trading season, their removal from Macao, William Henry's death, and the ships that carried weary voyagers away—some too soon, others frustratingly slow. Since leaving Macao, Harriett had grown more reflective, and she attempted to give some constructive meaning to her China years. The melancholy tone that she struck during this period was representative of many, perhaps most, American expatriates, who returned with a sense of failure, defeat, and loss. At the boardinghouse, the atmosphere was one of mourning, as black-creped widows tried to succor one another. They could do nothing for one woman who had buried her husband and three children in India and was inconsolable. Having lost "her all," she "goes home childless and alone," was all that Harriett could write. In a missive to Mary Ann in early April, just two weeks after their uncle's death, Harriett dismissed the narrow confines of her sister's Brooklyn world and rebuked Mary Ann's naïveté: "How little you know in America of the miseries of the rest of the world! India, I believe, is full of such. I could fill volumes with stories of unhappy marriages, of dreadful separations of parents and children; indeed of domestic misery in all its darkest colors. Ambition, envy, jealousy, and all the bad passions, are fully displayed there." The sole ray of light on which she commented was the ministrations of the Dutch populace, whom she called "the best and kindest of people, who have done everything for us."[52]

Harriett had become world-weary. Hearing of an expedition to the Mountains of the Moon in Africa, she responded that she now wished to travel only to civilized countries. The expatriate experience had left her feeling adrift, powerless, and alienated from everything that did not recall her youth in Salem. A signal element of the expatriate condition, accentuated because she was young and a woman, was the realization of her powerlessness. She described herself as "a travelling spinster," and as such, lacked the means to control her fate, buffeted between monsoons, mandarins, patriarchal constraints, and overbooked ships. She revealed this sense one morning in June, aboard another East India Company ship bound for London, after her plans for an industrious day of reading and reflection were once again disrupted. "So little can we control events and so much are we the creatures of circumstances that not for one little day can we pretend to say what we will or will not do." It was an attitude that she had, in fact, carried to the East with her, a reflection of the experience of Yankee travelers in the world that had not changed since the days of Samuel Shaw. They were, she described, still "strangers in a strange land."[53]

Finally, on the 5th of May 1834, almost five years to the day since she departed Salem, Harriett boarded the *Royal George* with Abigail to leave Cape Town. The voyage was a slow, uncomfortable jog, on a ship filled with "noisy French people" and cockroaches, and even now, they would not be heading home directly. She had ample opportunity to compare nationalities, but this time on an Atlantic stage. Not surprisingly, she enjoyed the celebrations of her countrymen. Aboard a British ship on the 4th of July, she noted, "the fifty-eighth anniversary, I believe, of our Independence" and toasted the "peace and prosperity of our country." Harriett Low closed her famous journal with an entry for 20 September 1834, aboard the *Montreal*, off Sandy Hook. She hoped to "stone raisins" for Thanksgiving. But she would not return to the familiarity of Salem. The family had relocated to yet another unfamiliar corner, and she would celebrate the holidays in Brooklyn.[54]

George Chinnery's portrait in miniature of Harriett Low, painted in Macao and now hanging in the galleries of the Peabody Essex Museum in Salem, pictures her in May 1833, at age twenty-four, suggesting a citizen of the world in the style described by Shaw, Delano, and Fanning. She appears confident, adorned in the high style of European gentry, and sophisticatedly holding a book. It is a misrepresentation. Harriett Low never adapted. She never became the cosmopolitan globetrotter that travel to the East had made of Delano or Fanning. Instead, her encounters reflected the values of another rising generation and a new definition of the national character. This American was more grasping, more materialistic, more confident, far less doubtful of her reputation, and certainly less tolerant of the diverse cultures that she encountered. In her five-year sojourn at Manila, Macao, and Cape Town, Low's dislike of all things English may have moderated with time and experience, but her views of others, the Spanish and Portuguese, the Chinese and Africans, in particular, remained caustic, from the outward voyage to the journey home.

"The Estimation of All Good Men"

THE YOUNG WOMAN who wept from the deck of the *Sumatra*, bound for Macao, in May 1829 was no innocent. At least, Harriett Low was not innocent to the moral complications of race and religion that had disturbed American politics since the founding of the colonies and were coming to a head in her lifetime. Her caustic nativism drew on developments that were coalescing during her adolescence and erupted while she was in Macao. In Low's day, the East was not a separate sphere of American life, nor was it immune to the disturbances developing at home. She imbibed her anti-Catholicism in a New England that had been steeped in a hatred of Church and pope and that filled its bookshelves with volumes such as *The French Convert* (London, 1696) and *A Protestant's Resolution* (Boston, 1746), its pulpits with "an unconquerable Aversion to Popery and Slavery and an ardent Love to Religion and Liberty," and its streets with protests against "Popish Tyranny, Superstition, Bigotry, and cruel Principles." Nor was this intolerance confined to Low's corner of the country. A notorious Christmas Eve riot exploded in New York City in 1806, when a mob attacked St. Peter's Church to stop its purportedly satanic rituals. It had erupted just three years before her birth and was one of many similar disturbances that framed her childhood. In August 1834, as Low was on her homeward voyage from the East, a Protestant mob of a thousand working men attacked the Ursuline convent in Charlestown, Massachusetts, forcing a dozen nuns and fifty Protestant students to flee for their lives.[1]

As a young girl in Salem, Low was no stranger to the speeches, sermons, and street gossip that warned of dangerous conspiracies and secret societies threatening the republican experiment. She knew of the slave rebellion led by Denmark Vesey in the Carolinas in 1822 and learned of Nat Turner's uprising in Virginia during her second year in China. "Indian troubles" developed during the years leading up to her passage abroad, and in 1830, Congress passed the Indian Removal Act, forcibly evicting the Chickasaw, Choctaw, and other tribes from their lands in Georgia, a provision that Andrew Jackson rationalized as an act of "Philanthropy" in his State of the Union address. She knew, also, of the assaults on Masons, and, two years before her departure to the East, learned that a national Anti-Masonic Party had formed and a state party in her own Massachusetts was organizing.

For all her scalding criticism of Macao's British expatriates, Low expressed the same haughty, paternalistic view of the world that they were in the process of conquering. She would have felt comfortable with the new generation of British expatriates who now carried this arrogance to China and India, particularly Thomas Macaulay, the future lord and historian who was making a splash with his strikingly Anglocentric views. Macaulay arrived in Calcutta in 1834, as Low was leaving Macao, to serve on the governor's council, at a time when India's colonial administration was in the hands of William Jones and his coterie of "Orientalists." Jones's scholar-administrators had formed the Asiatick Society dedicated to the study of Mughal India. Some had even gone native, sporting the banyans, turbans, and hookahs of Indian elites, even taking Indian wives and mastering indigenous languages. Macaulay was appalled to find that the Orientalists not only sang the praises of Mughal culture, but also even shaped East India Company policy to ensconce native languages and customs within the administrative apparatus of the emerging British Raj. Macaulay soon proceeded to impose his own sense of British superiority onto India's bureaucracy, gathering about him a cadre of "Anglicists," who challenged the Orientalists' notions of cultural sensitivity. The hallmark of his program was an English-style educational system that was intended to "civilize" a core of native-born civil servants. Macaulay famously observed that "all the historical information which has been collected from all the books written in Sanskrit language is less valuable than what may be found in the most paltry abridgments used at preparatory schools in England." Harriett Low no doubt concurred.

The debate between Britain's Asiaticks and Anglicists mirrored the republic's own ambivalence toward the world during its antebellum period. American books and newspapers, cupboards and parlors reflected an interest in the East that continued well after Low had returned to America. Across the country, in the pages of the *Alexandria Gazette*, New Orleans *Daily Picayune*, *Madison Enquirer*, and *Richmond Inquirer*, Americans read Hindu poetry, fretted over typhoons in the South China Sea and volcanic eruptions in Hawai'i, bragged about President Van Buren's Arabian horses (a gift from "the Imaum"), and lamented British abuses in the Opium War. In the bookshops, they purchased travelogues on South Africa, the Loo Choo (Ryukyu) Islands, and India, and in their parlors they laughed over Washington Irving's satirical *Salmagundi*. And, they continued to buy Indian bandanas, checkered muslins, and bombazines as well as Canton crepes. On the eve of Low's return to America, her fellow citizens' fascination with the Orient had blossomed into a complex new philosophy—transcendentalism. In packed athenaeums and tightly written essays, Ralph Waldo Emerson, Henry David Thoreau, and others filled the consciousness of antebellum America with the inspiration of the Ganges and the Bhagavad Gita.[2]

By the time of Low's China sojourn, her country's attitudes toward other peoples, whether the Indians of the subcontinent or the Indians of the Ohio Valley, were ambivalent. Some Americans held onto the Enlightenment vision of tolerant encounters revealed in the narratives of Delano and Fanning; others embraced the emerging ethnocentrism of Low. For its part, the government was changing its policies also, heralded in the bellicose democracy of President Andrew Jackson. Following George Washington's farewell address, Jackson's predecessors had cautiously held aloof from "entangling alliances" and had abjured official support for overseas adventurism. Jackson's democracy, however, brimmed with the bravado of a more assured and more assertive power. Perhaps the most notorious, and most controversial, episodes of Low's time involved Yankee gunboats in the Great South Sea: the *Essex*'s participation in the tribal wars on Nuku Hiva in the Marquesas in 1814, the *Potomac*'s attack on the village of Kuala Batu in northwest Sumatra in 1832, and assaults on Samoa and Fiji by the US Exploring Expedition during its 1838–1842 cruise.[3]

The voyage of the USS *Essex* during the War of 1812 heralded a shift in America's engagement with the world. When David Porter took the war into the Pacific, bringing the *Essex* around Cape Horn in the spring of 1813, his objective was to decimate the British whaling fleet, not to assert American hegemony nor to embroil the United States in local wars among indigenous peoples. Yet, this is what Porter did in the Marquesas, when he anchored his modest fleet of captured whaling ships off of Nuku Hiva, dubbing the cove Massachusetts Bay. Hundreds of American tars plunged ashore to set up a dock and shops for refitting his vessels, in effect taking possession of the island. Porter made no secret of his views of a people "much addicted to thievery [and] treacherous in their proceedings" or of his expectation that his men would find easy sexual gratification among the island's "handsome and well formed" women and girls.[4] By November, he had consummated the occupation, claiming the Marquesas for the United States, christening his village complex Madisonville, and dubbing Nuku Hiva Madison Island. Congress later disappointed the commodore by refusing to confirm American possession of the archipelago, reluctant to follow the course set by Porter's intervention in the island's politics. The *Essex* had arrived during a round of tribal wars, and Porter made the unfortunate decision to involve American interests, supporting the Te I'i people against the Happah. His second ill-considered decision was to turn over command of his expeditionary forces to Lieutenant John Downes, an officer whose colorless personality belied a spirit of bellicose adventurism. Downes led a squad of forty crewmen and hundreds of Te I'i into Nuku Hiva's lush valleys, assaulting a stronghold held by several thousand Happah warriors and their families. The invading force stormed the fortress, forcing their chiefs to submit to terms with both the Te I'i and the Americans. In November, Porter escalated the conflict, leading two hundred American sailors and some five thousand Te I'i and newly allied Happah in a second incursion, this time into the valley of the Tai Pi. His rationale—that his new allies had pleaded for protection from the more powerful Tai Pi—was compromised by his admission that he anticipated a bounty of cocoanuts and hogs from the invasion.[5] When the *Essex* raised anchor in December, she left in her wake the remains of fallen warriors on both sides and bitter memories from a populace who now "considered themselves a conquered people," prepared to rebel at an opportune moment. Nonetheless, Porter, Downes, and the crew had distinguished themselves as Yankee heroes and returned home to a triumphal reception that drowned out the discordant notes sounded in journals like the *Salem Gazette*, which cautioned that actions such as those of Porter in Nuku Hiva would give the national character a hegemonic cast similar to that of the European powers.[6]

Harriett Low had been a toddler when the Madison administration pressured Congress to declare a "second war of independence" on Great Britain in June 1812, yet her consciousness of the world and her country's place in it would be shaped by the tales of Yankee heroism that appeared in the republic's newspapers and conversations for decades after. Today, the War of 1812 is one of the country's "forgotten wars," and its hallmark event—an ill-conceived, ill-fated invasion of Canada—is recalled mainly by scholars and reenactors. Largely forgotten are the global dimensions of the conflict, with the few American victories won mainly across the expanse of the world's oceans. Yankee privateers roamed as far as the Indian Ocean and South China Sea, and at home American newspapers reported skirmishes off of Canton and Calcutta. When the East India Company demanded that China prohibit American privateers from access to the Pearl River, the Celestial government refused the imposition, and American readers celebrated the recognition of their nation's status. Even after the American victory at New Orleans and the Senate's ratification of the Treaty of Ghent in 1814, the nation's navy fought along the East Indies trade routes. Over the spring and summer of 1815, American ships continued their patrols. When the USS *Hornet* defeated HMS *Penguin* on 23 March 1815, the battle took place off of Ascension Island in the South Atlantic, where the *Hornet* lay in wait for British Indiamen. Likewise, when the USS *Peacock* won a handy victory over the East India Company's warship *Nautilus* on 30 June 1815, the skirmish was fought in the Sunda Strait. And, long after these battles, Americans continued to recall the struggle against British tyranny for "free trade and sailors' rights" in the waters off of Java, Sumatra, and Calcutta.[7]

America's Indies Trade faltered after 1815, the victim of its government's embargoes, its people's war fever, and its merchants' maverick success. The French Wars that had begun twelve years earlier virtually paralyzed Europe's overseas commerce and created an opportunity for the new nation to position itself as the only major neutral power. But Jefferson's hated embargo, Madison's inane nonintercourse policies, and the war itself devastated American seaports, bankrupting merchants and debilitating the country's shipyards, sail lofts, rope works, and instrument makers. On top of that, Napoleon's defeat at Waterloo in 1815 opened the world's oceans to Europe's merchant shipping again, and Americans now faced stiff competition that eroded their profits. Complicating their position further, Parliament had stripped the British East India Company of its monopoly over the India Trade the year before, and in the new world order British private traders poured into the subcontinent. Ironically, it was the Yankees' own success that contributed to the loss of the Company's hold over India. Astonished at the Americans' achievements in the Indies Trade and persuaded by Adam Smith's antimercantilist ideas in *The Wealth of Nations*, a free trade movement had grown up in England. In 1813, free trade proponents successfully pressured Parliament to rescind the Company's monopoly. They won the day by exploiting the Company's own records, revealing that it had steadily lost trade to American merchants, who operated without the benefits of a monopoly, hulking ships, a private army, and a costly bureaucracy. Ultimately, the Yankees knew, their Indies Trade had been predicated on artificial conditions that could not be sustained forever, and many had been eying opportunities beyond China and India and even outside the field of global trade altogether. Merchants such as Francis Cabot Lowell were lured by the new technological paradigm that became the Industrial Revolution, and, consequently, channeled their profits from the Indies Trade into textile mills, railroads, steamboats, and canals. In time, Lowell, Lawrence, and Manchester, Massachusetts, replaced Calcutta, Canton, and Bombay as the sites where American entrepreneurs made their fortunes.[8]

American merchants did not give up entirely on the Indies Trade. Instead, they adapted to new economic conditions, as they had after the Revolution, now scouring the distant seas for quotidian commodities like coffee, sandalwood, and pepper. Even birds' nests and sea slugs, the favored Asian delicacy known as *bêche-de-mer*, filled the holds of Yankee ships roaming the Pacific for anything that would sell in the marts of the East. New York and Philadelphia newspapers continued to report the departures of vessels named the *True American*, the *Canton*, and *Malay*, and Americans still read of their countrymen freighting calicoes, coffee, and pepper off the coasts of "Sillicat," "South Tallapow," and "Quallah Battoo." Even peripheral ports gained from this niche commerce, and in these desultory voyages the Indies Trade shaped a local as well as national identity. When Salem, the most famous of these secondary ports, incorporated in 1836, the city seal depicted a Sumatran villager sporting a parasol and surrounded by pepper plants against the background of a Yankee merchant ship drawing into an Acehan harbor.

Americans' encounters with the rajahs, mandarins, and chieftains of the Great South Sea remained cautiously civil, punctuated by lurid reports of piracy and the occasional bloody fracas over theft or bad bargaining. But the voyage of the ironically named *Friendship* shifted their vision of the East and raised fresh questions about their own evolving national character. In February 1831, the *Friendship*, a 316-ton Indiaman belonging to the prominent Salem firm of Silsbee, Pickman, and Stone, moored in the bay fronting the Sumatran village of Quallah Battoo (Kuala Batu, or "Rocky River"), as her captain negotiated an exchange for pepper. In the 1790s, Salem's merchants had discovered the bounty of pepper in the mountains above Sumatra's northwestern coast, and Captain Charles Endicott and a complement of seventeen officers and men had come to pack his ship with the profitable spice. This voyage would be different. On the overcast night of February 7, with Endicott and his officers bargaining ashore, pirates silently rowed out from the village and swarmed aboard the *Friendship*, overpowered the guard, and plundered the vessel. Three sailors were killed and another three wounded, but six managed to lower a boat, reach shore, and locate the captain. The next morning, Endicott made it to Muku to the north, where he found three Yankee ships moored in company, and with their assistance he recovered the badly damaged *Friendship*. When Endicott brought his vessel into Salem on July 16, he reported $40,000 in losses, five men dead, and six wounded.

The massacre aboard the *Friendship* infuriated President Andrew Jackson and his secretary of the navy, Levi Woodbury, who fretted that the incident could provoke more attacks and ultimately force American merchants to curtail their commerce in Southeast Asia. Ever sensitive to considerations of honor, whether national or personal, Jackson demanded retaliation, and Woodbury complied by rerouting an available warship that had been destined for the Pacific. This was the USS *Potomac*, and in command was the same John Downes who had served aboard the *Essex* in 1813 and had participated in the tribal wars on Nuku Hiva. The *Potomac* anchored off of Kuala Batu in February 1832, almost exactly a year after the massacre. Downes's orders had called for him to survey the scene, identify the culprits, and negotiate restitution for the *Friendship*'s losses. Instead, the impetuous commander ordered a dawn assault on the village and its outlying posts along the coast. Perhaps the intelligence he had received at Cape Town convinced him of the futility of negotiations; perhaps his experiences serving under Porter in the Marquesas had embittered him. Regardless, by the evening of February 6, one town was in flames, one village plundered, and as many as 150 Sumatrans killed.[9]

The *Potomac* returned to New York in May 1834, about the time Harriett Low was making her mournful homeward passage by St. Helena. If Downes had expected a heroes' reception similar to the one Porter had enjoyed in 1814, he was disappointed. The response to the *Potomac*'s assault on Kuala Batu in American news journals was mixed, in part reflecting the partisan divide over the Jackson administration generally, in part echoing the country's ambivalence about its expanding role in the world. No longer the anxious, insecure republic fretting over its legitimacy, by the 1830s the United States presented itself to the world as an economic and military power. How it would use that power now became a question for public debate. Fanning's *Voyages*, published in New York the year before and now available in London and Paris editions, reprised the idea of a commercial republic whose posture toward other peoples was one of tolerant amity. But other voices now challenged this cautious approach. A letter from the *Potomac*, published in the *New York Evening Post* on 5 July 1832 and then widely disseminated, celebrated the invasion and gave voice to this more bellicose posture. At the same moment, amidst the Black Hawk War, Americans were reading reports of how untrained Illinois militiamen had precipitated the Battle of Stillman's Run by ambushing Sauk negotiating parties. The incident left traditionalists from the first generation wondering what had happened to their enlightened republic.

The four-year voyage of the South Seas Expedition amplified the simmering controversy. There had been little in the navy's mission that should have induced conflict with the indigenous peoples of the Pacific. Secretary of the Navy James K. Paulding's instructions, dispatched to Lieutenant Charles Wilkes on 11 August 1838, underscored the idea that "the Expedition is not for conquest but discovery." Paulding had advised Wilkes to avoid conflict and to make arrangements with local rulers for provisioning American vessels and to provide shelter for shipwrecked crews.[10] Paulding was a Jackson appointee and a staunch believer in the idea of his country's manifest destiny, and his instructions assumed the superiority of American civilization. He counseled a paternalistic "courtesy and kindness toward the natives." Ten years after Harriett Low had departed Salem, however, Charles Wilkes carried his own ideas of the national character into the Pacific, with effects that were broader and more troubling. Low's depictions of the Chinese were echoed by those of Wilkes, possibly the most judgmental, most condescending of Yankee mariners who ventured into the Pacific. His own narrative describing the expedition, *Voyage Round the World*, carried a title resonant of the great travelogues of Cook, Delano, and Fanning, but its tone and sensibility recalled the swaggering impulsiveness of Porter.[11]

The commodore's own orders on leaving Callao, Peru, in July 1839 required his men to treat native peoples with "courtesy and kindness." But, at the first sign of resistance, on the beaches of the Pacific atoll of Reao, the inclination of the "Stormy Petral," as his men came to call him, was to fire birdshot into a crowd of Polynesians to prove the Americans' "prowess and superiority." A year later, when the fleet anchored in the Fiji Islands, Wilkes again took on the role of enforcer. At Viti Levu, he learned the details of a notorious incident that had taken place there in 1834, hearing an eyewitness account of the massacre of eight crewmen from the merchant ship *Charles Doggett*. Wilkes precipitously ordered the arrest of the leader, a chief and the king's brother, named Vendovi, roiling local politics. Things only got worse. In July, when islanders absconded with a survey boat, Wilkes ordered a village burned and friendly chiefs held hostage until the boat and its supplies were returned. Two weeks later, on Moala

Island, as two officers, one of them Wilkes's nephew, bartered for food, they were set upon and killed. Never one to let professional responsibilities outweigh his personal feelings, Wilkes ordered the destruction of two more villages, leaving them "a heap of smoking ruins," as he wrote, and some eighty-seven Fijians dead. Another year passed, and at Drummond's Island in April 1841, a landing party went to search for a sailor who had vanished, launching rockets and burning a village when they encountered resistance. In order to exact retribution and discourage future treachery, Wilkes then sent an armed expedition against the town of Utiroa. The islanders put up a brave fight, but in the end twelve were killed and their town was burned. By the time the South Seas Expedition had returned to the United States, Wilkes's encounters in the Pacific moved the country from the path marked out by Shaw and Delano and toward that of Porter, and, in time, George Custer, and Wounded Knee. By 1842, Americans had largely joined Europeans in a common sense that they had the authority to force their will on less civilized peoples around the globe. Missionary Robert Morrison, a favorite of Harriett Low, had asserted as much in 1823, when he observed that "the governments of Europe and America" were in a position to force the Chinese to accept their customs and that "affairs might be conducted in a manner much more reputable to the nations of the west than they now are." Such was "the estimation of all good men."[12]

Yet, many of Wilkes's men did not share his bellicose views. One was William Reynolds, a twenty-two-year-old midshipman from Lancaster, Pennsylvania, who secretly kept his own private journal during the voyage. Reynolds was cut from the same practical Enlightenment cloth as Delano and Fanning, and distinguished from explorers such as Charles Darwin. Darwin had observed of the people of Tierra del Fuego that "one can hardly make oneself believe that they are fellow creatures, and inhabitants of the same world." Yet, Reynolds's view was that of the American citizen of the world, and he challenged the emerging racism of his age, asking, "Who can judge one nation by another? What man can say, this people shall be my standard, by them I will judge all others." Where Reynolds was dumbfounded at the Tahitians' sexual promiscuity, like "beasts in the fields," he was more critical of the missionaries who had come to Christianize the native peoples and who seemed more concerned with enhancing their own authority than in conversion. Other shipmates worried over the practical effects of Wilkes's attacks. Surgeon John Whittle predicted that if a Western ship were wrecked on Reao in the future, the natives would massacre the crew in retaliation for the treatment they had received. Charles Pickering, one of the scientificks, was another whose views foreshadowed the cultural relativism of later generations of Americans. His sojourn among the Tahitians in the autumn of 1839 fostered an appreciation of the integrity of Tahitian culture. Having adapted to their natural environment in a way that impressed Pickering, he concluded, "These people are not to be judged precisely by the same rule as ourselves." With viewpoints that differed as widely as that of Wilkes on the one hand and Reynolds and Pickering on the other, the South Seas Expedition emerged as a microcosm of the tensions within the country.[13]

CHAPTER FIVE

Robert Bennet Forbes
and the First Opium War
1838-1840

I N THE EARLY EVENING HOURS of 26 February 1839, a party of American merchants—the cream of the Canton Yacht Club—returned from their sunset sail on the Pearl River, the regular diversion for young Boston, New York, and Philadelphia gentlemen from the trials of fourteen-hour days during Canton's furious tea season. The cheer of genteel camaraderie was shattered immediately upon their landing at the Hong wharves, however. They were "confounded to learn that a chinese implicated in some way with the opium trade had been executed in the public square in front of our factories." A further outrage, the victim had been strangled in the gruesome rite known as the *cangue*, in the plaza of the offices that housed such well-heeled firms as Russell & Company. The grisly spectacle disturbed Boston merchant Robert Bennet Forbes, especially, and he deplored the "insult." But Forbes and his colleagues were troubled less by the cruelty that the Celestial government perpetrated on its subjects than the mandarins' choice of a site for the ritualized performance of their authority. That gentlemen such as themselves should be forced to view such tawdry displays offended their sense of civility, Forbes's partner, William C. Hunter, admonished the presiding mandarin. And he warned the official that the expatriate community leased the factory plaza and consequently considered the space as their private property. The following day, every Hong lowered its flag in protest. The true affront lay elsewhere, however: Canton's expatriates did not wish to be reminded of their own involvement in the crime.[1]

Like Harriett Low, Forbes was part of a second cohort of Americans who had acquired Jacksonian democracy's obsession with individualism, materialism, and racial superiority. The South Seas voyagers and expatriates of this follow-ing generation were citizens of a steadier, more stable, more confident Amer-

Robert Bennet Forbes (1804–1889). Courtesy of the Forbes House Museum.

ica, a proud nation that had weathered the storms of the early republic. The America they left behind in the 1820s and 1830s had fought France to a draw in the Quasi-War of 1798–1799, defeated the Barbary pirates by 1815, and reaffirmed its independence from Britain in 1815. For these Yankees, the struggle to gain legitimacy within the community of civilized nations was completed. And the liberalism they embraced was an expression of "an individualistic and competitive America, which was preoccupied with private rights and personal autonomy." They largely eschewed the Federalism of Shaw and Delano, with its pretensions of civic consciousness, cultural tolerance, and "a decent respect to the opinions of mankind," pronounced in the Declaration of Independence. Where that generation of voyagers had seen the need to defend the integrity of their new republic and the reputation of their national character, the generation of Low and Forbes exuded the arrogance of a country that counted itself among the superior nations of the world and had license to travel to any land with impunity. And, where a Shaw or Delano would have considered the tragedy of 26 February as an alarming insult to Enlightenment ideals like the rights of man, virtuous freedom, and "the pride of human virtue," Forbes regarded it as an affront to personal rights and private property.[2]

On the surface, Robert Bennet Forbes epitomized the China trader as a romanticized, adventurous, larger-than-life figure, exploiting the exotic luxuries of the Orient. He sailed ships into nearly every ocean, battled pirates and weathered typhoons in the South China Sea, freighted opium through the Sea of Bengal, brought ice to Canton and carried food to Ireland during the Great Famine, volunteered his services during the Civil War, invented an ingenious kind of rigging, built shelters for needy sailors, and, not coincidentally, amassed a fortune. Beneath the glimmer of the conventional American rags-to-riches fable, however, Forbes's narrative exposed the harsh realities of Americans' early voyages in the Great South Sea—sacrifice and suffering, loss and loneliness. Like many Indies traders who came before him, Forbes recalled the events of a stormy life years after he had left the sea. In his *Personal Reminiscences* (1882), the mythology of the Old China Trade resembles the façades of the Western factories that once loomed imperiously over the Pei-ho River, their whitewashed classical formalism disguising dank brick warehouses and offices where clerks and coolies furiously sweated over chests of opium and teas. Significantly, the narratives they sent home along with cargoes of porcelain and silk redefined the maturing American character. Forbes's *Reminiscences* was not only a parable of astounding success, although that is a dominant chord in his writing. It was also an account of piercing sacrifice and loss that inspired in its author remarkable empathy for the suffering of others, yet little concern for the Chinese and Indians who appeared so different from his own race.[3]

As with Harriett Low, it is difficult to say that Forbes adapted to his surroundings in the East. Certainly, he accepted the factories and villas of the Pei-ho River as his domain. More than Low, however, and more like Thomas Macaulay's Anglicists, Forbes sought to make the East adapt to his beliefs. During a dozen voyages and two extended stays at Canton, in 1830–1832 and 1838–1840, Forbes's disdain for the East remained acutely acerbic. His views of Asian peoples did not soften or grow more enlightened or more tolerant. Rather, they hardened into orders of race, nationality, and gender. Forbes seems never to have tried to study the languages, survey the beliefs, or understand the customs of the Chinese and Indian peoples with whom he did business.

Forbes was born fifty years after Samuel Shaw, on 18 September 1804, in Jamaica Plain, then a rural suburb of Boston. He was born into the kind of middle-class family that, like the Shaws, Delanos, Fannings, and Lows, saw its fortunes fluctuate dramatically as wars, depressions, and treaties changed the rules of overseas commerce, always grasping for opportunity and as often beaten back. Bennet, as he became known, was the son of Boston merchant Ralph Bennet Forbes (1773–1824) and Margaret Perkins (1773–1856) and the second of eight children. Ralph Forbes was esteemed as a man of "great energy," but business had not favored him, and at age forty-five he suffered a stroke from which he was partially paralyzed. He died six years later, in 1824, when Bennet was twenty-one. Consequently, the wealth with which the family name is associated today lay well in the future and was scarcely a dream for young Bennet. Through the next decade, the orphaned Forbes children subsisted on the generosity of their mother's relations.

For Margaret Perkins Forbes, the character of a family, like the identity of a nation, necessarily evoked the principles of duty and responsibility, and she inculcated their importance in her children. Years later, Bennet recalled the difficult conditions of his childhood, attesting that his "most ardent desire" was to assist his mother, then to "deserve the very high confidence" placed in him by family members like his uncles and patrons Thomas Handasyd Perkins and John P. Cushing. In contrast to the expansive individualism that we associate with Jacksonian America, Forbes represented himself as a man who subsumed his interests within the family. Indeed, he believed, "all that I had and all that I could get belonged to my mother, and was only held in trust by me for her comfort." As for money, he claimed to be "entirely indifferent . . . except as a means for their [his family's] benefit." Ironically, the Perkins-Forbes clan resembled the exemplary household of Confucian philosophy, refracted through the New England Way, and the "strict economy" that governed the Forbes home required each member to make "little sacrifices" for the others.[4]

Ralph Forbes's repeated sorties into overseas commerce depended on the hope that he could somehow emulate his Perkins in-laws' successes in the Atlantic and Caribbean trades. In the wake of the several embargoes imposed by Jefferson and Madison after 1807, he left the country, relocating his import-export operations to France to take advantage of his country's neutral status. His prospects must have looked promising because, in 1811, when Bennet was seven years old, Ralph called his family to France. But the inevitable war with Britain that broke out in June 1812 betrayed this endeavor, too, and in 1814 a chastened

Ralph Forbes packed up his household for the return voyage to Boston. It was not, however, the end of the family's embarrassments. On three separate occasions, belligerent ships detained their vessel, boarding and searching the ships' papers and passengers' possessions. Bennet was born after the Revolution and was too young to go to war in 1812; consequently, he did not store away bitter memories of British hubris. But the future expatriate did harbor an abiding mistrust of "arbitrary" government, and his emerging views on the "tyranny" of petty officials would color his opinion of China's imperial bureaucracy.[5]

Despite its patriarch's reverses, the Forbes family was not destined for poverty, largely because of the fortunate marriage that Ralph had made. Margaret Perkins was the sister of James and Thomas Handasyd Perkins, who sat in the pantheon of Boston's most enterprising and esteemed merchants. The Perkins uncles installed them in a home in Milton, just south of Boston, and provided a handsome stipend of $1,200 per annum. The elder boys, Thomas and Bennet, were enrolled into the countinghouse of their uncles on Foster's Wharf, where they acquired the aspiring merchant's facility with ledgers, daybooks, bills of lading, and unremitting waves of correspondence. Gentle encouragement and ready assistance distinguished the careers of both boys, but the advantages they gained through kinship connections were complicated by lofty expectations.

As it expanded "eastward of Good Hope," the Indies Trade followed the eighteenth-century model that guided trade within the Atlantic and Caribbean. Convention directed the deployment of vessels into the South Seas, engaging knowledgeable navigators to sail the ships and capable supercargoes to manage the exchanges. A supercargo escorted the freight to its destination, sometimes calling for the captain to alter course if commercial conditions warranted, exchanged the outbound cargo for foreign goods, and usually accompanied these exotic wares back to the homeport. This was the position of Shaw and Randall when they traveled aboard the *Empress of China* in 1784. But they quickly learned the advantages of a China-based agency office, and in 1786, they set up the firm of Shaw & Randall as a commission house, where they served as general agents in Canton, representing a variety of merchants and taking a modest percentage of the profits. In 1803, the Perkins brothers improved upon their strategy, establishing a branch house in Canton and sending a partner to manage business there. After twelve years in Canton, they opened the first American branch house, E. Bumstead & Co., and soon American partnerships filled the Hong establishments. They included Benjamin C. Wilcocks of Philadelphia, Daniel Stansbury of Baltimore, John Jacob Astor of New York, and Edward C. Carrington of Providence. These enterprises mark a significant change in the way Americans conducted business in China. After 1815, they gradually replaced the supercargo, although one could find this figure throughout the Great South Sea throughout the period of the Old China Trade. Among the new entrants, the most significant was Samuel Russell & Company. Edward Carrington's Providence partnership had operated in Canton for several years before deciding to risk a branch house there. On 26 December 1818, the firm contracted with Samuel Russell of Middletown, Connecticut, to serve as resident agent. Russell did business both on behalf of the partners and on his own account. He rented a factory space and chose Consequa to represent the firm as its Hong. As Bennet Forbes later described, "You must know the Hong merchants are responsible for the good conduct of the foreigners, they own the houses we live in & let them to us & if any one does wrong the Hong are called to account—notwithstanding all this responsibility—the merchants have no power to enforce their orders therefore when they have any thing to complain of they talk to us & we obey or not as suits our convenience."[6]

This was a young man's world. Thomas Perkins was just twenty-three when he sailed aboard Elias Hasket Derby's *Astrea* for Canton. In 1818, Perkins called his nephew, Robert Bennet Forbes, to his factory in China—at age thirteen. There, Forbes was reacquainted with his cousin John Perkins Cushing, who was in charge of the Perkins China office—at age sixteen. Another member of Canton's expatriate community, William C. Hunter, arrived at Macao in 1829—also at age thirteen. Dudley Leavitt Pickman was a teenager when he went to work at the Salem Custom House. When he turned twenty, he sailed for Madras as supercargo in John Crowninshield's *Belisarius*. At age twenty-two, he voyaged to Sumatra, and at age twenty-four he sailed for Calcutta in the *Derby*. Harriett Low left Salem aboard the *Sumatra*, bound for Macao on her twentieth birthday. Three brothers from the Silsbee family of Salem offer particular insight into the youthful nature of the Indies Trade. Each started out as a clerk in a counting-house: Nathaniel at fourteen, William at fifteen, and Zachariah at sixteen. Each commanded a vessel before the age of twenty: Nathaniel at eighteen, William at nineteen, and Zachariah at nineteen. And each retired from the sea at the ripened age of twenty-eight.[7]

It was into this world of young men and family connections in 1816, at age twelve, that Bennet entered as a clerk in the Perkins's Boston countinghouse at Nos. 52 and 54, Central Wharf. Young Forbes must have demonstrated great promise, because the next year, at age thirteen, he found himself aboard the Per-

William John Huggins's (c. 1824) romanticized depiction of opium ships anchored off Lintin Island evokes Forbes's stint as overseer of the opium trade for Russell & Company. Courtesy of the Peabody Essex Museum.

kins ship *Canton Packet*, bound for China. There he met up with his cousin John Perkins Cushing, who had been managing the Perkins factory there since he had arrived three years earlier. In Canton, Bennet found an extended network of kin, with the Canton branch managed by Forbes's cousin John and later by his brother Thomas, while cousin Samuel Cushing managed the Calcutta end of things. In 1830, his seventeen-year-old brother John Murray Forbes would arrive. And it was through the hands of a web of young cousins, brothers, and uncles that Chinese silks, porcelain, and teas, Indian madras and calico, Hawai'ian sandalwood, Nootka furs, and Turkish opium all moved. The real money was not to be made in voyages but in commission work. Here was a chance for young men with little capital but the right connections—opportunities closed off to a shipwright such as Delano or a mariner such as Fanning.[8]

Forbes made perhaps a dozen voyages in and about China, operated Russell's opium station at Lintin Island for nearly two years, and experienced storms, captivity, privation, and loss. In 1828, the twenty-three-year old salt confided, "During the ten years of my sea-going life, I had not been on shore more than six

months, and much of that time had been spent at Canton,—very little at home."
By 1834, at age thirty, he was a gray-haired old man and ready to settle down.
Leveraging his experience and Perkins connections, he established himself in
Boston in 1832, and on 20 January 1834 he married Rose Greene Smith. But
the mercurial dynamics of emergent industrial capitalism and political economy
tripped up his plans. He would return to China.

Bennet Forbes did not go back to Canton for adventure, glory, or the allure
of opulent wealth; he did not want to go there at all. He had been at sea for so
much of his life, so often in Eastern waters that drew him half a world away
from the family and home that he treasured, that the letters he sent back from
Canton, Lintin, and Manila were filled with complaints. For most Americans,
the experience in China was less an adventure than a sacrifice, made often in
desperation, to gain a competency and entrance into the commercial community at home. As Forbes described his dilemma for Rose, waiting back in Boston,
in April 1839, "I sometimes think the ship I have taken was not justified by any
state of affairs, that it was a cruel sacrifice. Then a pain comes to me & the
reflection that I could only have remained home in a state of dependence, that I
must have incurred obligations which could never cancel. By coming here I have
done all I could to retrieve my fortunes & procure an independence." Forbes's
experience in the 1830s was no different from his countrymen's experience a
generation earlier. In 1800, another Bostonian, Sullivan Dorr, made the same
point. He was in China, he wrote, because he knew of "no business bringing in
more prompt and great profit." Even so, "all the Chinese dominions would not
induce" Dorr to remain for more than a few years. He was confident that the
climate would eventually break his health.[9]

Like so many Yankee travelers to the East, Forbes was driven there by ill
winds. In March 1837, the business world fell into "wild confusion" as a result
of President Andrew Jackson's refusal to renew the charter of the Bank of the
United States. The three major English banks that managed most of America's
Indies Trade had failed. Russell & Company's books showed $400,000 of debt.
Forbes himself was overextended. He had lent money to friends and invested
in the Farrandsville Coal and Iron Company, in Pennsylvania, a producer of
nails, his one foray into manufacturing. He estimated that he lost $100,000 in
that venture alone. Fortunately, younger brother John Murray returned from
his posting at Russell's Canton office in December 1836 to manage the firm's
affairs from Boston's Central Wharf, anticipating a less feverish pace than that

of China's tea season. Over the next two years, John Murray tried to revive his brother's bankrupt company, but unsuccessfully. Pursued by creditors, Forbes was left without resources.[10]

Eventually, there was an opening, one available to him that was closed to men such as Delano and Fanning. It was back in China. A generational shift was shaking up several of the long-standing American firms in Canton; old men such as the Perkins's John P. Cushing, Philip Dumaresq, and Charles Pearson, as well as Russell's Samuel Russell and John Cleve Green, made plans to retire from trade. After William Henry Low had died in South Africa in 1834, stranding Harriett and Abigail, and Samuel Russell himself withdrew from the company in 1836 and returned to the United States, an opening developed in Russell & Sturgis for a capable hand to guide the concern through the churning waters of a global economy. The unstable conditions triggered an effort to consolidate several of the great houses of the Indies Trade—Russell, Sturgis, Perkins—bringing them together in a single entity. Forbes again turned to his more prosperous family scions and asked to return to China to take over his brother's position in the reorganized Russell & Company.[11]

On 8 June 1838, Forbes boarded the *Mary Chilton* in Boston for yet another voyage to China. He abandoned any immediate hope for a settled life and left behind Rose, who had moved into modest quarters on Boston's Beacon Hill, and his eight-month-old son, Bob. In his absence, Rose wrote long, reassuring letters that boasted of her careful household economy. Even after his fortunes had declined, Forbes had chided his wife that she did not need to be so penny-wise, but Rose was determined to do her part. There were other reasons why the thought of returning to Canton repelled Forbes. His arrival under such desperate circumstances brought a poignant sense of personal failure and, he feared, public embarrassment. Deeper still, he had neither resolved his testy relationship with his older brother Thomas, who had been both role model and rival, nor had he reconciled himself to Thomas's death in a typhoon off Lintin Island in 1829. "That when he died we were just beginning to feel like Brothers, has always been a source of great uneasiness to me," Forbes confided, and he marked every anniversary of Tom's death. The prospect of sailing past Lintin Island, where the older Forbes had lost his life, was chilling.

Forbes missed others from his Boston community as well. A cousin, Thomas Handasyd Cabot, had sailed to Canton in 1833 with John Murray Forbes at age nineteen but died of smallpox and was buried in China two years later. His remains were disinterred and returned home to Brookline; "The superstitious ideas of the chinese prevented them from aiding [him]," Forbes noted. Even when he came to the assistance of others, death seemed to stalk his efforts. He was haunted by the fate of a favorite shipmate aboard the brig *Nile*, his first officer Mr. Gillespie. Anchored at Manila in 1825, Forbes learned that a British ship had lost its captain and needed a capable commander. He immediately arranged for his mate to take the helm of the British brig. Gillespie did well in the Pacific trade and eventually saved enough capital to buy his own vessel, the brig *Telemacus*. Some time later, he, too, was lost at sea, in a hurricane off Mazatlán. As Forbes remembered the events, his own "kind act was the indirect cause of his death."[12]

Bennet arrived at Canton in October, as a junior partner in Russell & Sturgis, located in the Swedish Hong, No. 2. He joined Russell's chief John Cleve Green of Trenton, New Jersey, and junior partners Edward King of Newport, Rhode Island, William C. Hunter of New York, Warren Delano, Jr., of Fairhaven, Massachusetts (a distant relation of Amasa Delano), and Abiel Abbott Low of Salem, Massachusetts (a nephew of William Henry Low), as well as clerks Daniel Nicholson Spooner of Plymouth, Massachusetts, and Joseph Taylor Gilman of Exeter, New Hampshire. One partner, the cantankerous Joseph Coolidge of Boston, protested Forbes's admission on the specious grounds that Forbes was too young and inexperienced. Fortunately, Coolidge was then absent in London, and his generally unpleasant disposition soon led to his own ouster from the company.

Forbes thought the prospects for recouping his losses by going East were good. He described Russell & Company's business as "enormous." He calculated that Green would retire with $300,000, his brother John Murray with $160,000, and Coolidge with $120,000. For his part, Forbes could expect to earn $40,000 from even a half year of business, and he had been promised a full partnership at the end of that year. The work was not unpleasant, "the accounts & hard work being done by the clerks & the younger members." And, so, he would reacquaint himself with the finer distinctions between Wo-Ping, Fokeen Bohea, Congo, Tankay, and Hyson teas, the various grades of silks, and the rhythms of a life that he considered a temporary exile in China.[13]

Despite his reluctance to return to Asia, there were some aspects of life abroad that Forbes anticipated with pleasure. For one thing, the expatriate community of some three hundred Westerners and Parsees contained familiar faces. In fact, the Americans constituted a virtual gentlemen's club of friends, shipmates, and kin. When another distant relation, Charles Tyng, arrived at Whampoa in 1838

The offices that Forbes supervised as head of Russell & Company in Canton likely looked like this 1888 depiction of a tea taster's office by an unknown artist. Courtesy of the Peabody Essex Museum.

as first mate aboard the *Cordelia*, he was enmeshed in a web of relations that included Cabots, Perkinses, Forbeses, and Cushings. Complementing the contingent of a couple dozen Americans who filled the offices of Russell & Company, Russell & Sturgis, J. P. Sturgis, Gordon & Talbot, and Wetmore & Co. was a vibrant, cosmopolitan community that included nearly two hundred English in Macao and Canton. The East India Company was there, hosting dinners and sponsoring races that filled the hours. The Company had forfeited its monopoly four years earlier, and the Scottish firm of Jardine, Matheson now dominated trade, but social life had lost little of its capacity for diversion. Perhaps Forbes did not wish Rose to think his absence was some sort of lark, for he lamented the scarce opportunities for enlivening conversation: "Here the mind is constantly fixed on business subjects & there are no wits here abouts."[14]

The pleasures of reacquaintance extended beyond the American quarter. Forbes looked forward to renewing his relationship with Wu Ping-Chien, known as Houqua, the most renowned of the Hong merchants and someone whom he had come to consider a dear friend. In his letters to Rose, he referred

This *View of the American Garden*, by an unknown artist, shortly after Forbes's departure, documents American dominance within Canton's expatriate community around the time of the First Opium War. Courtesy of the Peabody Essex Museum.

affectionately to this savvy, astute trader as "the old Gent." As for other people of color, Forbes's attitudes were curiously complicated. His letters home sometimes complimented African Americans, Chinese, and others who occupied the margins of Canton's expatriate society. At one point, as he lay ill in Canton from tropical fever, he praised one "china man" who had brought him a package as a "sweet creature." Like other Americans, and unlike Low, he could extoll the virtues of his "faithful Chinese servant." And, when Major, his Indian valet, fell ill, Forbes "had the pleasure of attending on him." Yet, Forbes threw around the racist language of his times cavalierly. He described, for instance, falling in with "a very honest 'niggar'" at Hong Kong and engaged the man to bring his dog home to Boston. He did not care to learn the man's name, referring to him only as "Sambo." He ridiculed his chief nurse as a "curious specimen . . . resembling an orangutan." In this, he was typical of the expatriate community, whose members also described the Chinese as "a very peculiar people" and made no

Forbes's Chinese counterpart, "the old Gent," Hong merchant Wu Ping-Chien (1769–1843), known as Houqua. Courtesy of the Peabody Essex Museum.

complaint when Russell Sturgis denigrated a ball hosted by Indian merchants as "a Quadroon party."[15]

Forbes may have been comforted by the familiar faces and accustomed rhythms of Canton's trading seasons that greeted him in October 1838, but China had changed in the eight years that had elapsed since his last sojourn in the East. In Macao, St. Paul's Cathedral still reined over the main plaza, but now only its eminent façade was left standing. One of the raging typhoons that attacked the South China Sea with cruel regularity had razed the main structure three years earlier. Forbes would have noticed a curious amalgam of carvings and statues adorning the ruins: an image of the Virgin Mary flanked by a peony (representing China) and a chrysanthemum (representing Japan), a Chinese dragon, a Portuguese ship, and a demon of indeterminate origin. At the factories in Canton, remodeling had improved Peter Parker's Ophthalmic Hospital in Hog Lane. Changed, too, were the Celestial Empire's policies toward the *fan quai* and especially toward a product on which the Western trading companies had come to depend—opium.[16]

With Cushing, Green, and other old guard residents departing China, Canton presented unusual opportunities for a seasoned trader who hoped to recoup his fortunes. Yet, in autumn of 1838, 1,400 miles to the north, forces were being unleashed that would not just compromise his fortune but threaten his life. Unhappy with the increased flow of opium smuggled along the coast and the consequent loss in silver revenues that flowed into the imperial treasury, the Daoguang Emperor issued a new, strident set of policies designed finally to reign in the insidious activities of the *fan quai.* At the end of December, as Forbes settled into the rhythms of the tea season, the emperor appointed a *ch'in-ch'ai ta-ch'en,* or imperial commissioner endowed with plenipotentiary authority, to put an end to the opium smuggling. He was Lin Zexu (Lin Tse-shü, 1785–1850), the highly regarded former governor of Hu-Huang province, noted throughout the empire for bringing effectiveness and efficiency to a corrupt political system. The "incorruptible" Confucian scholar, whose nickname was "Clear Sky," was known for unusual probity. As Lin's caravan moved south toward Guangzhou province, rumors of his mission agitated the closed world of provincial officials.

Lin seems to have understood the challenge he was taking on. At least since 1729, when the emperor Yongzheng had issued an edict to prohibit opium smoking and trafficking, imperial officials had struggled to limit the infestation of the drug in the Middle Kingdom. Yongzheng's proclamation had been followed by a similar decree from Emperor Kia King in 1799 and echoed in periodic warnings thereafter. Opium constituted multiple threats to the Manchus' control over China. The drug presented a moral threat to the fundamental institution of Confucian society, the family. Authorities in Peking feared that it could turn China "into a nation of hopeless addicts, smoking themselves to death while their country descended into chaos." Manchu officials saw the narcotic as a political threat as well. Some reports asserted that the ranks of the imperial bureaucracy, and even the army itself, were rife with opium smoking and even complicit in the trafficking of the drug. And, by the 1830s, opium sales triggered an economic crisis. There were signs that the dramatic increase in opium sales had begun to drain the treasury of silver, the foundation of the imperial tax system.[17]

Yet, each thrust against the pernicious drug by Beijing had been parried by the East India companies and private traders. Portuguese merchants are credited with the introduction of Malwa opium throughout the East China Sea in the 1500s. A century later, they directed cargoes of the narcotic from their Indian possessions to Macao and began to channel its distribution along the coast. In the 1700s, the Dutch also began to export shipments of Indian opium to China and the islands of Southeast Asia. It was they who introduced the practice of mixing a concoction of tobacco and opium called *madak*, inhaled through a pipe, to the Chinese. After midcentury, British merchants, particularly those of the East India Company, discovered the economic benefits that could accrue from linking the farmers of India to the consumers of China. In 1750, the Company asserted its control over Bengal and Bihar, two of India's prime poppy-growing provinces. The occupation enabled British merchants to substitute the mild, high-quality Patna for the unreliable and often harsh Malwa. The Company's directors made a significant strategic decision as well. They decided that it was more economical to focus on opium production in India than to pay for the small, fast ships needed to distribute the drug. Thus, private traders came to dominate the opium trade out of Calcutta and into the South China Sea, a system known as the "country trade." After independence, American traders found that their nimble, swift ships gave them an advantage in the new arrangement, and the British establishment found it useful to employ them. By 1767, British traders were carrying two thousand chests of the drug to China each year. To sew up its monopoly, in 1793 the Company banned other nations' East India companies from selling opium in Bengal.[18]

Over forty years later, as Lin trekked south from Beijing, delayed by the snowstorms of the north country and the innumerable ceremonies requisite for an imperial official at every small town, panic filled Guangzhou officialdom. Provincial governor Teng T'ing-chen broke with precedent to write directly to the expatriate community, warning the *fan quai* to desist. His courier was the Hong merchant Houqua. To shield their own complicity in the trade, Governor Teng and the Hoppo had been staging arrests and executions of Chinese smugglers throughout the previous autumn. It was rumored that by the spring of 1839, Canton's jails held some two thousand opium users.

The consequences of Lin's visit swept over the expatriate community in waves. Some took it seriously, and the *Chinese Repository*, the Canton newspaper edited by American missionary Elijah Bridgman, warned of the "extraordinary changes and reverses" that were imminent. William Jardine, the Scottish physician who had gained fabulous wealth in the opium trade, predicted that 1839 imports would be half of what they had been in recent years. Others sneered at what they regarded as another display of imperial impotence and continued to do business in the drug. Within the confines of Russell & Company's Hong, the strains of trade—the frenzy of the tea season, the insistence of customers, the impatience of sea masters, the admonitions of partners, the need to make one's *lac*—followed rhythms that had been established twenty years earlier, when the founders had turned to opium trafficking. January marked a moment of particular achievement for one junior member of the firm. On the first day of the new year, Forbes was named a full partner in Russell & Company and set on a path to restoring his financial position. He could not have suspected that his reinstatement would coincide with the last days of the Old China Trade.[19]

It was in this context in the early evening hours of 26 February 1839 that Canton's mandarins carried out the ritual execution that left the Russell partners deeply troubled and the expatriate community in a state of agitation. The next day, shaken from their complacency, the partners voted to withdraw the house from opium trafficking. Their reasons appear to have been largely economic, partly political, and, to a degree, moral. Forbes wrote to Rose, explaining, "When the dreadful effects are brought before our very eyes we cannot compromise ourselves by dealing in it & thus perishes one of our most important sources of business." Clerks Daniel Spooner and Joseph Gilman hurriedly dashed off letters to notify the firm's "constituents" that Russell & Company would honor its commitment to manage the opium cargoes that were then in transit but would accept no further orders. Green, as senior partner, ordered the company ship *Rose* to cease its smuggling along the coast and return to Whampoa. The Hong merchants likewise reduced their orders of opium.[20]

Yet, Yankee merchants did not react as Chinese peasants and kowtow completely before Lin's authority. The merchants would demonstrate their objection, and this defiance would reinforce their own sense of community. On the 27th, Forbes wrote to Rose, "A parting of the English was holden last night & they agreed not to hoist the British flag again. This morning our Consul Mr. Snow called a meeting of the Americans & I was nominated secretary & we voted that the American flag shall not be hoisted until Mr. Snow should receive orders from his Government to hoist it."[21]

Taken together, the firm's actions of February 26 and 27 were ambiguous but not inconsistent. At their deepest level, they demonstrated the distance that the national identity had traveled since Yankees had first arrived in the East. The new generation of American expatriates was self-consciously redefining a sense of the national character that grounded the principle of liberty in antebellum notions of property and propriety. In rejecting Lin's edicts, they asserted the position that China's policies violated the fundamental dictums of a society that considered itself capitalist, civil, and progressive. And yet, the crisis over China's new program of enforcement recalled America's revolutionary legacy. In the commissioner's edicts, the Celestial Empire was asserting something similar to the 1766 Declaratory Act, in which Parliament insisted that its imperial administration had authority over every aspect of colonial society, "in all cases whatsoever." Lin's decrees likewise were intended to awe the *fan-quai* and instill a respectful appreciation of its power. And, like Parliament, Chinese officials were incapable of gauging the resolve that followed the expatriates' initial wave of dismay. Lin's policies only stiffened the bonds that held the expatriate community together. He had managed to replicate the effects of Lords Grenville, Townsend, and North, whose policies united the disparate classes of British America in concert against a common foe—the imperial government of George III. As Forbes described it, "Every one was quiet & shocked in the greatest degree & a good deal of excitement prevailed but as the residents could do no more than talk they did not interfere." The commissioner's demands now put the Americans in the position of the revolutionaries of the 1760s. Their response demonstrated that the urgent sense of republicanism that inspired Shaw and Delano had not vanished. Rather, this element of the American character had been absorbed into the fabric of the culture and remained latent until challenged by a force that the expatriates perceived as morally and politically inferior.[22]

Other concerns disturbed the genteel apartments of the factories. This new round of instability further threatened the partners' reputations as responsible businessmen, already fragile in the mercurial global economy of the nineteenth century. This Forbes knew too well from his own recent financial embarrassments. He argued that the Russell partners were obligated to their clients for the security of any cargoes over which they took charge. He fretted, also, for the safety of their friends in the Chinese community. "Although we are under no fears for our own safety," Forbes wrote, the partners worried about the safety of the Hong merchants, especially for Mouqua and the "old Gent," Houqua, who seem to have been singled out by the commissioner for public ridicule. As the imbroglio continued, Forbes documented the toll that Lin's intimidation took on Houqua, in particular. In March, he wrote to Rose, "I found the old Gent almost exhausted & the very picture of despair, he had eaten hardly for a week, his feet & legs much swollen, his house filled with soldiers, horses, &c." For their part, the Hong traders realized that the friendship and interest that bound them to the *fan quai* were stouter than their loyalty to the Manchu conquerors, and several of them took risks to protect the expatriates. Forbes could reassure Rose that "Houqua told me the other night to give myself no uneasiness on account of safety . . . & he would see us protected even if a riot should take place from the imprudence of any of the English men—I am well known to all his men & should fear nothing under any emergency."[23]

By early March, when Lin was expected to arrive, the expatriate community had had two months in which to consider how to respond to his demands. But the architecture of a common response was a complicated matter. For one thing, there appeared to be too much government in China, too many layers of authority, formed by the accretions of the imperial apparatus in distant Beijing, the provincial government, Canton's customs office, the Hong syndicate, and the Portuguese administration in Macao. Each issued its edicts and decrees, and these often garbled the commands and demands of one or more of the others. Westerners such as Hugh Hamilton Lindsay suspected that local officials used "ingenuity and fraud" to further their own interests while cloaking their deception in imperial guise. A regime of long-standing tradition, local custom, and the outlaw rule of pirates and smugglers heightened the confusion.[24]

A few expatriates took Lin's appointment as a sign that it was time to get out of China, and even before the commissioner's arrival in Canton in early March many had booked passage on outbound ships. The most active of the British traders, the Scotsman William Jardine, known as "Old Rat," had cashed in his stake and left the factories in February. A few Americans likewise packed up their affairs and returned home. Forbes believed that they were abandoning considerable investments built up over many years of sacrifice. Russell Sturgis had spent nearly six years in China and had moved his family to Macao. When he left Canton in mid-March 1839, Forbes observed, he had "lost his wife & gained only gray hairs." Russell's chief partner, John Cleve Green, was also planning to retire, and he would also depart Canton in March, leaving Forbes, the newest partner, in charge. For his part, Forbes had not yet made his *lac* and could not afford to return to Boston. Instead, he mustered his resolve to lead Russell & Company through the crisis, employing the strategy that the merchants of the first generation had mastered. Russell would take advantage of a vacuum left by less adventurous competitors.[25]

Lin came to Canton on March 10. The oppressive heat and humidity carried in by the winter monsoon was beginning to build, and the commissioner found that it disturbed his concentration. It was the end of the tea season, and the expatriate community's annual retirement to Macao was well underway. Charles Eliot, the Royal Navy officer who had taken over the position of chief superintendent and plenipotentiary of Britain's China Trade in December 1836, had already repaired to his offices downriver. He was in Macao on the day Lin arrived at Canton. Several of the Western traders, including Forbes's partner William C. Hunter, had remained in Canton to complete their ledgers, however. They observed the commissioner's procession up the Pei-ho into the city, noting little pomp as Lin was virtually whisked into the inner city, avoiding the factory site.[26]

The *ch'in-ch'ai ta-ch'en* undertook his task with both force and directness. He had carried with him a list of sixty-two known participants in the opium trade, both Celestial and *fan quai*, and he set about interrogating as many as he could reach, from Hong merchants to compradors to fast crab pilots. He ordered sweeps, arrests, and executions on a scale never before seen in the province. But the key to his strategy hinged on a tactic that Manchu officials had been reluctant to employ before this. Lin planned to threaten the expatriate community directly, anticipating that he could force their compliance through intimidation. On the 18th of March he sprang, ordering the twelve Hong merchants to report immediately to Yueh-hua Academy, where the Confucian scholar had established his offices. As the old men sat bent over on their knees in a position of contrition, Lin blasted them for their betrayal of the empire and their association with the wicked *fan quai*. He warned the merchants of the Co-hong that if they continued to shield the barbarians from the laws of China, Lin would make an example by selecting one or two of the elders for execution. He then ordered them to carry his words to the factories. In a sweeping proclamation addressed to "the Barbarians of every nation," he demanded they deliver "every particle of opium" to him for destruction. Furthermore, the foreign merchants would be required to post bonds, promising that they would no longer smuggle opium into the Middle Kingdom. If any failed to comply, they would suffer "the extreme penalty of the law." To emphasize the seriousness of his edict, he allowed the Westerners only three days in which to assent. What Lin could accomplish, with the trading season suspended and most merchants downriver, was anyone's guess.[27]

The next day, March 19, he ordered Houqua and Mouqua to carry yet another edict from Consoo House—the "extensive and handsomely built series of buildings" that constituted the headquarters of the Hong merchants—even more ominous than the order of the previous day, forbidding the departure of the *fan quai* from Canton. That the command came through the office of the Hoppo, and not the viceroy or governor, perplexed the expatriates. More startling still, was the dangerous precedent that Lin's order implied. For his part, the commissioner seems to have anticipated immediate obedience and was unprepared for the response of the expatriate community. The forty-member Chamber of Commerce, the body authorized to govern the affairs of the community, did not meet until Thursday, March 21, under the gavel of William Wetmore, an American merchant from Connecticut and Rhode Island. Wetmore and others argued that Western concepts of commerce and property trumped the arbitrary demands of a backward tyranny. In true parliamentary fashion, the merchants agreed that they could not provide an answer until the following Wednesday, March 26, after a subcommittee had studied the proposal.[28]

The Hong elders returned that evening. The commissioner was furious, they reported, and their own lives were threatened if he did not receive an immediate response. Most of the Chinese servants had already fled the factories, but the few who remained now rounded up outraged merchants and supercargoes. Forbes had been "dining at the club" when "the summons came to meet at the Chamber of Commerce," and he was irritated to have his repast disturbed by more nonsense from the official he now styled the Yum-chi (the term was a corruption of the Chinese word for "commissioner"). "The foreign community were so much deceived by this real or imaginary danger to their friends," he complained. When the chamber reconvened at 10 p.m., the members reconsidered the plight of the Hong men and voted to surrender a token of 1,036 chests, worth one-third of a million dollars. Forbes's cynicism was contagious. Most expatriates calculated that this feint would be enough to placate the *ch'in-ch'ai ta-ch'en*, who would no doubt present the emperor with an affirmation of his success and pocket the proceeds of the confiscated opium. They remained doubtful that another Manchu official sincerely intended a radical departure from the old ways of corruption and self-enrichment. And they expected the "Imperial Robber" would cloak his private avarice behind a veil of official sanctions.[29]

The expatriate community misjudged the commissioner's resolve, just as Lin had misjudged them. He rejected their token offer out of hand and demanded instead that they turn over every chest of opium they held. Within days, the effects were apparent. The factory square filled with "a body of police belonging to our friends the Hong merchants," Forbes reported. The sense of mutual interest and regard that had melded this cosmopolitan world of *fan quai*, Hong merchants, compradors, and local shopkeepers and artisans fostered a mutual bond in defiance of the imperial officials. Houqua and his colleagues sent a force of men brandishing spears and sporting the caps of their respective houses, positioned throughout the square to protect the expatriates. Lin retaliated. He ordered the Hoppo's dragon boats to close the river to the *fan quai*'s watercraft, intercepting one yacht as it attempted to leave the factories and capturing another at the Bocca Tigris. Then, ominously, soldiers appeared, filling the streets and alleys—Hog Lane, Old China Street, and New China Street—and preventing escape from the factory compound. By Friday, March 22, Lin commanded British opium trader Richard Dent, whom he considered among the chief culprits, to appear before him.[30]

The blockade of vessels, confinement of the merchants, and the threat to Dent prompted Superintendent Charles Eliot to rush back from his headquarters at San Francisco Green on Macao. The "imprisoned" Americans painted an amusing description of his entrance in the early evening of Sunday, March 24. Eliot had appropriated the jolly boat from the sloop HMS *Larne*, the sole Western warship in the vicinity, and stood defiantly at the stern in full naval dress, with the British ensign flying abeam, pursued by four dragon boats "who were taking especial good care to keep behind." It was all "gallant style" but little substance. The ceremony glossed over Eliot's embarrassment, when he had first taken up his post at the end of 1836 and Governor Teng had ignominiously spurned his request for permission to establish his headquarters at Canton. Now, parading into the grounds of the English Lungshun factory on the early evening of Sunday, March 24, his men could find no flag to hoist and not even a flagstaff to support one. His first act was to write directly to Lin, a breach of imperial protocol, demanding that the commissioner clearly state his intentions and assert whether these inclined toward war.

Within hours, a colorful conclave of English, Parsee, American, and Hong merchants crowded the resplendent grand hall of the New English factory in a sort of town meeting, with all looking to the superintendent for guidance. Eliot announced his view that Lin had escalated a minor disagreement into a full-blown international crisis. Worse, the Chinese had insulted British honor. To the astonished merchants, he then announced that they would all immediately remove their possessions from Canton and make plans to follow. Eliot reassured them, somewhat disingenuously, that the HMS *Larne* was ready to aid their departure, and he called upon the entire factory community to comply. To ensure their cooperation, he again overreached, promising that the British government would compensate for any losses. Everyone in the hall knew that he did not have the authority to offer such guarantees, and everyone now intended to hold him to his word.[31]

Recognizing the sprinkling of Americans in the hall, Eliot expressed his delight for their tacit cooperation and assured them, too, of the protection of the British government. Perhaps the superintendent did not realize—perhaps no one in the room fully appreciated—the import of his next words. Proclaiming what everyone already knew, that two American warships, the imposing USS *John Adams* and the *Columbia*, were expected soon, he hoped that he could count on their assistance. "Yes, you may," someone shouted back. On the one hand, the highest official representing the British Empire in China had offered the empire's protection to the lesser states of the international community. Yet, by invoking the aid of the American navy, he tacitly acknowledged the authority of the new nation. The action amounted to recognition of the Americans as full partners alongside the British as members of the community of civilized nations. It was the moment that Shaw and Delano had anticipated in their day. All in all, it was "a very pretty speech," Forbes observed.[32]

The celebratory spirit of ecumenical cooperation evaporated when the merchants returned to their apartments. At the American factory, Forbes, Green, and the others found mayhem, as the remaining servants, compradors, and washers frantically scooped up their belongings and fled. By the morning of Monday, March 25, the factories of Canton were emptied of Chinese. Lin had been busy overnight as well, and the Westerners awoke to find the streets and alleys blocked by wooden bars nailed across the gates and Chinese soldiers surrounding the entire compound. Some five hundred guards, armed with pikes and staves, filled the square. In the river fifty yards beyond, two or three sweeping arcs of sampans—house boats, river boats, duck boats, crab boats, and fast boats—crammed the waterside, further confining the factory site and blockading communication with Whampoa and Macao. From the hundreds of river craft rose a constant, deafening braying of horns, "resting on the extremities of our limits," and unnerving the expatriates. "We were really prisoners," Forbes wrote in disbelief, finally acknowledging the severity of his situation.[33]

Forbes wrote of this confinement as he did of much of his China experience, with melodramatic flair. Men who had never entered their own kitchens, laundered their own clothes, cooked their own meals, or drawn their own water were now left to their own devices, and the results of this "very serious" situation were comical. Boat crews on liberty from Whampoa were commandeered to serve as replacement cooks, washers, and servants, but they could not replace the dozens of Chinese who customarily attended to the men of the factories. Forbes and company shanghaied "a sailor boy and a lascar." They sent away their cows, which grazed in a small backyard enclosure, because "we could not well act servants & grooms." It appears that none of them, in fact, knew how to milk a cow. Forbes himself described the situation as "ludicrous." He thought that Rose "would have been much amused to have seen me making fire, splitting wood & boiling the Tea Kettle." After he found Warren Delano, Abiel Low, and Edward King struggling to cook "in the very *worst* style," his partners appointed him chef, with even worse results. He conjured a pan of scrambled eggs that resembled shoe leather and tasted worse, his incompetence cost him the job, and he was relegated to the position of dishwasher and furniture polisher. In desperation, Forbes and consul Peter Snow left the American factory to subsist at Sturgis's residence in the Swedish establishment.[34]

By and large, the American community considered the clumsy gavotte between Lin and Eliot to be a "farce," Forbes wrote to Rose. A few moralists—he was thinking of David Olyphant and Charles King, who refused to trade in opium on religious grounds—took the whole affair too seriously, but most of the men kept their heads and regarded John Bull and the Yum-chi as hopelessly constrained by the antiquated regulations of their respective bureaucracies. Between the puffery of the Briton and the tyranny of the Celestial, the Americans imagined their national character emerging as the paragon of common sense, enterprise, and adaptation. Their "imprisonment" took on a particularly farcical cast as carts of provisions and coal poured into the factories. Houqua sent them a cook, and his guards smuggled in hams and capons. Their Parsee neighbors sent such an abundance of food that the tables in the American apartments and in Swedish factory No. 2 were "groaning with solids." Forbes boasted that the Russell gourmands were "more likely to suffer from repletion than starvation." As to their safety, confined to a small island and surrounded by thousands of soldiers and militia, Forbes reassured Rose that he was not particularly concerned. To the contrary, he insisted, the merchants were worried solely about the possibility of exaggerated reports needlessly alarming loved ones in the United States, who were "not acquainted with the Chinese character." When the Yum-chi demanded an audience with Richard Dent, Forbes offered to accompany the British smuggler into the city, as "there was not the least personal danger." The Bostonian pretended disappointment when he learned that his partner John Green "had applied for the same *privilege*." Yet, they were "all well & merry as crickets."[35]

Even so, serious matters required Forbes's attention. It was left to him, as the new head of Russell & Company, to safeguard investors' property through the crisis and to articulate the company's position in the fracas. On May 25, the Russell partners, calling themselves the American "Merchants in Canton, China," voted to send a memorial to Congress to protest their conditions and call for the Van Buren administration to intervene. The petition broke with a tradition begun when Samuel Shaw and Thomas Randall came to Canton. Randall had articulated their position toward China in 1791, emphasizing, "The idea of a representation, concerning the frauds and impositions of the Chinese to the Emperor, would deserve attention were there not the danger of making things worse." The second generation of American China traders was less consistent. On the one hand, they framed the crisis as a disagreement solely between China and Britain. On the other hand, they called "for the dispatch of a suitable naval force to protect American lives and property." They hoped, too, that Van Buren would send an agent to negotiate a commercial treaty that would protect American interests in the future.[36]

Russell & Company's 1839 memorial presented a view of China that superseded the romanticized vision that held sway in Shaw's day. That Enlightenment view imagined an ancient civilized order governed by a wise, patient, but disciplined overseer. In Russell's petition, the Chinese emperor emerged instead as a tyrant who, like the pashas of Barbary, wielded arbitrary power and whose lust for power and treasure drained the energy and fortunes of the kingdom, channeling it all to feed the indolence and luxury of an indifferent court. The language of the petition framed a distinctly American perspective, however. This republican view recalled the country's revolutionary heritage and, especially, Jefferson's depiction of George III in the Declaration of Independence sixty years earlier. Where Jefferson had chronicled "a long train of abuses and usurpations" and "a history of repeated injuries and usurpations, all having in direct object the establishment of an absolute Tyranny over these States," the Americans in Canton complained that they had been "made prisoners in our factories, and surrounded by armed men and boats." They faced both "the threatened forfeiture of life if his arbitrary exactions were not complied [with]" and "severe but undefined penalties."

Like the memorials of the revolutionary era, the 1839 complaint included economic grievances that portrayed the petitioners as innocent victims. At the core of the Russell partners' argument was the pretense that they were nothing more than commercial intermediaries whose involvement in opium trafficking was incidental. Acting as agents on behalf of clients who were the real owners of the drug, American merchants in China could not be directly linked to the product or implicated in its consequences. To some degree, they argued, Western merchants could not even be expected to know about the physical effects of opium on its users, as they were not allowed beyond the wall that separated the factories from Canton's population. Yet, they were responsible for their clients' property, and they feared the Chinese might confiscate "British owned opium, which may be valued at more than ten millions of dollars," a sum they would be required to reimburse. The thesis was serviceable for other audiences as well, and Forbes appropriated it when Eliot asked the Americans to join the British flight out of Canton. He rebuffed the chief superintendent, insisting the Americans must remain at their factory in order to protect their clients' goods. Declaring that he was merely "a sort of public servant," Forbes developed the argument in more detail in a letter to Rose in October. "We are fortunate in being only agents & having nothing but the interests of Constituents at stake," he insisted. Indeed, he complained, there were others more directly involved in the trade—the Chinese themselves. This point was central to the argument that excused Americans from culpability. "Formerly," Forbes wrote, "the trade was considered legalized by the connivance of the mandarins & local authorities."[37]

Indeed, the Russell partners staked their claim to the moral high ground. Asserting they had "no wish to see a revival of the opium trade," the opium traders reminded Congress that, "believing in the sincerity of this Government in their efforts to destroy the trade, we would in future abstain from dealing in the drug." Opium use, they admitted, "has been productive of much evil and of scarcely a single good to the Chinese." It had "degraded the foreign character in the estimation of the better portion of the Chinese." But they decried "the violent measures that have given occasion for the present memorial" and that profaned the rules of decorum embraced by the truly civilized nations. There was little sincerity in the claims of the American merchants, but they did offer some signals of newly discovered compunction. Since returning to the East, Forbes himself had begun to feel misgivings about his involvement in the opium trade. He confessed to Rose, "Perhaps Providence took away my fortune because I made it in Opium," and he promised, "What I make this time will be free from that stain."[38]

As the American community awaited a response from Congress, Forbes's mood soured. The novelty and excitement of the crisis faded, the continued inconveniences stopped up trade, and the isolation of the Hongs grew more strained. Lin tightened his stranglehold on the factories by sealing off the side streets and alleys. Although Forbes thought things would soon return to their customary state, he was not, as he told Eliot, there for pleasure. After Lin ordered the residents' pleasure boats removed from the plaza and dragged across the rough paving of the factory square—another violation of their property rights, the Americans complained—Forbes took a more adamant tone. He confided to Rose that he wished Eliot to delay the release of the opium trove until Lin had first restored the residents' liberty. "I shall go to church today & pray for a blessing on you & confusion to all the China Gov.," he wrote home to Boston. Detaining some two hundred defenseless residents, demanding the surrender of the opium without a reciprocal promise that their liberty would be restored, and expecting Eliot to guarantee that there would be no repercussions from his nation, the Chinese were a "mean and despicable people." Forbes was always more a man of action than a great thinker, and he was prepared to take the necessary step. If he had not been a husband and father, he would "volunteer under any flag" to make the imperial government pay for its ruthless behavior. "They should be punished for their incivility," he protested.[39]

Superintendent Charles Eliot was less sanguine. His resumé had included extended postings in colonial Guiana and the West Indies, but he had not encountered anything like the opium standoff. Beneath the bravado that he showed before Canton's expatriates, Eliot recognized the weakness of the British position. Lacking an effective naval force in the China Sea—the British East India Company confined the bulk of its fleet to the Indian Ocean—he ordered Britain's merchant ships to the inlet of Hong Kong and placed them under the command of the senior naval officer there. More serious was the perceived threat to lives and property, and Eliot overreached.[40]

When the superintendent met with the chamber again on Wednesday, March 27, he ordered the British merchants to surrender the entirety of their opium stores to him. These he would convey to Lin. As the Crown's representative in Canton, he promised that everyone who complied, of whatever nationality, would be indemnified for their losses. Most of the British merchants met Eliot's demand with equanimity. Ironically, the action of their government, effectively subsidizing their illegal trade and guaranteeing them against losses, satisfied the merchants who had imbibed the drink of free trade and had lobbied for the removal of the East India Company's monopoly in 1834. Forbes, however, was outraged by this governmental appropriation of private property. "Twenty Thousand Chests of Opium value *Ten Million dollars*," wrote the astonished

Bostonian the next day. Still, Russell & Company complied, cognizant that the 1,400 chests that it turned over to Consul Peter Snow, the property of British owners, now fell under the protection of the British government, and the company would be held blameless. The diplomatic crisis might well bring on war—Forbes thought as much on March 28, the day that the full complement of 20,283 chests of opium were delivered to Lin—but if so, the Americans would either profit as neutrals or return to the United States a bit sooner than they had anticipated and carry no losses. For his part, Forbes was adamant that if he could not earn his *lac* in China, he would "cut & run."[41]

Following Eliot's direction, the British residents evacuated their factories, some removing themselves to Macao, others relocating to their ships anchored off of Hong Kong. Their motives were an amalgam of economic interest and national honor. Forbes recalled that as early as April 11, some had already begun "to talk as if they should leave Canton. They consider their national dignity hurt." The superintendent hoped to demonstrate a defiant national character, and he convinced the British community that their removal would "alarm the Chinese as to the effects of their seizure." To Forbes, however, the retreat showed neither unity nor discipline, but rather signaled a lack of fortitude, sacrificing both their own needs and, more importantly, the interests of their constituents. He had written to Rose in March, "We cannot of course consent to give away the property of our customers." The Americans agreed among themselves that they would not deign to such ignoble behavior, despite Eliot's repeated pleas. They would stand their ground as long as there was an ounce of tea to trade. Putting a nationalistic gloss on the American position, Forbes reminded the superintendent, "We Yankees had no Queen to guarantee our losses." Besides, there were profits to be made in the vacuum left by the British houses, a great deal of profit if Russell & Company played its cards right. He ordered the partners to disperse their cargoes of cotton and linen to other ports throughout the East, trying the markets in Singapore, Thailand, and India.

The opium transfer took place at Lankit, an isle some five miles below the Bocca Tigris. On April 11, Lin watched as Alexander Johnston, Eliot's deputy superintendent, delivered the first fifty crates. By the end of June, 20,283 chests had been destroyed; Forbes estimated their value at $10 million. Yet, Lin feared that his measures were not strong enough. On May 12, he received a censor's report that criticized him for assuming that the destruction of one season's opium ended the problem. Instead, the report directed the commissioner to ensure that no future shipments would reach China. Nonetheless, when Lin began the destruction of the opium on June 3, he believed that he had humiliated the foreigners, and he indicated as much in a memorial to the emperor on June 13. Lin's hazy understanding of the West extended to the United States. He had hoped to communicate directly with Western rulers as the permanent solution to the opium-silver crisis. But he believed that the Americans had no national ruler, that instead, twenty-four headmen ruled separate provinces, making a unified policy unlikely. Curiously, he seems to have been unaware that Martin Van Buren was serving as the eighth American president at this time or that in July 1832 President Andrew Jackson had sent the USS *Potomac* to Sumatra to bombard the villages of Quallah Battoo in retaliation for the loss of the *Friendship*.[42]

The confinement of the *fan quai* at Canton ended in early May, as more than 20,000 chests of opium made their way to Lankit. Familiar routines quickly resumed. For Forbes, this meant that "trade was opened; servants came back, and all breathed freely again." Not everything fell into their normal rhythms, however. John Cleve Green was gone, along with a number of other familiar faces, having been placed on Lin's list of proscribed *fan quai*. Green had planned to leave China in March but now found he was expelled from the country, and he departed on June 2 "much annoyed" but very wealthy after five years in Canton. Forbes would miss his mentor's acumen, but he relished the opportunities that attended his own ascension as the head of the premier American company in the East. Furthermore, in the absence of British merchants, the opium troubles had indirectly accelerated the pace of business for American factors who filled the vacuum. The leisurely rhythms of the summer months in Macao now were broken, punctuated by the urgent press of business that now washed over the American firms.[43]

The suppression of the opium trade kept Forbes, a remarkably active man in ordinary times, busier than he had ever been in his life, the pace rising to a frenetic crescendo throughout the hot, fetid summer of the South China coast. Within days of Lin's arrival, even before his March 19 edict, the factories had buzzed with activity as merchants and clerks were flurrying to get their ships out of Whampoa before the trade was stopped. Forbes was not hopeful that they would accomplish the task before the deadline, and, at a time when everyone would usually decamp for the long summer holiday at Macao, merchants and clerks burned the midnight oil to fill cargoes and complete invoices. Personal letters, journals, recreation, and the like must wait until the late hours of the evening. As Forbes told Rose, "I have no other time so easily at my disposal."[44]

By early June, Russell & Company was taking on more work, managing consignments for British captains desperate to fill their ships for the homeward voyage and even taking business away from their American rivals, Wetmore & Co. As Green and others had departed, Forbes recognized that the firm was "more likely to have too much to do than too little this summer." The partners needed more clerks to process the avalanche of correspondence, invoices, and bills of lading, and Forbes brought in clerk David Eckley. Forbes made regular forays to Macao to maintain contact with newly acquired English constituents and ensure that cargoes were loaded. Forbes left Canton on August 9, expecting to spend most of the month in Macao. Amidst the sweeping beauty of the Praya Grande, his accommodations were ample, offering an opulence that eluded him in Boston or Milton. Overlooking the Typa Bay, the villa offered him eight expansive rooms on its upper floor, with two verandahs to the rear. From these, he gazed down upon graceful gardens filled with newly planted fruit trees. On the ground floor offices and servants' quarters gave him even more room. But trouble—in the form of the imperial commissioner himself—followed him to Macao.[45]

Within a day of his arrival downriver, Forbes learned that "the Imperial Robber" would soon follow with a thousand soldiers. Lin was coming to Macao, Forbes believed, "to get up a secret negotiation" with Superintendent Eliot. The Americans expected that he would attempt to restore the trade in tea and cotton that the British had abandoned and that China needed. Lin had overplayed his hand, however. "It is now too late," Forbes wrote, and Eliot must wait for London's decision. On August 15, Lin embarked for Macao, as he had been ordered to do the previous April. At this point, the crisis worsened. Lin came not to negotiate trade but to find satisfaction for a crime stemming from July 7, when parties of English and American sailors on liberty had landed at a village near Hong Kong and fell into a brawl with local villagers. In the aftermath, a peasant named Lin Wei-his lay dead. Eliot made a sincere effort to satisfy the Chinese government, as the expatriate community saw it, but his hands were tied. He had held a trial "or some sort" and invited Chinese observers, but Lin doubted that justice would be done, and he refused to send anyone. The court of inquiry found five British sailors culpable and sent them home in chains, but "no proof could be brought against any one as the murderer." Lin's doubts were justified when the authorities in London released the tars, rejecting the superintendent's judicial authority. When Eliot failed to produce the murderer, the commissioner took steps to force the British out of China. On August 16, the mandarins issued a *chop* that prevented any provisions from reaching the English residents in Macao and demanded that they evacuate the peninsula within ten days. Again, Lin's grasp exceeded his reach. Forbes dismissed the whole affair as "quite amusing" and wrote to Rose: "It is very unfortunate for this great rascal that he did not rest content with the suppression of the Opium trade, that was a good cause, but now to make such row to carry out the bloody laws of China which demand life for life is a great mistake & his late conduct will attract the attention of England more than the other trouble."[46]

Even so, the Americans clung to the trappings of neutrality. And, despite the stakes, Forbes's letters continued their lighthearted tone. He wrote home, "The Portuguese & Americans are not involved & it is looked upon as a good joke rather than a case of starvation." The English community, he added, would now have to retreat to Hong Kong. Again underscoring his nation's privileged position, he noted, "The Americans will keep entirely aloof from the quarrel & I do not anticipate any trouble to our business." In keeping "aloof," they flew the flag of a neutral power, the strategy that Delano, Fanning, and other Indies traders had employed a generation earlier, and so reaped the benefits of the Anglo-Chinese disagreement. British merchants, in particular, used the Stars and Stripes as a flag of convenience for getting their goods through Canton. Russell's clipper *Lintin* racked up incredible profits shuttling cargoes between Canton and Macao, earning as much as she would have on a voyage to the United States, and by late August Forbes could hope that his "warmest expectations" for the year's revenues would be realized. In mid-August, British firms sold two vessels to Russell & Company and consigned another cargo to the American firm. Even the preeminent houses that had replaced the East India Company, Jardine and Matheson, and the Dents asked for American coverage for their agents. Cargoes came in from every point in the East—Singapore, Java, India—and ships departed China filled with cotton, teas, and porcelain, most under the imprimatur of Russell & Company. The Yankees would "keep entirely aloof from the quarrel," and with good reason, Forbes observed. Freight now brought $4 per bale of cotton, earning almost as much as a Pacific voyage. In fact, he boasted, "the Americans are reaping a rich harvest out of the English & I hope their ships will be kept out of Port a good while."[47]

There were limits to collusion with the Americans, of course, and British merchants bristled over the advantages that their Yankee cousins had gained in a trade they had dominated just months before. Although Eliot admitted the subterfuge to be a useful arrangement, and many British merchants availed

themselves of the benefits that the Americans provided, there lingered the sentiment that any firm that did not follow the English to Hong Kong had "bent the
neck to the Chinese." Worse, it was said, through their proximity to the sources
of Chinese products, they were in a position to take the cream of the trade.
"The Americans sacked the commissions and other perquisites, the government the duties, and the Hong merchants the profits," lamented the East India
Company supercargo Hugh Hamilton Lindsay when he returned to London.
"Jonathan has dipped into his brother's pockets," privileging profits over character, and sullied his honor, unlike the British merchants who had "preserved
their reputation.[48]

There was little they could do to end the crisis, however. And so, in anticipation of Lin's August 26 deadline, the British community fled again, this time
across the strait to Hong Kong, and Forbes followed. He continued to adapt to
the circumstances of the Anglo-Chinese conflict, conditions that he could not
control but of which he could take advantage. On August 21, Forbes reported
that many of the English were taking residence aboard ships at Hong Kong.
Four days later, with the British evacuation nearly complete, Lin was confident
that he had the upper hand. What he did not realize—one of the many factors
that he misjudged—was the arrival off Hong Kong of HMS *Volage*, a twenty-
eight-gun frigate, sent by India governor-general Aukland. In London, British
leaders prepared for war.[49]

Forbes arrived at Hong Kong aboard Russell & Company's *Canton Packet* at
the beginning of September and for the next six weeks lodged aboard a British ship consigned to his company. He found it to be a "fatiguing campaign,"
confined to a stifling cabin, bringing cotton into Canton and teas out. Business
was hectic, and at one point in October Russell had fourteen vessels consigned
to it. Things changed dramatically again on September 4. Hearing the booming
of cannon in Kowloon Bay, Forbes grabbed a telescope and jumped in a gig to
observe a pitched battle between four junks and a small flotilla of English vessels. Eliot had had enough of Lin's starvation policy. He demanded provisions
from local villages, and when Lin refused these, the superintendent ordered
English warships to fire on Chinese warships stationed nearby. Forbes described
the battle as "fun" and a "farce." The Americans were not able to appreciate the
historic consequences of what became known as the Battle of Kowloon and the
commencement of the first of the Opium Wars.[50]

The onset of military operations did not sway the Americans' position that
they should remain "aloof," however. In response to the sinking of the *Bilbaino*,

a Spanish vessel that the Chinese navy mistook for a British opium clipper, Captain H. Smith of HMS *Volage*, under Eliot's direction, threatened to blockade the Pei-ho, employing the only two men-of-war at his disposal. For Yankee merchants, Smith's decree undermined the whole point of coming to China, and they issued a remonstrance in defense of their national rights. On September 11, the day that Smith had appointed for the commencement of the blockade, ten of them dispatched a formal note of protest to Superintendent Eliot. It was another remarkable document from the "younger brother." They wrote that the blockade infringed upon their legal right as Americans to trade freely throughout the world. The Yankees lectured Britain's superintendent of trade that the edict violated international law, and they warned him that they would hold the British government responsible for any loss of life or property sustained "by any American citizen." Under the combined weight of the expatriate community, Eliot soon rescinded the "insane order."[51]

But it was Lin's policies, recalling the dystopian qualities of an earlier British and now Chinese tyranny—arbitrary, resistant to negotiation, insensitive to the needs of the people—that alienated the Americans more. They used the commissioner's thrusts and Eliot's parries to further hone an understanding of their national character. Toward the end of August, the commissioner had banned the Portuguese from allowing their slaves to aid the English and demanded they assist in forcing the English out of Macao. In September, he turned on the Americans, threatening to cut off their provisions if they continued to "entertain" the English. In October, Lin issued another decree that required all Western ships to leave China and then return. To circumvent what was, to them, another irrational edict, English merchants sold their ships to the Americans. In sum, Forbes said, "everything was done to get all goods into market." The "system of annoyance" was, he complained, "an old custom with the Chinese." "We Yankees," he wrote, feel different and superior, but it was the Chinese position that seemed particularly imperious.[52]

Forbes does not seem to have given much thought before this to China's place on the scale of civilization that constituted the conventional wisdom of the Western world, but by autumn 1839 he was writing that the commissioner's actions had fallen outside the pale of civilized nations. When fighting broke out again in early November, this time at the Bocca Tigris, he justified the preemptive attack launched by British forces. "It is always admitted among civilized nations as proper," he insisted, that states enjoyed the right to defend their citizens overseas. Furthermore, the "Chinese deserve punishment & must have it & if

John Bull does not do it effectively now, he will never have so good a chance again." For Forbes, as for Shaw and Delano earlier, there was a distinct community of civilized nations; for the second generation of China traders, however, the place of the new nation within this community was unquestionable. As Forbes wrote, "I have always contended that the Chinese would never get into the list of civilized nations until fairly flogged into the list." It was a prejudice shared by most members of the British community and that bound them to each other as it separated them from the Chinese. "They are still barbarians" only on the verge of civilization, it was asserted in British books and journals of the time, and the American traders agreed.[53]

The "imbecility of the Chinese Govt" continued until the end of the year, when Lin ordered that after December 6 English cargoes could not be transferred to American merchants, nor could English flag ships be sold to American buyers. Although the edict would have disrupted business considerably, Forbes was dismissive of the consequences of yet another order from the Yum-chi. He observed that the edict might be negotiated, and even if the English removed themselves to Manila, American merchants would follow them there to continue the flag of convenience subterfuge. At all events, Americans would ply their "regular" trade, "disconnected from the English outside trade." Either way, it brought little credit to the authority of the imperial government.[54]

Despite the disruption in trade brought by the officials of both empires, a year into Forbes's second stay in China, conditions for the recovery of his fortune looked promising again. In October, the director of Russell & Company observed that he had been in Canton for a year and marked the halfway point of his time there. By October 6, he could write to Rose from Hong Kong that his prospects were "brilliant." He had tallied the firm's commissions for the year at $200,000, and his share as $41,000; with another year ahead in China, and through careful management of the family finances at home, he would be rich again.[55]

By October 21 he was back at Canton. Forbes returned from Hong Kong "when the outside work was fully organized." His partners were "getting quite anxious" to see him, he was finding the work at Kowloon exhausting, and partner Joseph Coolidge's arrival from London was anticipated at any moment. Yet, he found no respite from the frenzied pace of work at the factories. He had much to do and little time for sleep, "and shall be glad when the work is over." The planning and "extensive correspondence" necessary to oversee offloading and reloading fourteen vessels "often makes my head snap," and the weather was "oppressively hot." The temperature reached 86 degrees, but without modern air conditioning, it felt much worse. The work kept the merchants and clerks up past midnight, and Forbes complained that he was getting about five hours of sleep each night. But, because no one could predict when—or if—conditions would return to normal, it was in the firm's interest to continue to service the British firms.[56]

It was not the opium crisis that sent Forbes home in July 1840, nor had he made his *lac*, although he had earned a great deal of money. Ominously, as with William Henry Low six years earlier, the urgency of business and climate of the South China Sea had damaged his health. The fevered pace, the rapid shifts in temperature from intensely hot days to cool nights, even the medical remedies recommended by the best physicians in Macao—leeches, to draw off impurities in his blood—had weakened him to exhaustion, and a fall off his pony left him so incapacitated that Forbes feared he would soon join his brother in the Protestant cemetery. As early as mid-March, he complained that he had been working to exhaustion, writing by candlelight into the small hours of each night, and compromising his eyesight, the common complaint of Canton merchants. Others noticed how he had aged—in Boston his family and friends commented on a miniature portrait that he had sent home. He admitted, "I dare say I have grown old—my hair is much grayer," and he warned his wife that he had aged two years for every one that he spent abroad. By early March, Forbes recognized the signs: he must depart or die in the East. The *Niantic* was available, and, joined by the famed American medical missionary, Dr. Peter Parker, he departed Canton for the second time.[57]

Forbes returned to Boston on 11 December 1840, after a sojourn of two-and-a-half years, with his body intact and finances restored, "blessed with success beyond my most ardent hopes." He had been spared the fate of Samuel Shaw and William Henry Low and the penury of Amasa Delano. He was well aware of his good fortune. On the eve of his homeward voyage, he had anticipated a fortune of half a million dollars and the restoration of his reputation. He was aware, as well, of the many who had sailed "eastward of Good Hope" and were not as fortunate. Encountering the captain of the *Lehigh*, a former schoolmate who had sailed into Whampoa with him nearly twenty years earlier, Forbes found him now "a married man & poor into the bargain" who hoped to earn a modest $1,500 per year "as the acme of human felicity."[58]

Unlike so many others who followed the South Sea winds, in later years Forbes became the kind of larger-than-life figure emblematic of the roman-

American ships like the clipper *Wild Pigeon*, out of Portsmouth, New Hampshire, continued to pay visits to China after the First Opium War but were more likely to anchor off of Hong Kong rather than Canton. Attributed to the Chinese artist Sunqua. Courtesy of the Portsmouth Athenaeum.

ticized China Trade. Like Fanning, he invested in more than seventy vessels, some of them the first American steamships in the East Indies Trade, and reaped the rewards that built the family fortune. But his reputation extended beyond his wealth. He manifested the values of civic responsibility, learned at an early age, and in the kind of paternalistic generosity that typified the Guilded Age. He acquired a medal for heroism for saving passengers in an accident at sea, conveyed supplies to Ireland during the tragic famine of 1846–1847, and earned the sobriquet "the seamen's friend" for his generous support of retired sailors.[59]

His first concern, Forbes never tired of asserting, had been "to form a character" as an honest and competent seaman, and he achieved this and much more. His efforts were contemporaneous with the country's continuing efforts to form its own identity. This national character had been undergoing dramatic alteration from the days of Samuel Shaw. By the demise of the Old China Trade in the mid-1840s, the United States had become regarded as a confident and capable member of the community of civilized nations. In 1844, it memorialized its great power status by imposing on China the Treaty of Wangxi, exacting the same privileges of commerce and extraterritoriality that Great Britain had demanded from the defeated Manchu kingdom two years earlier. As Charles Eliot had attested, the other powers now looked to the erstwhile rebel republic to provide stability and order in a changing world.

Postscript

Aمericans traveled around several worlds between 1784 and 1844, and their "voyages of commerce and discovery" in the Great South Sea excited the imaginations of their countrymen. From the journals, ship logs, newspaper accounts, and books of Samuel Shaw, Amasa Delano, Edmund Fanning, Harriett Low, Robert Bennet Forbes, and hundreds of other voyagers there emerged new understandings of the national character. This true Yankee represented multiple meanings, shaded in subtly different ways, each showing a different side of how Americans imagined themselves.

Their discoveries revealed much about this imagined character through the first decades of the American experience. For one, Yankee travelers arrived in Arabian, Indian, and Pacific waters three centuries after Europeans had first sailed there; when Delano or Fanning employed the term "discovery" in their writing, they were referencing the experience of contact rather than an original encounter with a previously unknown land. Second, consistent with Crève-coeur's construction of "this new man, the American," the writings of the Indies Trade introduced a new figure on the world stage, and so an element of the "discovery" invokes the construction of Americans by Europeans and other peoples. Third, and most important, the central experience of encounters with Eastern lands, waters, and peoples constituted an act of "discovering" their own national identity.

Samuel Shaw, Amasa Delano, and Edmund Fanning were representative, but not alone, among a first generation of American travelers who described them-selves as republican patriots, defending their country's honor and reputation. Yet, they also depicted Americans as citizens of the world. Yankees were, they fancied, genteel, polite, educated, cosmopolitan, and refined, and not at all the coarse bumpkins that Europeans often portrayed.

This self-image took another turn by the 1830s. Antebellum Americans imagined the national character differently from the ways in which the first generation had thought about it. On the eve of the First Opium War, their country had assumed the role of one of the world's leading commercial powers. One could find its flag on every sea and ocean, and the country's concern with the "the reception its citizens met" was in eclipse. In their telling of the China Trade story, Harriett Low and Robert Bennet Forbes wrote of the national character as something superior to the peoples of both Europe and the East. The true Yankee exemplified the spirit of familial duty, commitment to economic gain, and concern with material goods, a vibrant mixture of Confucian devotion and capitalist enterprise.

The American who was fashioned in the literature of exotic worlds was pointedly exceptional. Yankee travelers who returned from Canton, Calcutta, and Cape Town described themselves as a distinct expatriate community, separate from the residents of other nations and decidedly superior to them. The letters of Low, Forbes, and other expatriates are filled with the designation, "we Yankees." This sense of navigating a middle course between Europe and Asia had been the hallmark of the first generation's construction of their national identity, and it continued into the second generation. For both, the historic importance had a spiritual dimension, captured in the metaphor of the transit of civilization from East to West. In an early issue of the *Chinese Repository*, China trader Charles King wrote, "Ever since the dispersion of man, the richest stream of human blessings has, in the will of Providence, followed a western course." The First Opium War, which began in 1839, solidified this sense of a manifest destiny, the term coined in the same year by the editor of the *United States Democratic Review*, John L. O'Sullivan.[1]

NOTES

Introduction

1. *Salem Gazette*, 24 May 1785; *New Hampshire Gazette*, 27 May 1785; and *Columbian Herald*, 24 June 1785.

2. Samuel Shaw, *The Journals of Major Samuel Shaw, the First American Consul at Canton*, ed. Josiah Quincy (Taipei: Ch'eng-Wen, 1968), appendix, 43 and 200.

3. Linda Colley, *Britons: Forging the Nation, 1707–1837* (New Haven: Yale University Press, 1992), and *Captives: Britain, Empire, and the World, 1600–1850* (New York: Random House, 2002); Shaw, *Journals*; Amasa Delano, *A Narrative of Voyages and Travels, in the Northern and Southern Hemispheres: Comprising Three Voyages Round the World; Together with a Voyage of Survey and Discovery, in the Pacific Ocean and Oriental Islands* (Boston: E. G. House, 1817); Edmund Fanning, *Voyages Round the World; with Selected Sketches of Voyages to the South Seas, North and South Pacific Oceans, China, etc., Performed under the Command and Agency of the Author. Also, Information Relating to Important Late Discoveries; between the Years 1792 and 1832, Together with the Report of the Commander of the First American Exploring Expedition, Patronised by the United States Government, in the brigs Seraph and Annawan, to the Southern Hemisphere* (New York: Collins & Hannay, 1833); Harriett Low, Journal, 1829–1834, 9 vols., Phillips Library, Peabody Essex Museum, 7–8 September 1829; Robert Bennet Forbes, *Personal Reminiscences* (Boston: Little, Brown, 1878).

4. Quoted in Timothy Sweet, review of "The First West: Writing from the American Frontier, 1776–1860," by Edward Watts and David Rachels, *Early American Literature* 38, no. 3: 536.

5. Fisher Ames, "Eulogy of Washington," 8 February 1800, *Works of Fisher Ames*, ed. W. B. Allen (Indianapolis: Liberty Fund, 1983), 1:523.

6. Isaac Kramnick, "The 'Great National Discussion': The Discourse of Politics in 1787," *William and Mary Quarterly* 3rd ser., 45, no. 1 (January 1988): 5.

CHAPTER 1: Samuel Shaw's Polite Reception, 1784–1794

1. Samuel Shaw, *The Journals of Major Samuel Shaw, the First American Consul at Canton*, ed. Josiah Quincy (Taipei: Ch'eng-Wen, 1968), appendix, 43.

2. Josiah Quincy, "Memoir," in Shaw, *Journals*, 3–5; *Historical Researches of Gouldsboro, Maine* (Bar Harbor, ME: W. H. Sherman, 1904), 8.

3. Amasa Delano, *A Narrative of Voyages and Travels, in the Northern and Southern Hemi-*

spheres: Comprising Three Voyages Round the World; Together with a Voyage of Survey and Discovery, in the Pacific Ocean and Oriental Islands (Boston: E. G. House, 1817), 21.

4. Quincy, "Memoir," in Shaw, *Journals*, 9–10, 14, 23, 43, 11–12, 87.

5. Quoted in Philip Chadwick Foster Smith, *The Empress of China* (Philadelphia: Philadelphia Maritime Museum, 1984), 46.

6. Hamilton Andrews Hill, "The Trade, Commerce, and Navigation of Boston, 1780–1880," in *The Memorial History of Boston, including Suffolk County, 1630–1880*, ed. Justin Winsor (Boston: Ticknor, 1881), 4:201–204; Franklin, quoted in Benson J. Lossing, *The Pictorial Field-Book of the War of 1812* (1869; Whitefish, MT: Kessinger, 2010).

7. Jean Gordon Lee, *Philadelphians and the China Trade* (Philadelphia: Philadelphia Museum of Art, 1984), 23; Thomas M. Doerflinger, *A Vigorous Spirit of Enterprise: Merchants and Economic Development in Revolutionary Philadelphia* (Chapel Hill: University of North Carolina Press, 1986), passim; Stanley Elkins and Eric McKitrick, *The Age of Federalism: The Early American Republic, 1788–1800* (New York: Oxford University Press, 1993); James R. Gibson, *Otter Skins, Boston Ships, and China Goods: The Maritime Fur Trade of the Northwest Coast, 1785–1841* (Montreal: McGill–Queen's University Press, 1992); James Rogers Sharp, *American Politics in the Early Republic: The New Nation in Crisis* (New Haven: Yale University Press, 1993); Gordon S. Wood, *The Radicalism of the American Revolution* (New York: Vintage, 1993).

8. *President Dwight's Decisions of Questions Discussed by the Senior Class in Yale College, in 1813 and 1814* (New York, 1833), 73, quoted in Larzer Ziff, *Writing in the New Nation: Prose, Print, and Politics in the Early United States* (New Haven: Yale University Press, 1991), 132.

9. T. H. Breen, "An Empire of Goods," *Journal of British Studies* 25 (October 1986): 267–299; David Jaffee, "The Ebenezers Devotion: Pre- and Post-Revolutionary Consumption in Rural Connecticut," *New England Quarterly* 76, no. 2 (June 2003): 249–251.

10. Lee, *Philadelphians and the China Trade*, 12.

11. *Salem Gazette*, 4 March 1784; *Virginia Journal and Alexandria Advertiser*, 11 March 1784.

12. This may have been the same Thomas Randall who in June 1774 sent the ship *Amiable Louise* under Captain Malaharde from New York to New Orleans. Aboard as first mate was the future Philadelphia tycoon, Stephen Girard. Shaw, *Journals*, 133, 149; *Virginia Journal and Alexandria Advertiser*, 11 March 1784.

13. Dirk J. Struik, *Yankee Science in the Making* (New York: Macmillan, 1948; Collier, 1962), 97; Lee, *Philadelphians and the China Trade*, 24.

14. *Virginia Journal and Alexandria Advertiser*, 11 March 1784; *New Hampshire Mercury and General Advertiser*, 19 July 1785.

15. See, for instance, Benjamin Goodhue to Elias Hasket Derby, 5 April 1789, and notes, *Essex Institute Historical Collections* 1, no. 3 (July 1859): 111; Magnús T. Gudmundsson and Thórdís Högnadóttir, "Volcanic Systems and Calderas in the Vatnajökull Region, Central Iceland: Constraints on Crustal Structure from Gravity Data," *Journal of Geodynamics* 43, no. 1 (January 2007): 153–169; Leonard Blussé, *Visible Cities: Canton, Nagasaki, and Batavia and the Coming of the Americans* (Cambridge: Harvard University Press, 2008), 60; Lee, *Philadelphians and the China Trade*, 11. Morris intended the *Empress* to depart from Philadelphia but opted for the deeper waters of New York because of the freezing of the Delaware River.

16. Smith, *Empress*, 3; Henri Cordier, "Américains et Français à Canton au XVIIIe siècle," *Journals de la Société des Américanistes* 2 (1898): 1–13; David Taylor, "Getting to the Root of Ginseng," *Smithsonian Magazine* (July 2002): 100. Ginseng was known for its appeal in the East, and in Virginia William Byrd II had experimented with it and sent a cargo of it to England as early as 1738.

17. Smith, *Empress*, 93, 96.

18. Smith, *Empress*, 128–129, 138.

19. Shaw, *Journals*, 153–157; Shaw to Jay, 19 May 1785, in Shaw, *Journals*, 337–338; Cordier, "Américains et Français," 1–13.

20. Smith, *Empress*, 159, 160, 167.

21. Smith, *Empress*, 150.

22. Shaw, *Journals*, 163–164.

23. Shaw, *Journals*, 173.

24. Shaw to John Jay, 19 May 1785, in Shaw, *Journals*, 338.

25. Shaw, *Journals*, 183; *Worcester Magazine*, 1 May 1787; Samuel Patterson, *Narrative*, 1817 (Fairfield, WA: Ye Galleon Press, 1967), 23–24; Shaw to Jay, 19 May 1785, in Shaw, *Journals*, 338.

26. Shaw, *Journals*, 176–177; Smith, *Empress*, 152–153.

27. Shaw, *Journals*, 181.

28. D. E. Mungello, *The Great Encounter of China and the West, 1500–1800* (New York: Rowman & Littlefield, 2005), 3.

29. G. A. Starr, "Defoe and China," *Eighteenth-Century Studies* 43, no. 4 (Summer 2010): 435–454.

30. Shaw, *Journals*, 167–168; Mungello, *Great Encounter*, 77, 82; Jonathan D. Spence, *The Chan's Great Continent: China in Western Minds* (New York: W. W. Norton, 1998), chs. 4 and 5.

31. C. Toogood Downing, *The Fan-Qui in China in 1836–7*, 3 vols., 1838 (New York: Barnes & Noble, 1972), 1:v. Downing explains: "The term of reproach, therefore, if such it still be, expresses in China, not only the English, but all Europeans, Americans, Parsees, Arabs, Malays, and the inhabitants of every other quarter of the globe, excepting their own Celestial Empire" (v–vi). Although in time Americans better appreciated the rest of Downing's sentence—"but having been so long accustomed to the epithet, and hearing it so often pronounced, we are willing to hope that it is now generally used without intention to insult, and may be fairly translated 'Foreigner,'"—in the early days of their involvement in the China Trade, they were more sensitive to the original meaning of the term.

32. Jacques M. Downs, *The Golden Ghetto: The American Commercial Community at Canton and the Shaping of American China Policy, 1784–1844* (Bethlehem, PA: Lehigh University Press, 1997), 39, 61, 73; Dorothy Shurman Hawes, *To the Farthest Gulf: The Story of the American China Trade*, ed. John Quentin Feller (Ipswich, MA: Ipswich Press, 1990), 110; Robert E. Peabody, *The Log of the Grand Turks* (Boston: Houghton Mifflin, 1926), 79; Shaw, *Journals*, 178–179.

33. Shaw, *Journals*, 184; Jonathan Goldstein, *Philadelphia and the China Trade, 1682–1846* (University Park: Pennsylvania State University Press, 1978), 42.

34. Downs, *Golden Ghetto*, 73–74; Hawes, *To the Farthest Gulf*, 111.

35. Shaw, *Journals*, 184–185.

36. Shaw, *Journals*, 235.

37. Shaw, *Journals*, 181.

38. Shaw, *Journals*, 180.

39. Shaw, *Journals*, 180–181.

40. As a man who prided himself on his republican honor, Shaw was obliged to amend his self-gratifying anecdote: "Thus far, it may be supposed, the fellow's remarks pleased me. Justice obliges me to add his conclusion: 'All men come first time China very good gentlemen, all same you. I think two three time more you come Canton, you make all same Englishman too.'" Shaw, *Journals*, 199–200; Robert Morrison, *Notices Concerning China, and the Port of Canton. Also, a Narrative of the Affair of the British Frigate Topaz, 1821–1822: with Remarks on Homicides, and an Account of the Fire of Canton* (Malacca: Mission Press, 1823), vii.

41. David Sanctuary Howard, *New York and the China Trade* (New York: New York Historical Society, 1984), 73–74.

42. Peabody, *Log of the Grand Turks*, 43–35.

43. Shaw, *Journals*, 209–210.

44. Hawes, *To the Farthest Gulf*, 130; Tyler Dennett, *Americans in Eastern Asia: A Critical Study of United States' Policy in the Far East in the Nineteenth Century* (New York: Barnes & Noble, 1922), 7–8; Foster Rhea Dulles, *The Old China Trade* (Boston: Houghton Mifflin, 1930), 4–12.

45. *Salem Gazette*, 24 May 1785, 7 June 1785, 30 August 1785; *Massachusetts Centinel*, 17 October 1787.

46. W. Grayson to James Madison, 28 May 1785, Madison Papers, vol. 14, cited in Dennett, *Americans in Eastern Asia*, 7.

47. Blussé, *Visible Cities*, 60; Hawes, *To the Farthest Gulf*, 112, 132, 141.

48. James R. Fichter, *So Great a Proffit: How the East Indies Trade Transformed Anglo-American Capitalism* (Cambridge, MA: Harvard University Press, 2010), 82–83.

49. *Independent Chronicle*, 29 July 1785.

50. Randall's plans were less clear. He wrote that he hoped "to settle in America."

51. Shaw, *Journals*, 219.

52. Shaw, *Journals*, 221–225.

53. Shaw, *Journals*, 221.

54. Shaw, *Journals*, 227–228, 233–235.

55. Shaw, *Journals*, 317, 234.

56. Shaw, *Journals*, 114, 218–219, 228–232; Smith, *Empress*, 93.

57. Peabody, *Log of the Grand Turks*, 80, 84–85, 89.

58. Shaw, *Journals*, 232.

59. Shaw, *Journals*, 234–235.

60. Shaw, *Journals*, 233.

61. Shaw, *Journals*, 235.

62. Shaw, *Journals*, 236–237.

63. Shaw, *Journals*, 240–241.

64. Shaw, *Journals*, 239–241.

65. Shaw, *Journals*, 242–243.

66. Shaw, *Journals*, 227.

67. Shaw, *Journals*, 252–253.

68. Smith, *Empress*, 20–23; Shaw, *Journals*, 263.

69. Shaw, *Journals*, 263–267.

70. Shaw, *Journals*, 262, 265, 271.

71. Shaw, *Journals*, 269, 284.

72. Shaw, *Journals*, 287–288.

73. Shaw, *Journals*, 288–291.

74. Shaw, *Journals*, 295, 297.

75. Shaw, *Journals*, 333–334.

76. *Massachusetts Magazine*, July 1790; *Columbian Centinel*, 18 September 1790.

77. Quincy, "Memoir," in Shaw, *Journals*, 177–118; Dennett, *Americans in Eastern Asia*, 12; *New Hampshire Gazette*, 7 April 1790.

78. Quincy, "Memoir," in Shaw, *Journals*, 111. A cash-strapped Congress sold the *Alliance*, the last ship in the Continental navy, on 1 August 1785 to Philadelphia merchants. Robert Morris purchased the vessel, converting her for the Indies Trade. On the outward leg of her voyage, June to December 1787, the *Alliance* reached Canton by a new route through the

Dutch East Indies and the Solomon Islands. She returned to Philadelphia with a cargo of tea on 17 September 1788. Lee, *Philadelphians and the China Trade*, 11.

79. Delano, *Narrative*, 38–42; Dennett, *Americans in Eastern Asia*, 15.

80. *Columbian Centinel*, 29 August 1792; *American Apollo*, 5 October 1792.

81. *New-York Daily Gazette*, 26 August 1794; *Columbian Gazetteer*, 25 August 1794; *Columbian Centinel*, 16 August 1794.

INTERLUDE 1: "Tempestuous Seas of Liberty," 1785–1790

1. Quoted in Michael Warner, *The Letters of the Republic: Publication and the Public Sphere in Eighteenth-Century America* (Cambridge: Harvard University Press, 1990), 204.

2. Rhys Richards, "United States Trade with China, 1784–1814," *American Neptune* 54 (1994): 5–18; Robert J. Allison, *The Crescent Observed: The United States and the Muslim World, 1776–1815* (Chicago: University of Chicago Press, 2000), 107, 110; Caroline Frank, *Objectifying China, Imagining America: Chinese Commodities in Early America* (Chicago: University of Chicago Press, 2011), 1–11, 30–43, 54; Eric Jay Dolin, *When America First Met China: An Exotic History of Tea, Drugs, and Money in the Age of Sail* (New York: Liveright, 2012), 107.

3. [Goberdhan] Bhagat, "America's First Contacts with India, 1784–1785," *American Neptune* (January 1971): 40; Susan Bean, *Yankee India: American Commercial and Cultural Encounters with India in the Age of Sail, 1784–1860* (Salem, MA: Peabody Essex Museum, 2001), 17; Holden Furber, "The Beginnings of American Trade with India, 1784–1812," *New England Quarterly* 11, no. 2 (June 1938): 235–236; Joseph Ingraham, *Joseph Ingraham's Journal of the Brigantine hope on a Voyage to the Northwest Coast of North America, 1790–92*, ed. Mark D. Kaplanoff (Barre, MA: Imprint Society, 1971), xii; Robert G. Albion, William A. Baker, and Benjamin W. Labaree, *New England and the Sea* (Middletown, CT: Wesleyan University Press, 1972), 57; Jacob E. Cooke, *Tench Coxe and the Early Republic* (Chapel Hill: University of North Carolina Press, 1978), 272; Dorothy Shurman Hawes, *To the Farthest Gulf: The Story of the American China Trade* (Ipswich, MA: Ipswich Press, 1990), 112, 141; Alexis de Tocqueville, *Democracy in America: Historical-Critical Edition of De la démocratie en Amérique*, ed. Eduardo Nolla, translated from the French by James T. Schleifer (Indianapolis: Liberty Fund, 2010), 2.

4. Magdalen Coughlin, "Commercial Foundations of Political Interest in the Opening Pacific, 1789–1829," *California Historical Quarterly* 50, no. 1 (Mar. 1971): 16. These figures compare with estimated GDP of $556 million in 1805 and $699 million in 1810. See www.usgovernmentrevenue.com/year_revenue.

5. John D. Forbes, "European Wars and Boston Trade, 1783–1815," *New England Quarterly* 11, no. 4 (December 1938): 711–715.

6. Bean, *Yankee India*, 7, 17; Richard E. Winslow, III, *"Wealth and Honour": Portsmouth During the Golden Age of Privateering, 1775–1815* (Portsmouth, NH: Portsmouth Marine Society, 1988), 73. The statistical tables cover the period from 1 October 1802 through 30 September 1803. John Adams to Robert Livingston [?], 18 July 1783, Langdon Papers, MS 92, Box 1, Folder 13, Strawbery Banke Museum, Portsmouth, NH.

7. Jean Gordon Lee, *Philadelphians and the China Trade* (Philadelphia: Philadelphia Museum of Art, 1984), 11.

8. Gardner W. Allen, *Our Naval War with France* (Boston: Houghton Mifflin, 1909), 41; Langdon Papers, MS 92, Box 1, Folder 13, Strawbery Banke Museum, Portsmouth, NH; Joseph J. Ellis, *Founding Brothers: The Revolutionary Generation* (New York: Alfred A. Knopf, 2001), 93. Historians have estimated the number of American prisoners in North African prisons during the period 1785–1815 as between 500 and 700. The numbers were comparatively small. Robert G. Davis estimates that between 1530 and 1780, 1 million to 1.25 million Europeans were captured and taken as slaves to North Africa, principally Algiers, Tunis, and

Tripoli, but also Istanbul and Salé. In 1800, 1 million African Americans were held in bondage in the United States. See Robert J. Allison, *The Crescent Obscured: The United States and the Muslim World, 1776–1815* (Chicago: University of Chicago Press, 1995), 107, 110; Lawrence A. Peskin, *Captives and Countrymen: Barbary Slavery and the American Public, 1785–1816* (Baltimore: Johns Hopkins University Press, 2009); Charles Hansford Adams, *The Narrative of Robert Adams: A Barbary Captive* (New York: Cambridge University Press, 2005), xlv–xlvi; Martha Elena Rojas, "'Insults Unpunished': Barbary Captives, American Slaves, and the Negotiation of Liberty," *Early American Studies: An Interdisciplinary Journal* 1, no. 2 (Fall 2003): 165.

9. Forbes, "European Wars and Boston Trade," 722; Winslow, *"Wealth and Honour,"* 76; *Salem Gazette,* 12 January 1802.

10. Christopher Kingston, "Marine Insurance in Philadelphia during the Quasi-War with France, 1795–1801," *Journal of Economic History* 71, no. 1 (2011): 6–7; Donald R. Hickey, "The Quasi-War: America's First Limited War, 1798–1801," *Northern Mariner* 18, nos. 3–4 (July–October 2008): 67–68; Forbes, "European Wars and Boston Trade," 710; and Allen, *Naval War,* 716.

11. Edmund Fanning, *Voyages Round the World; with Selected Sketches of Voyages to the South Seas, North and South Pacific Oceans, China, etc., Performed under the Command and Agency of the Author. Also, Information Relating to Important Late Discoveries; between the Years 1792 and 1832, Together with the Report of the Commander of the First American Exploring Expedition, Patronised by the United States Government, in the brigs Seraph and Annawan, to the Southern Hemisphere* (New York: Collins & Hannay, 1833), 31–34.

12. Richard Morton Smith, *Patriarch: George Washington and the New American Nation* (Boston: Houghton Mifflin, 1993), 270–276; Allen, *Naval War,* passim; James Duncan Phillips, "Salem's Part in the Naval War with France," *New England Quarterly* 16 (December 1943): 543–566; Winslow, *"Wealth and Honour,"* 74–76; Kingston, "Marine Insurance," 7; and Hickey, "The Quasi-War," 74.

13. Allen, *Naval War,* 249, 267.

14. Phillips, "Salem's Part in the Naval War with France," 565; Captain Edward Preble to Secretary of Navy, 25 March 1800, quoted in Allen, *Naval War,* 156.

CHAPTER 2: Amasa Delano Opens the Great South Sea, 1790–1820

1. Amasa Delano, *A Narrative of Voyages and Travels, in the Northern and Southern Hemispheres: Comprising Three Voyages Round the World; Together with a Voyage of Survey and Discovery, in the Pacific Ocean and Oriental Islands* (Boston: E. G. House, 1817), 23.

2. Throughout the *Narrative,* Delano offered his readers apologies for his "want of an early and academic education." See, for instance, Delano, *Narrative,* 17.

3. "Biographical Sketch," in Delano, *Narrative,* 577, 580.

4. For example, John Green, captain of the *Empress of China* on her first voyage to Canton, had been a prisoner of war, as had two of Edmund Fanning's brothers, one of whom died aboard a British prison ship, while the other fought under John Paul Jones. When the Revolution began, Richard Cleveland's father Stephan returned the favor of his own earlier impressment into the Royal Navy, building and fitting out privateers. On one of his first voyages, as a twenty-two-year-old seaman aboard an Indiaman, Cleveland observed how the war had affected the character of another veteran, Captain Chipman of Salem, who had "seen severe and even cruel service at sea." Delano, *Narrative,* 202–204, 256, 561, 571–572, 576, 583, and Cleveland, *A Narrative of Voyages and Commercial Enterprises* (Boston: H. Pierce, 1850), 36.

5. Delano, *Narrative,* 21.

6. Delano, *Narrative,* 21, 25, 26–39; Paul E. Fontenoy, "An 'Experimental' Voyage to China, 1785–1787," *American Neptune* 55, no. 4 (Fall 1995): 289–300; and Mary A. Y. Galla-

gher, "Charting a New Course for the China Trade: The Late Eighteenth-Century American Model," in *The Early Republic and the Sea: Essays on the Naval and Maritime History of the Early United States*, ed. William S. Dudley and Michael J. Crawford (Washington, DC: Brassey's, 2001), 55–82.

7. Delano, *Narrative*, 38–42.

8. Delano, *Narrative*, 44. Richard Henry Dana used the term "Yankee land" in his classic memoir, *Two Years Before the Mast* (Boston, 1840). The term "Jonathan" was used commonly in Britain to denote an American; within colonial and postrevolutionary America, the term described a humble everyman or country bumpkin, often a New Englander, whose most telling trait was a humorous naïveté. See Winifred Morgan, *An American Icon: Brother Jonathan and American Identity* (Newark: University of Delaware Press, 1988).

9. Delano, *Narrative*, 50, 157. One certainly can make the case that other merchants and mariners, such as Samuel Shaw or William C. Hunter, participated in the China Trade as historians and museum scholars have constructed it, based in China and India. Hester Blum distinguishes "the more widely read sea writing of the antebellum period" from the Barbary narratives, for instance, which she sees as "addressed to fellow seamen." Hester Blum, "Pirated Tars, Piratical Texts: Barbary Captivity and American Sea Narratives," *Early American Studies* 1 (Fall 2003): 134.

10. Delano, *Narrative*, 47, 89, 166, 525–526, 151, 156, 177, 264; Matthew McKenzie, "Salem as Athenaeum," in *Salem: Place, Myth, and Memory*, ed. Dane A. Morrison and Nancy L. Schultz (Boston: Northeastern University Press, 2004), and David Jaffee, "The Village Enlightenment in New England, 1760–1820," *William and Mary Quarterly* 3rd ser., 47, no. 3 (July 1990): 327–346.

11. John Smith, *A Description of New England* (1616); William Wood, *New England's Prospect* (1634); John Josselyn, *New England's Rarities, discovered in Birds, Beasts, Fishes, Serpents, and Plants of that Country* (1671); and Delano, *Narrative*, 221, 313, 337, 366, 397.

12. Delano, *Narrative*, 182.

13. Delano, *Narrative*, 153, 158, 53–54.

14. Delano, *Narrative*, 57–68.

15. Delano, *Narrative*, 91–95, 81, 99.

16. Delano, *Narrative*, 200–202.

17. Delano, *Narrative*, 235–236.

18. Delano, *Narrative*, 203, 211, 227, 229, 250.

19. Delano, *Narrative*, 256.

20. Delano, *Narrative*, 265–267, 271, 283–286. The term "green Yankee" was in common usage throughout the period. Edmund Fanning described himself as a young man as "but a green Yankee" in his 1833 *Voyages Round the World; with Selected Sketches of Voyages to the South Seas, North and South Pacific Oceans, China, etc., Performed under the Command and Agency of the Author. Also, Information Relating to Important Late Discoveries; between the Years 1792 and 1832, Together with the Report of the Commander of the First American Exploring Expedition, Patronised by the United States Government, in the brigs Seraph and Annawan, to the Southern Hemisphere* (New York: Collins & Hannay, 1833), 38. See, also, *Spirit of the Times; A Chronicle of the Turf, Agriculture, Field Sports, Literature and the Stage* 15, no. 23 (2 August 1845): 265. It is not clear how much of Delano's reading was done after his retirement from the sea, which occurred sometime after 1810, but he seems to have consulted others' travelogues regularly in planning his voyages.

21. Delano, *Narrative*, 298, 354, 369.

22. Delano, *Narrative*, 259, 360.

23. See, for example, Samuel Shaw, *The Journals of Major Samuel Shaw, the First American*

Consul at Canton, ed. Josiah Quincy (Taipei: Ch'eng-Wen, 1968); Fanning, *Voyages Round the World;* and Richard Jeffry Cleveland, *Narrative.*

24. Delano, *Narrative,* 275, 387, 405, 410; James Duncan Phillips, *Pepper and Pirates: Adventures in the Sumatra Pepper Trade of Salem* (Boston: Houghton Mifflin, 1949), 8–14; Charles Corn, *The Scents of Eden: A Narrative of the Spice Trade* (New York: Kodansha, 1998), ch. 19; Rev. William Rees, *The Cyclopædia; or, Universal Dictionary of Arts, Sciences, and Literature* (Philadelphia, 1806).

25. Five years later, his brother Samuel was especially successful at the Galápagos Islands, where he "procured between twelve and thirteen thousand skins, with which they arrived safe at Canton, though some of the skins were damaged by being wet, in consequence of the schooner being upset while entering the China seas." The reader must be cautious in reading the *Narrative,* as Delano's writing moves between episodes and across time throughout the text. In this section, particularly, descriptions of events that occurred in 1805 interrupt the narrative of the 1799–1802 voyage. As he wrote, "I have made no difference whether it was during my first or second voyage; as it could be of no consequence to the reader." Delano, *Narrative,* 259, 270, 306–307, 366–368, 309. Wage estimates are notoriously difficult to make. In 1820, C. S. Van Winkle estimated that laboring wages for New York were $1.00 per day; Danny Vickers and Winifred Rothenberg, however, offer monthly estimates of $5.00–$5.50 for New England farm hands and $7.50–$8.80 for mariners. C. S. Van Winkle, *A Review of the Trade and Commerce of New York from 1815 to the Present Time, with an Inquiry into the Causes of the Present Distress and the Means of Alleviating It, by an Observer* (1820); Danny Vickers, with Vince Walsh, *Young Men and the Sea: Yankee Seafarers in the Age of Sail* (New Haven: Yale University Press, 2005), 178; Winifred Barr Rothenberg, "The Invention of American Capitalism: The Economy of New England in the Federal Period," in *Engines of Enterprise: An Economic History of New England,* ed. Peter Temin (Cambridge, MA: Harvard University Press, 2000), 106.

26. Cook was killed at Kealakekua Bay on the island of Kaua'i on 14 February 1779. Delano, *Narrative,* 288, 395–397.

27. There is some confusion over the date of the marriage, with some genealogies placing it in 1785 or c. 1788 in Boston. However, the Providence vital records and Boston newspapers report the marriage on 21 June 1803. It appears that Hannah operated a boardinghouse on Atkinson Street and then Beacon Street in Boston whose patrons later included William Emerson's Anthology Society and a young Daniel Webster. *United States Chronicle,* 23 June 1803; Delano, *Narrative,* 420–421; and Randall L. Holton and Charles A. Gilday, "Sarah Goodrich: Mapping Places in the Heart," *Antiques* (July 2013).

28. Delano, *Narrative,* 472.

29. Delano, *Narrative,* 265, 296, 510 507, and John L. O'Sullivan, "Annexation," *United States Magazine and Democratic Review* (July/August 1845).

30. Delano's first visit in 1800 had been much more friendly. Delano, *Narrative,* 309–311.

31. Delano, *Narrative,* 496–497.

32. Delano, *Narrative,* 496–497, 318, 329. Some of these accounts were reprinted from the *Gazette of the United States. Newburyport Herald,* 21 August 1807; *Salem Gazette,* 21 August 1807; *Portsmouth Oracle,* 22 August 1807; *Mercantile Advertiser,* 24 April 1806 and 27 August 1807; *Public Advertiser,* 22 August 1807; *Republican Watch-Tower,* 1 September 1807; *New-York Spectator,* 26 April 1806; *Democratic Press* 28 August 1807; *Poulson's American Daily Advertiser,* 25 August 1807; *Vermont Centinel* (Burlington), 2 September 1807; *Alexandria Daily Advertiser,* 28 April 1806; and the *Enquirer* of Richmond, Virginia, 6 May 1806. Melville published "Benito Cereno" in serial form in *Putnam's Monthly* in 1855 and a year later revised it for *The Piazza Tales.* A number of literary critics have wrestled with the moral ambivalence they find in Melville's classic short story. See, for instance, Andrew Delbanco, *Melville: His World and*

Work (New York: Knopf, 2005); Rosalie Feltenstein, "Melville's Benito Cereno," *American Literature: A Journal of Literary History, Criticism, and Bibliography* 19, no. 3 (1947): 245–255; Dan McCall, *Melville's Short Novels: Authoritative Texts, Contexts, Criticism* (New York: Norton, 2002); Lea Bertani Vozar Newman, "Benito Cereno," in *A Reader's Guide to the Short Stories of Herman Melville*, ed. Lea Bertani Vozar Newman (Boston: G. K. Hall, 1986); Maggie Montesinos Sale, *The Slumbering Volcano: American Slave Ship Revolts and the Production of Rebellious Masculinity* (Durham, NC: Duke University Press, 1997); Sterling Stuckey, "The Tambourine in Glory: African Culture and Melville's Art," in *The Cambridge Companion to Herman Melville*, ed. Robert S. Levine (New York: Cambridge University Press, 1998), 37–64; and Eric J. Sundquist, *To Wake the Nations: Race in the Making of American Literature* (Cambridge, MA: Belknap Press of Harvard University Press, 1993).

33. Delano, *Narrative*, 89, 64–65, 347–348.

34. Phillip Ammidon, Edward Carrington, Thomas Perkins, and H. W. Wilcocks were in operation in Canton by 1807. Jacques M. Downs, *The Golden Ghetto: The American Commercial Community at Canton and the Shaping of American China Policy, 1784–1844* (Bethlehem, PA: Lehigh University Press, 1997); Delano, *Narrative*, 529–530.

35. Delano, *Narrative*, 530–542, 412. The actual phrasing in this passage reads, "For the purpose of showing with what dread, punishments for violations of the laws of this empire are held, I shall insert an anecdote." The phrase "master mariner" entitles James Brendan Connolly's biography of Delano, *Master Mariner: The Life and Voyages of Amasa Delano* (Garden City, NY: Doubleday, Doran, 1943).

36. In describing his 1810 voyage to St. Bartholomew's, Delano emphasized the impositions of "sharpers" and "all those little mean dishonorable practices that are at the present day." Connolly suggests that he was able to get a job as a clerk in the Boston Custom House. Connolly, *Master Mariner*, 309; C. Hartley Grattan, "Preface," in Delano, *Narrative* (reprint; New York: Praeger, 1970), vii; and Delano, *Narrative*, 559, 563, 422, 593.

37. A tearful Harriett Low left Salem about her twentieth birthday for a five-year stint in Macao because her family could not afford her upkeep; likewise, Rebecca Kinsman accompanied her husband Nathaniel there in part because of the family's precarious finances. John Beaglehole, *The Life of Captain James Cook* (Stanford: Stanford University Press, 1974), 290; Robert Foulke, *The Sea Voyage Narrative* (New York: Twayne, 1997), 103–104; and Delano, *Narrative*, vii, 15–16.

38. The opening pages of Delano's *Narrative* are very similar to the beginning of John Bartlett's *A Narrative of Events in the Life of John Bartlett of Boston, Massachusetts, in the Years 1790–1793, During Voyages to Canton and the North-West Coast of North America*. Little is known of Bartlett or the provenance of his work, which was not published until 1925 as an excerpt in *The Sea, the Ship and the Sailor: Tales of Adventure from Log Books and Original Narratives* (Salem, MA: Marine Research Society). Delano, *Narrative*, 16, 197, 318, 320, 569, 17.

39. "The Origin of Melville's 'Benito Cereno'" appeared in the *New York Evening Post* for 9 October 1855 and recounted Delano's achievements. On the 1818 edition of the *Narrative*, see Robert K. Wallace, "Fugitive Justice: Douglass, Shaw, Melville," in *Frederick Douglass & Herman Melville: Essays in Relation*, ed. Robert S. Levine and Samuel Otter (Chapel Hill: University of North Carolina Press, 2008), 43, 61; *North American Review* 5, no. 14 (1817): 244–257. Richard Hakluyt's popular treatments of exploration, *Divers Voyages Touching the Discovery of America* (1582) and *The Principal Navigations, Voyages, Traffics and Discoveries of the English Nation* (1589–1600), continued to inspire American mariners into the nineteenth century.

40. *Independent Chronicle & Boston Patriot*, 30 April 1823; *Salem Gazette*, 2 May 1823; and Delano, *Narrative*, 497.

INTERLUDE 2: "The Strangers Were Americans"

1. The concept of a "citizen of the world" is thought to have originated with Oliver Goldsmith, whose letters in the *Public Ledger* beginning in 1760 popularized the idea of a sophisticated world traveler who used one's global encounters to gently critique the customs of one's own and other societies. See also, Peter Linebaugh and Marcus Rediker, *The Many-Headed Hydra: Sailors, Slaves, Commoners, and the Hidden History of the Revolutionary Atlantic* (Boston: Beacon Press, 2000), 247–248, and Sam W. Haynes, *Unfinished Revolution: The Early American Republic in a British World* (Charlottesville: University of Virginia Press, 2010), passim.

2. Caroline Frank, *Objectifying China, Imagining America: Chinese Commodities in Early America* (Chicago: University of Chicago Press, 2011), chs. 1–2; Guillaume Vandenbroucke, "The U.S. Westward Expansion," University of Southern California (November 2006), http://papers.ssrn.com/sol3/papers.cfm?abstract_id=1014941, accessed 4 December 2006.

3. James W. Gould, "American Imperialism in Southeast Asia before 1898," *Journal of Southeast Asian Studies* 3, no. 2 (September 1972): 306–307.

4. Frank, *Objectifying China*, passim; Marcus Rediker, *Between the Devil and the Deep Blue Sea: Merchant Seamen, Pirates, and the Anglo-American Maritime World, 1700–1750* (New York: Cambridge University Press, 1987), 36–41 and 44–48; Maya Jasanoff, *Liberty's Exiles: American Loyalists in the Revolutionary World* (New York: Vintage, 2012), 6; on the concept of Orientalism, see Edward Said, *Orientalism* (New York: Vintage, 1978), and A. L. Macfie, *Orientalism* (New York: Longman, 2002).

5. William C. Hunter, *Bits of Old China* (1855; reprint, Taipei: Ch'eng-Wen, 1966), 3–7; Harriett Low, Journal, 1829–1834, 9 vols., Phillips Library, Peabody Essex Museum, 7–8 September 1829.

6. Ralph D. Paine, *The Ships and Sailors of Old Salem: The Record of a Brilliant Era of American Achievement* (Boston: Charles Lauriat, 1924), 144–145; John Crowninshield, "Journal of Capt. John Crowninshield at Calcutta, 1797–1798, When Master of the Ship 'Belisarius,'" *Essex Institute Historical Collections* 81, no. 18 (1945): 355; Cleveland, *A Narrative of Voyages and Commercial Enterprises* (Boston: H. Pierce, 1850), 40; John White, *History of a Voyage to the China Sea* (Boston: Wells and Lilly, 1823), 5; Thomas N. Layton, *Voyage of the "Frolic": New England Merchants and the Opium Trade* (Darby, PA: Diane Publishers, 1997), 141, and Susan Bean, *Yankee India: American Commercial and Cultural Encounters with India in the Age of Sail, 1784–1860* (Salem, MA: Peabody Essex Museum, 2001), 109.

7. *Salem Gazette*, 1 November 1791 and 6 March 1792; Edmund Fanning, *Voyages Round the World; with Selected Sketches of Voyages to the South Seas, North and South Pacific Oceans, China, etc., Performed under the Command and Agency of the Author. Also, Information Relating to Important Late Discoveries; between the Years 1792 and 1832, Together with the Report of the Commander of the First American Exploring Expedition, Patronised by the United States Government, in the brigs Seraph and Annawan, to the Southern Hemisphere* (New York: Collins & Hannay, 1833), 306.

8. Robert E. Peabody, *The Log of the Grand Turks* (Boston: Houghton Mifflin, 1926), 79, 48; Paine, *The Ships and Sailors of Old Salem*, 148–150, 278; Bean, *Yankee India*, 102; and White, *History of a Voyage to the China Sea*, 6–7.

9. Dorothy Shurman Hawes, *To the Farthest Gulf: The Story of the American China Trade*, ed. John Quentin Feller (Ipswich, MA: Ipswich Press, 1990), 24.

CHAPTER 3: Edmund Fanning's "Voyages Round the World," 1792–1833

1. Edmund Fanning, *Voyages Round the World; with Selected Sketches of Voyages to the South Seas, North and South Pacific Oceans, China, etc., Performed under the Command and Agency of the Author. Also, Information Relating to Important Late Discoveries; between the Years 1792 and 1832,*

Together with the Report of the Commander of the First American Exploring Expedition, Patronised by the United States Government, in the brigs Seraph and Annawan, to the Southern Hemisphere (New York: Collins & Hannay, 1833), 68–69.

2. Walter Frederic Brooks, *History of the Fanning Family: A Genealogical Record to 1900 of the Descendants of Edmund Fanning,* 2 vols. (Worcester, MA: n.p., 1905), 250–251.

3. Fanning, *Voyages,* iii, x–xii.

4. Fanning, *Voyages,* 13–16; Walter Barrett, *The Old Merchants of New York City* (New York: Thomas R. Knox, 1885), 3:167.

5. Fanning, *Voyages,* 31.

6. Fanning, *Voyages,* 48–49.

7. Fanning, *Voyages,* 69.

8. Fanning, *Voyages,* 17–18.

9. Fanning, *Voyages,* 23–25.

10. Fanning, *Voyages,* 18–19, 20.

11. Fanning, *Voyages,* 29; *Daily Advertiser* (New York), 16 November 1793.

12. Fanning, *Voyages,* 66.

13. Fanning, *Voyages,* 66–68.

14. Fanning, *Voyages,* 70–71.

15. Fanning, *Voyages,* 75–76, 81–82.

16. Fanning, *Voyages,* 73, 75.

17. Fanning, *Voyages,* 77–78, 81–82, 90–91, 99–100.

18. Fanning, *Voyages,* 118.

19. Fanning, *Voyages,* 19, 218.

20. Fanning, *Voyages,* 84–90, 119.

21. Fanning, *Voyages,* 19, 88, 90–91, 127.

22. Fanning, *Voyages,* 96, 92.

23. Fanning, *Voyages,* 105–108.

24. Fanning, *Voyages,* 96, 105, 103.

25. Fanning, *Voyages,* 103, 107–111, 115–118.

26. Fanning, *Voyages,* 118–121.

27. Fanning, *Voyages,* 189–190.

28. Fanning, *Voyages,* 117, 152, 216–217.

29. Fanning, *Voyages,* 123–125.

30. Fanning, *Voyages,* 125–129.

31. Fanning, *Voyages,* 131–134.

32. Fanning, *Voyages,* 137–138.

33. Fanning, *Voyages,* 145–147, 158; Ernest S. Dodge, *Islands and Empires: Western Impact on the Pacific and East Asia* (Minneapolis: University of Minnesota Press, 1976), 8.

34. Fanning, *Voyages,* 155–158.

35. Fanning, *Voyages,* 159–167.

36. Fanning, *Voyages,* 172–177.

37. Fanning, *Voyages,* 208.

38. Fanning, *Voyages,* 209, 157–158, 201, 182, 178, 194, 201, 145.

39. Fanning, *Voyages,* 198–200.

40. Fanning, *Voyages,* 137, 152, 168–172, 204–206.

41. Fanning, *Voyages,* 218–226.

42. Fanning, *Voyages,* 226–228.

43. Fanning, *Voyages,* 235–237.

44. Fanning, *Voyages*, 238–248.

45. Fanning, *Voyages*, 250–253; James Horsburgh, *The India Directory, or, Directions for Sailing to and from the East Indies*, 6th ed. (London: William H. Allen, 1852), 2:385.

46. Fanning, *Voyages*, 254–257.

47. Fanning, *Voyages*, 254–260; Samuel Shaw, *The Journals of Major Samuel Shaw, the First American Consul at Canton*, ed. Josiah Quincy (Taipei: Ch'eng-Wen, 1968), 180–181.

48. Fanning, *Voyages*, 261–262.

49. Fanning, *Voyages*, 262–264.

50. Patrick Conner, *The Hongs of Canton: Western Merchants in South China, 1700–1900, as Seen in Chinese Export Paintings* (London: English Art Books, 2009), 225–226; Sullivan Dorr, "Letters of Sullivan Dorr," ed. Howard Corning, Massachusetts Historical Society *Proceedings*, 3rd ser., 67 (October 1941–May 1944): 215.

51. Fanning, *Voyages*, 265–267.

52. Fanning, *Voyages*, 266.

53. Fanning, *Voyages*, 268.

54. Fanning, *Voyages*, 282; Joseph Ingraham, *Joseph Ingraham's Journal of the Brigantine hope on a Voyage to the Northwest Coast of North America, 1790–92* (Barre, MA: Imprint Society, 1971), 11.

55. William Marsden, *The History of Sumatra*, 3rd ed. (1811; reprint, New York: Oxford University Press, 1966), 13.

56. John White, *History of a Voyage to the China Sea* (Boston: Wells and Lilly, 1823), 12–15, 22–23: Harriett Low to Abiel Abbott Low, 16 March 1829, *The China Trade Post-Bag of the Low Family of Salem and New York, 1829–1873*, ed. Elma Loines (Manchester, ME: Falmouth Publishing House, 1953), 19.

57. Fanning, *Voyages*, 193; White, *History of a Voyage to the China Sea*, 28.

58. Fanning, *Voyages*, 269–272. Four-pounders were cannon that could fire a four-pound shot of metal. These were small guns compared to the 28- and 32-pounders in common use in Western navies.

59. Fanning, *Voyages*, 272–273.

60. Fanning, *Voyages*, 273–275.

61. Fanning, *Voyages*, 278, 281.

62. Fanning, *Voyages*, 203–204.

63. *New York Gazette and General Advertiser*, 8 May 1799; *Albany Centinel*, 4 June 1799; *Daily Advertiser* (New York), 4 May 1799; Fanning, *Voyages*, 282.

64. *Baltimore Patriot*, 22 October 1829.

INTERLUDE 3: "How T'other Side Looked"

1. In the figures of Captain Jack Aubrey and surgeon-spy Stephen Maturin, Patrick O'Brian's celebrated fictional series depicting the Royal Navy during the Napoleonic Wars captures the spirit of the age. See, for instance, *Master and Commander* (New York: J. B. Lippincott, 1969).

2. Maritime travelogues from the early republic and antebellum periods can be found in a host of archives, including the Phillips Library at the Peabody Essex Museum, John Carter Brown Library at Brown University, G. W. Blunt White Library of Mystic Seaport, and any number of local historical societies. Nathaniel Philbrick, *Sea of Glory: America's Voyage of Discovery: The U.S. Exploring Expedition* (New York: Penguin, 2003), xvii.

3. Thomas Jefferson, confidential message to Congress, 18 January 1803; Brett Mizelle, "Displaying the Expanding Nation to Itself: The Cultural Work of Public Exhibitions of Western Fauna in Lewis and Clark's Philadelphia," in *The Shortest and Most Convenient Route: Lewis and Clark in Context*, ed. Robert S. Cox (Philadelphia: American Philosophical Society,

2004), 215–235; Michael F. Robinson, "Why We Need a New History of Exploration: Lewis and Clark, Alexander von Humboldt, and the Explorer in American Culture," *Common-Place: The Interactive Journal of Early American Life* 10, no. 1 (October 2009): common-place.org/vol-10/no-01/robinson; William H. Goetzmann, *New Lands, New Men: America and the Second Great Age of Discovery* (New York: Viking, 1986). Although American historians have begun to incorporate a Pacific horizon into their work, Robinson's essay suggests the limitations of the current trend; his interpretation of exploration and American culture omits the pervasive influence of American overseas travelers and expatriates, focusing instead on the influence of von Humboldt.

  4. Ralph D. Paine, *The Ships and Sailors of Old Salem: The Record of a Brilliant Era of American Achievement* (Boston: Charles Lauriat, 1924), 150; Edmund Fanning, *Voyages Round the World; with Selected Sketches of Voyages to the South Seas, North and South Pacific Oceans, China, etc., Performed under the Command and Agency of the Author. Also, Information Relating to Important Late Discoveries; between the Years 1792 and 1832, Together with the Report of the Commander of the First American Exploring Expedition, Patronised by the United States Government, in the brigs Seraph and Annawan, to the Southern Hemisphere* (New York: Collins & Hannay, 1833), 282, 218.

  5. In the *North American Review*, readers were regularly treated to reviews of their countrymen's travelogues, including Porter's *Journal of a Cruise* in 1, no. 2 (July 1815): 247–275; travels to the American settlements on the Northwest Coast in 2, no. 6 (March 1816): 301; a survey of the Sandwich Islands, or Hawai'i in 3, no. 7 (May 1816): 42–54; Delano's *Narrative* in 5, no. 14 (July 1817): 244–257; Riley's *Narrative* of his capture off the North African coast in 5, no. 15 (September 1817): 389–409; John White's *History of a Voyage to the China Sea* in 18, no. 42 (January 1824): 140–157; and Richard Henry Dana's *Two Years Before the Mast* in 52, no. 110 (January 1841): 56–75.

  6. Porter, in fact, claimed the Marquesas for the United States and renamed them the Madison Islands, in honor of then-President James Madison. David Porter, *Journal of a Cruise Made to the Pacific Ocean* (New York: Wiley and Halsted, 1822), 2:5, 71, 74, 80–81.

  7. *Richmond Enquirer*, 11 December 1840; *Times Picayune* (New Orleans), 19 July 1840.

  8. William Reynolds, *The Private Journal of William Reynolds: United States Exploring Expedition, 1838–1842*, eds. Nathaniel Philbrick and Thomas Philbrick (New York: Penguin, 2004), 11.

  9. *New-Bedford Mercury*, 10 July 1840.

CHAPTER 4: Harriett Low in Manila and Macao, 1829–1834

  1. Harriett Low, Journal, 1829–1834, 9 vols., Phillips Library, Peabody Essex Museum, 7–8 September 1829.

  2. It is difficult to gauge the influence of a private journal such as that of Harriett Low, often intended for a few family members and friends. Throughout the period of the Indies Trade, Americans dispatched homeward thousands of letters and journals, conservatively estimated. In addition to Low's nine-volume manuscript journal in the Phillips Library, Peabody Essex Museum, one can find published versions of the journal, some heavily edited, in *My Mother's Journal: A Young Lady's Diary of Five Years Spent in Manila, Macao, and the Cape of Good Hope from 1829–1834*, ed. Katherine Hillard (Boston: George H. Ellis, 1990); *The China Trade Post-Bag of the Low Family of Salem and New York, 1829–1873*, ed. Elma Loines (Manchester, ME: Falmouth Publishing House, 1953), and *Lights and Shadows of a Macao Life: The Journal of Harriett Low, Travelling Spinster*, ed. Nan Hodges and Arthur William Hummel (Woodinville, WA: The History Bank, 2002).

  3. Loines, *Post-Bag*, 11–14.

4. Susan Geib, "Landscape and Faction: Spatial Transformation in William Bentley's Salem," *Essex Institute Historical Collections* 113 (July 1977): 163–175.

5. Low, Journal, 24 May and 24 August 1829; Loines, *Post-Bag*, vi, 19; Harriett to Seth Low, 16 March 1829; Seth Low to Harriett, 17 May 1829.

6. Richard Henry Dana, *Two Years Before the Mast* (New York: Harper, 1840); Alison Games, *The Web of Empire: English Cosmopolitans in an Age of Expansion, 1560–1660* (New York: Oxford University Press, 2008), ch. 1.

7. Low, Journal, 24 May, 16 June, and 20 August 1829.

8. Harriett Low to Mr. and Mrs. Seth Low, 5 September 1829; Low, Journal, 19–22 July and 6–22 August 1829.

9. Low, Journal, 5 and 7 June 1829.

10. Low, Journal, 11 August 1829.

11. Low, Journal, 5 June and 21 July 1829; Harriett Low to Seth and Abigail Low, 5 September 1829.

12. Low, Journal, 25–26 August 1829.

13. Harriett Low to Seth and Abigail Low, 5 September 1829.

14. Low, Journal, 9–12 September 1829.

15. Low, Journal, 7–8 September 1829.

16. Low, Journal, 12 September 1829; Nancy L. Schultz, *Fire and Roses: The Burning of the Charlestown Convent, 1834* (New York: Free Press, 2000); Games, *Web of Empire*, 34; Owen Stanwood, "The Protestant Moment: Antipopery, the Revolution of 1688–1689, and the Making of an Anglo-American Empire," *Journal of British Studies* 46 (2007): 481–508; Daniel Kilbride, *Being American in Europe, 1750–1860* (Baltimore: Johns Hopkins University Press, 2013); and "The Dilemma of Anti-Catholicism in American Travel Writing, circa 1790–1830," Society of the Early American Republic conference, 15 July 2011.

17. Low, Journal, 12–14 September 1829; Francis J. Bremer, *Puritanism: A Very Short Introduction* (New York: Oxford University Press, 2009), 65–66.

18. Low, Journal, 10–14 and 20 September 1829.

19. Harriett Low to Seth Low, 16 March 1829; Low, Journal, 7 May 1833.

20. Low, Journal, 27 October 1830, in Loines 131–133.

21. Low, Journal, 27 October and 6 November 1830.

22. Low, Journal, 15–17 November 1833 and 25 January 1834.

23. William C. Hunter, *Bits of Old China* (1855; reprint, Taipei: Ch'eng-Wen, 1966), 2; Harriett Low to Mary Ann Low, 8 January 1831; Low, Journal, 25 January 1831.

24. Harriett Low to Mary Ann Low, 8 January 1831; Low, Journal, 25 January 1831 and 27 November 1831.

25. Low, Journal, 17 February 1833.

26. Low, Journal, 23 and 25 February 1833 and 28 January 1834; *Freeman's Journal, or The North-American Intelligencer*, 22 June 1785; Treavor Colburn, *The Lamp of Experience: Whig History and the Intellectual Origins of the American Revolution* (Chapel Hill: University of North Carolina Press, 1995), 3–39; David W. Conroy, *In Public Houses: Drink and the Revolution of Authority in Colonial Massachusetts* (Chapel Hill: University of North Carolina Press, 1995), 243–245; Caroline Robbins, *The Eighteenth-Century Commonwealthmen: Studies in the Transmission, Development, and Circumstance of English Liberal Thought from the Restoration of Charles II until the War with the Thirteen Colonies* (Cambridge, MA: Harvard University Press, 1959), 44–45, 106–107, 309–310.

27. Resolutions of the Gloucester town meeting, 15 December 1773, reported in the *Essex Gazette*, 25 January 1774; Low, Journal, 17 November 1830, 25 January 1831, and 17 October 1832.

28. Low, Journal, 25 January 1831 and 17 March 1833.

29. Low, Journal, 19 October 1829, 15 November 1831, 8 and 25 January 1831, 17 October 1832, and 20 May 1834; Drew R. McCoy, *The Elusive Republic: Political Economy in Jeffersonian America* (Chapel Hill: University of North Carolina Press, 1980), 87.

30. Low, Journal, 23 February 1833 and 13 November 1832.

31. Low, Journal, 30 October 1833, 11 October and 6 October 1832, and 2 December 1829.

32. Low, Journal, 10 October 1829.

33. Low, Journal, 28 February 1830 and 28 March 1830.

34. Low, Journal, 10 and 12 September 1829 and 17 February 1833.

35. See, for instance, Laurence Bergeen, *Over the Edge of the World: Magellan's Terrifying Circumnavigation of the Globe* (New York: Perennial/HarperCollins, 2003), 61, 70, 71, 102–103, and 111.

36. Low, Journal, 28 February 1830.

37. Low, Journal, 28 February 1830 and 28 August 1833.

38. Low, Journal, 23 January 1830 and 17 March 1833.

39. Low, Journal, 6 March 1830.

40. Low, Journal, 26 July and 15 October 1829.

41. Low, Journal, 25 December 1829 and 11 April 1830.

42. Low, Journal, 1 February 1833.

43. Low, Journals, 11 March 1833, 16 August 1832, 2 June 1830, 29 August and 16 November 1833.

44. Low, Journal, 9 September 1833.

45. Low, Journal, 9 September and 9 November 1833.

46. Low, Journal, 14 and 19 November 1833, 19 January 1834, 11 and 28 December 1833.

47. Low, Journal, 13–19 January and 24 February 1834.

48. Low, Journal, 6 December 1833, and 12, 13, 22, 23, and 26 January 1834.

49. Low, Journal, 15 and 16 January, and 2 and 9 February 1834.

50. Low, Journal, 15 and 16 January, and 2 February 1834.

51. Low, Journal, 17 and 19 January, 27 February 1834, 12, 15, and 30 March 1834, and 30 April 1834; *South African Commercial Advertiser*, 26 March 1834.

52. Low, Journal, 3 and 7 April 1834.

53. Low, Journal, 8 June 1834.

54. Low, Journal, 5 May and 4 July 1834. Removing seeds from raisins by setting them in a bowl of hot water was a traditional practice in Low's day.

INTERLUDE 4: "The Estimation of All Good Men"

1. Quoted in Norman O. Hatch, "The Origins of Civil Millennialism in America: New England Clergymen, War with France, and the Revolution," *William and Mary Quarterly*, 3rd ser. 31, no. 3 (July 1974): 425–426.

2. *Alexandria Gazette*, 22 February 1820; the *Daily Picayune* (New Orleans), 19 February 1840, and the *Richmond Inquirer*, 2 April 1839; Susan Bean, *Yankee India: American Commercial and Cultural Encounters with India in the Age of Sail, 1784–1860* (Salem, MA: Peabody Essex Museum, 2001), 21.

3. David F. Long, "'Martial Thunder': The First Official American Armed Intervention in Asia," *Pacific Historical Review* 42, no. 2 (May 1973): 145; James W. Gould, "American Imperialism in Southeast Asia before 1898," *Journal of Southeast Asian Studies* 3, no. 2 (September 1972): 306.

4. David Porter, *Journal of a Cruise Made to the Pacific Ocean* (New York: Wiley and Halsted, 1822), 2:4.

5. Porter, *Journal of a Cruise*, 2:86.

6. Porter, *Journal of a Cruise*, 2:100.

7. Porter, *Journal of a Cruise*, 2:4; *Essex Register*, 13 July 1814.

8. James R. Fichter, *So Great a Proffit: How the East Indies Trade Transformed Anglo-American Capitalism* (Cambridge, MA: Harvard University Press, 2010), 184–185.

9. Long, "'Martial Thunder,'" 148–149.

10. Terence Whalen, *Edgar Allan Poe and the Masses: Political Economy of Literature in Antebellum America* (Princeton: Princeton University Press, 1999), 166–167; Richard Drinnon, *Facing West: The Metaphysics of Indian-Hating and Empire Building* (Minneapolis: University of Minnesota Press, 1980), 129–130.

11. Charles Wilkes, *Voyage Round the World, Embracing the Principal Events of the Narrative of the United States Exploring Expedition* (Philadelphia: George W. Gorton, 1849).

12. Nathaniel Philbrick, *Sea of Glory: America's Voyage of Discovery: The U.S. Exploring Expedition* (New York: Penguin, 2003), 122–124, 129; Herman J. Viola and Carolyn Margolis, eds., *Magnificent Voyagers: The U.S. Exploring Expedition, 1838–1842* (Washington, DC: Smithsonian Institution Press, 1985), 200, 206, 217–218; Wilkes, *Voyage Round the World*, 450; and Robert Morrison, *Notices Concerning China, and the Port of Canton. Also, a Narrative of the Affair of the British Frigate Topaz, 1821–1822: with Remarks on Homicides, and an Account of the Fire of Canton* (Malacca: Mission Press, 1823), iv.

13. Philbrick, *Sea of Glory*, 102, 124, 133, and 135; William Reynolds, *The Private Journal of William Reynolds: United States Exploring Expedition, 1838–1842*, ed. Nathaniel Philbrick (New York: Penguin Classics, 2004). 9.

CHAPTER 5: Robert Bennet Forbes and the First Opium War, 1838–1840

1. Robert Bennet Forbes to Rose Forbes, 27 February 1839, Robert Bennet Forbes, *Letters from China: The Canton-Boston Correspondence of Robert Bennet Forbes, 1838–1840*, ed. Phyllis Forbes Kerr (Mystic, CT: Mystic Seaport Museum, 1996), 98–99; Maurice Collins, *Foreign Mud* (New York: New Directions, 1946), 198–199; Jacques M. Downs, *The Golden Ghetto: The American Commercial Community at Canton and the Shaping of American China Policy, 1784–1844* (Bethlehem, PA: Lehigh University Press, 1997), 144–145; Peter Ward Fay, *The Opium War, 1840–1842: Barbarians in the Celestial Empire in the Early Part of the Nineteenth Century and the War by Which They Forced Her Gates* (Chapel Hill: University of North Carolina Press, 1997), 140.

2. As George Dangerfield wrote, "Nationalism during this period transformed from an illusion of unity into the harsher and more testing realm of interest, prejudice, and appetite." George Dangerfield, *The Awakening of American Nationalism, 1815–1828* (New York: Harper & Row, 1965), 32. *Essex Gazette*, 4 and 11 January 1774.

3. Robert Bennet Forbes, *Personal Reminiscences* (Boston: Little, Brown, 1878), passim.

4. Forbes, *Reminiscences*, 91; J. Richard Olivas, "'God Helps Those Who Help Themselves': Religious Explanations of Poverty in Colonial Massachusetts, 1630–1776," in *Down and Out in Early America*, ed. Billy G. Smith (University Park: Pennsylvania University Press, 2004), 262–288; John Murray Forbes, *Letters and Recollections of John Murray Forbes*, ed. Sarah Forbes Hughes, 2 vols. (Boston: Houghton Mifflin, 1899), 41.

5. Leverett Saltonstall, "Memoir of Robert Bennet Forbes," Massachusetts Historical Society *Proceedings*, 2nd ser., 6 (1890–1891): 198.

6. Forbes to Rose Forbes, 6 December 1838, *Letters from China*, 74–75.

7. Dane Morrison, "Teaching the Old China Trade: A 'Glocal' Approach in Early Ameri-

can Travelogues," *World History Connected* 10, no. 2 (June 2013), http://worldhistoryconnected .press.illinois.edu/10.2/forum_morrison.html.

8. Forbes, *Reminiscences*, 3–4; Saltonstall, "Memoir," 197; Forbes, *Letters and Recollections*, 39, 55.

9. Sullivan Dorr, "Letters of Sullivan Dorr," ed. Howard Corning, Massachusetts Historical Society *Proceedings*, 3rd ser., 67 (October 1941–May 1944): 213; Forbes to Rose Forbes, 14 April 1839, *Letters from China*, 118.

10. Forbes, *Reminiscences*, 124, 135, 137; Forbes, *Letters and Recollections*, 90–91.

11. Forbes to Rose Forbes, 6 October 1838, *Letters from China*, 57; Forbes, *Reminiscences*, 150–151.

12. Forbes, *Reminiscences*, 141, 89–90; Forbes to Rose Forbes, 12 August 1839, *Letters from China*, 157, 67.

13. Forbes to Rose Forbes, 6 January and 17 August 1839, *Letters from China*, 84, 162; Forbes, *Reminiscences*, 142; Fay, *Opium War*, 150.

14. Forbes to Rose Forbes, 5 October 1838 and 16 August 1839, *Letters from China*, 56; Charles Tyng, *Before the Wind: The Memoir of an American Sea Captain, 1808–1839*, ed. Susan Fels (New York: Viking, 1999), 100; Collins, *Foreign Mud*, 210; and Downs, *Golden Ghetto*, 144–145.

15. Forbes to Rose Forbes, 10 April 1840, 1, 6, and 17 October 1839, Forbes, *Letters from China*, 218, 171, 175, 68; Forbes, *Reminiscences*, 156.

16. Fay, *Opium War*, 136.

17. Frank Dikötter, " 'Patient Zero': China and the Myth of the 'Opium Plague,' " Inaugural Lecture, School of Oriental and African Studies, University of London, 24 October 2003.

18. Dikötter, "Patient Zero," 7.

19. Fay, *Opium War*, 138–139; Forbes to Rose Forbes, 16 August 1839, *Letters from China*, 161.

20. Fay, *Opium War*, 131; Forbes to Rose Forbes, 27 February 1839, *Letters from China*, 98.

21. Fay, *Opium War*, 140; Forbes to Rose Forbes, 27 February 1839, *Letters from China*, 98.

22. Forbes to Rose Forbes, 27 February 1839, *Letters from China*, 98.

23. Fay, *Opium War*, 143–144; Forbes to Rose Forbes, 27 March 1839, *Letters from China*, 112.

24. [Hugh] Hamilton Lindsay, *Remarks on Occurences in China, Since the Opium Seizure in March 1839 to the Latest Date* (London: Sherwood, Gilbert, and Piper, 1840), 27.

25. Forbes to Rose Forbes, 11 March 1839, *Letters from China*, 105.

26. Collins, *Foreign Mud*, 194, 210; Fay, *Opium War*, 142; *Chinese Repository* 7 (August 1838), 231.

27. Collins, *Foreign Mud*, 212–214.

28. William C. Hunter, *The "Fan Kwae" at Canton before Treaty Days, 1825–1844* (London: 1882), 23.

29. Fay, *Opium War*, 145–147; Forbes to Rose Forbes, 25 March 1839, *Letters from China*, 109.

30. Forbes to Rose Forbes, 25 March 1839, *Letters from China*, 110; Collins, *Foreign Mud*, 212–215; Fay, *Opium War*, 145–146.

31. Fay, *Opium War*, 81, 148–149; Forbes to Rose Forbes, 25 March 1839, *Letters from China*, 110; Forbes, *Reminiscences*, 145–146.

32. Fay, *Opium War*, 149.

33. Fay, *Opium War*, 151; Forbes to Rose Forbes, 25 March 1839, *Letters from China*, 110–111.

34. Forbes to Rose Forbes, 25 March 1839, *Letters from China*, 111.

35. Forbes to Rose Forbes, 27 March 1839, *Letters from China*, 112–113.

36. Forbes, *Reminiscences*, 149; "A Memorial from the American Merchants at Canton" (25 May 1839) US House Document no. 40, 26th Cong., 1st sess., serial no. 364, in *United States*

Policy toward China: Diplomatic and Public Documents, 1839–1939, ed. Paul Clyde (New York: Russell and Russell, 1964), 3–6; Forbes, *Reminiscences*, 42; William T. Donahue, "The Caleb Cushing Mission," *Modern Asian Studies* 16, no. 2 (1982): 194.

37. Forbes to Rose Forbes, 27 October, 27 February, 11 April, 19 March, 27 October 1839, *Letters from China*, 182, 98, 117 108, 181; Forbes, *Reminiscences*, 149.

38. Forbes to Rose Forbes, 1 October 1839, *Letters from China*, 171.

39. Forbes, *Reminiscences*, 147–148; Forbes to Rose Forbes, 31 March and 19 April 1839, *Letters from China*, 114–115, 119.

40. Collins, *Foreign Mud*, 220.

41. Collins, *Foreign Mud*, 227; Forbes to Rose Forbes, 27 March 1839, *Letters from China*, 112–113.

42. Arthur Waley, *The Opium War through Chinese Eyes* (Stanford: Stanford University Press, 1958), 47–49, 50, 58; *Portsmouth Herald* (New Hampshire), 14 July 1832.

43. Forbes to Rose Forbes, 27 May and 3 June 1839, *Letters from China*, 128, 130.

44. Forbes to Rose Forbes, 20 March and 4 June 1839, *Letters from China*, 109, 131.

45. Forbes to Rose Forbes, 7 June and 17 August 1839, *Letters from China*, 131, 162.

46. Forbes to Rose Forbes, 16, 17, and 23 August 1839, *Letters from China*, 161–163; *Southern Patriot* (Charleston, SC), 19 May 1840; *New Bedford Mercury*, 22 May 1840.

47. Forbes to Rose Forbes, 14, 21, and 17 August 1839, *Letters from China*, 159, 163, 162; Forbes, *Reminiscences*, 151.

48. Lindsay, *Remarks*, 39, 43, 53–58.

49. Lindsay, *Remarks*, 6; Forbes to Rose Forbes, 17 August and 2 September 1839, *Letters from China*, 162 and 166; Waley, *Chinese Eyes*, 65.

50. Forbes to Rose Forbes, 5 and 6 September 1839, 9 and 17 October 1839, *Letters from China*, 167, 175, 177, 179.

51. Lindsay, *Remarks*, 17–18.

52. Forbes, *Reminiscences*, 150–151; Forbes to Rose Forbes, 21 August 1839, *Letters from China*, 163.

53. Forbes to Rose Forbes, 9 November 1839, *Letters from China*, 185; Lindsay, *Remarks*, 29–33.

54. Forbes to Rose Forbes, 1 December 1839, *Letters from China*, 188.

55. Forbes to Rose Forbes, 6 September and 9 October 1839, *Letters from China*, 175, 177.

56. Forbes to Rose Forbes, 9 and 17 October and 22 November 1839, *Letters from China*, 177–178, 186.

57. Forbes to Rose Forbes, 9 October and 19 March 1839, *Letters from China*, 177, 108; Forbes, *Reminiscences*, 156.

58. Forbes, *Reminiscences*, 164; Forbes to Rose Forbes, 9 and 22 November 1839, *Letters from China*, 185, 187.

59. Forbes, *Reminiscences*, 177–178.

Postscript

1. Peter Ward Fay, *The Opium War, 1840–1842: Barbarians in the Celestial Empire in the Early Part of the Nineteenth Century and the War by Which They Forced Her Gates* (Chapel Hill: University of North Carolina Press, 1997), 84; Forbes to Rose Forbes, 1–6 November 1839, Robert Bennet Forbes, *Letters from China: The Canton-Boston Correspondence of Robert Bennet Forbes, 1838–1840*, ed. Phyllis Forbes Kerr (Mystic, CT: Mystic Seaport Museum, 1996), 183–184; John L. O'Sullivan, "The Great Nation of Futurity," *United States Democratic Review* 6, no. 23 (1839): 426–430; Charles King, "Intercourse with China," *Chinese Repository*, 1 (August 1832): 144.

INDEX

Houqua (Wu Ping-Chien), 204, **206**, 208, 210–12, 214, 216

Hunter, William C., 52, 95, 97, 136, 164, 194, 199, 203, 212

Île de France (Mauritius), 29, 52, 59, 73, 95, 97; in imagining American identity, xvi

Ingraham, Capt. Joseph, 115–17, 120, 139, 143

Jardine, William, 204, 208, 211, 223

Java: description of, 69; as European colony, 33; exploration of, 66; in imagining American identity, xiv, 91, 188; as South Seas stopover, 13, 46, 131, 133, 156–57, 178; in South Seas trade, 223

Jay, 43–46

Jay, John, vii–viii, 3, 6–7, 20, 37, 46, 58, 94, 140

Jefferson, Thomas: anti-trade policies of, 54–55, 87, 188, 197; fighting Barbary piracy, 31, 57; parochialism of, xv; presidential policies of, 94, 139, 144; republicanism of, xvii, 81, 174, 217; self-fashioning of, 61

Jones, William, 140, 185

Journal of a Cruise Made to the Pacific Ocean, A (Porter), x, 142; as China Trade writing, x–xi, 142; in imagining American identity, 121, 142, 146, 187, 190, 192; referencing history, 142–43, 146, 187, 190, 192. *See also* Porter, Capt. David

Journal of Harriett Low, 155, 182: anti-Catholicism of, 158–60, 171–75, 184; on Canton Chinese, 162–68; on Cape Town Africans, 179–80; on Cape Town Dutch, 178–79, 181; as China trade writing, x, xii; on Chinese mandarins and Hong merchants, 165, 167, 169; describes homesickness, 156–57; on Europeans abroad, 161, 165, 175–77, 181; imagining the American in, xvii, 154–55, 157, 161, 165–67, 178, 230; imagining other peoples, 151, 156, 165, 185; on Indians, 156; on Macao Chinese, 160, 169–71,

177, 205; in Manila, 151, 158; on scales of civilization, 165–68; on slavery, 180; in Sumatra, 157

Journals (Shaw): imagining the American, xvi–xvii, 38, 45, 66; as Indies trade writing, x, 21, 23–25, 33–35, 38, 50; nationalist language in, 25, 27–28, 32, 34–36, 46, 60, 62; and Portuguese colonialism, 38–39; representing Chinese, 40; representing expatriate communities, 25, 34, 39, 41–42; representing Indians, 42. *See also* Shaw, Samuel

Juan Fernández Island, 78, 82, 112

Kaffirs (Caffres), 179

Kinsman, Nathaniel, 68, **161**

Kinsman, Rebecca Chase, 52

Knox, Henry, 5, 7, 31, 35, 42, 115

Ladrone Islands, xiii, 79, 124

Lady Hughes affair, 25–26, 33, 126

Lady Washington, 44, 53

Laki volcano, 11

Lam Qua, **161**, **163**

La Pérouse, Comte de, 39, 76, 142

Ledyard, John, 9, 12

Lintin, 223

Lintin Island, **200**, 200–202

Lin Zexu (Lin Tse-shū), 207–16, 219–26

Low, Abigail Knapp, 154, 162–63, **163**, 168, 178, 181–82, 202

Low, Harriett, **152**; economic needs and gains of, xii, xv, 154; as second generation, xvii, 146, 151, 162, 194–95; youth of, 152–54. *See also* Journal of Harriett Low

Low, Mary Ann, 151, 155, 157, 165, 170, 177, 181

Low, William Henry, 154, 162–64, 170, 177–78, 180–81, 202–3, 227

Lowell, Francis Cabot, 189

Macao (Macau), **125**, **160**, **161**, **166**; Americans buried at, 64; Americans in, x, xi, 39–40, 48, 52, 72, 124; Catholicism in, 160, 172–75, 206; English in, 37, 214, 220, 222–23, 225; entrance to Pearl River, 14, 26, 33, 37, 45, 47,

86, 123–24, 131; as global city, 14, 34, 69, 159, 161; in imagining American identity, 39, 95, 97, 175; as Portuguese colony, 14, 38–39, 211; as seasonal refuge, 39, 221; Sturgis in, 206, 211, 216; in writing, 67
Macaulay, Thomas, 185, 196
Madison, James, 187–88, 197
Magee, Capt. James, 32–33
Magellan, Ferdinand, 109, 113
Malabar Coast (India), 55, 67, 73–74, 159
Manila: Americans in, xi, 52, 69, 95, 151, 157, 179, 183, 201, 203; Catholics in, 158–60, 172–74; description of, 157–58; trade, 140, 151, 157
Manila galleons, 114, 121, 123
Marquesas Islands, xvii, 114–15, 121, 141–42, 186–87, 190
Mary Chilton, 202
Màs Afuera, 52, 73, 78, 112
Massachusetts, 46–47, 61–66, 68, 75, 80, 95
McClure, Commodore John, 65, 69–70, 76, 90
Melville, Herman, xi, xvii, 85, 91, 116, 121, 144
Moluccas (Maluku Islands), xvii, 86
Montreal, 182
Morris, Robert, 9–11, 28, 30–31, 53
Morrison, Rev. Robert, 27, 192
Mowqua, 167

Narrative of Voyages and Travels, A (Delano), **89**; Batavia, 69; Catholics, 83–84; Ceylon, 74; China, 87; as China trade writing, x–xi, 61–62, 76–77, 80, 84; the East, xvii, 67, 69, 83, 85, 87–89, 98; European expatriates, 70–72, 81–84, 87; imagining American identity, xi–xiii, xvii, 61–65, 69–70, 76–78, 81–85, 91; influence on American identity, 61–63, 66–71, 76, 81, 91–92; mortality chart in, 63–64; as navigational guide, 76; New Guinea, 72; Palau Islands, 70; referencing history, 66, 70–71, 76–78, 91; reviews of, 91; on slavery, 85–86; on South Seas beauty, 68; on South Seas bounty, 68, 81. *See also* Delano, Amasa

New Guinea, xvii
newspapers, reporting contact, ix, xii–xiii, xiv
Nexsen, Elias, 102–5, 107, 114, 135
Nexsen, Capt. William, 102
Nexsen Island, 122
Nuku Hiva, 116–19, 121, 123, 143, 186–87, 190

O'Donnell, Capt. John, 28, 42, 94
Ontario, 105, 131
Opium trade: American opposition to, 216, 218–19; Americans in, 42, 96, 194, 196, 200, 209, 217–18; American use, 67; British in, 208, 218–19, 221; Chinese policies toward, 207–8, 212–14, 219–21; introduction into China, 208; at Lintin, 43, 200
Opium War, x–xi, 94, 224–25, 231; American opposition to, 145, 186
O'Sullivan, John, 145, 231
Otaheite (Tahiti), 66, 145, 192–93
Owhyhee (Hawai'i): Americans in, 52, 79, 97; in China trade writing, 66, 76; Cook in, 139; in imagining American identity, xvii, 66, 86, 98, 186; as Indies stopover, 78, 86; trade, 97, 200

Paddock, Capt. Obed, 112
Pallas, 28–29, 42
Palmer, Capt. Nathaniel Brown, 136
Palmyra Island, 136, 140
Panther, 65–66, 68–69, 71–72, 75, 78, 80, 90
Paulding, James K., 191
Peabody Essex Museum, 182
Pearl (Pei-ho) River: Americans at, viii, 3, 23, 124–25, 128, 194; American trade at, 35; English at, 175; in European wars, 188, 225; flooding of, 177; location of, 14, 16, 21, 37, 79, 128, 131, 162, 196, 212
Pelew (Palau) Islands, xvii, 66, 69–70, 86, 90
Pendleton, Capt. Benjamin, 136
penguins, 108, 110–12
Perkins, Thomas Handasyd, 197–98, 199
Pernambuco (Chile), 140